Park Güell, Camp Nou
& La Zona Alta
(p173)

Barceloneta &
the Waterfront
(p107)

La Sagrada Família
& L'Eixample
(p125)

La Ribera
(p87)

El Raval
(p71)

La Rambla &
Barri Gòtic
(p47)

Montjuïc
(p155)

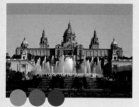

Montjuïc (p155)

Home to manicured
parks and gardens,
excellent museums and
cinematic views over the
city.

Don't Miss Museu Nacional
d'Art de Catalunya

Park Güell, Camp
Nou & La Zona Alta
(p173)

Take in Gaudí's fairy-tale
woodlands, a medieval
monastery and lofty
Tibidabo – followed by
football excitement at
hallowed Camp Nou.

Don't Miss Park Güell

Day Trips (p193)

Frolic on scenic beaches,
see Roman ruins and
explore monastic shrines
just outside Barcelona.

Contents

Plan Your Trip   Discover Barcelona

Discover
Barcelona

Experience the best
of Barcelona

This edition written and researched by

**Regis St Louis,
Vesna Maric, Anna Kaminski**

Discover
Barcelona

La Rambla & Barri Gòtic (p47)

Stroll Barcelona's famous boulevard, then lose yourself in the Gothic quarter.

Don't Miss La Rambla, La Catedral

El Raval (p71)

A once-seedy quarter that's home to cutting-edge museums and bohemian bars and eateries.

La Ribera (p87)

The trendiest part of the Ciutat Vella, with first-rate tapas bars and restaurants, medieval architecture and a stunning Modernista concert hall.

Don't Miss Museu Picasso

Barceloneta & the Waterfront (p107)

Bountiful plates of seafood, a long waterfront promenade and pretty beaches make for a memorable day on the Mediterranean.

La Sagrada Família & L'Eixample (p125)

Modernisme rules in Barcelona's 19th-century 'extension', crowned by masterpieces by Gaudí and others.

Don't Miss La Sagrada Família

**Park Güell,
Camp Nou &
La Zona Alta** 173

Welcome to Barcelona

A city of fabled architecture, inspiring museums and a world-class dining scene, Barcelona has long enchanted visitors. This is a city of narrow medieval lanes, elegant boulevards lined with sculpted buildings and sun-kissed beaches fronting the deep-blue Mediterranean. Galleries showcase Catalonia's renowned artistic heritage, while inventive chefs carve a name for themselves in colourful dining rooms all across town. Barcelona is no less enchanting by nightfall, with its vintage 19th-century bars, historic concert halls and buzzing nightclubs and lounges.

Barcelona's architectural heritage dates back more than 700 years. At its core lies one of Europe's best-preserved medieval centres. Centuries later, that heritage lent Gaudí and his Modernista contemporaries the historical foundation and inspiration for some of their wildest architectural creations. Their adventurousness is in the city's DNA, and local and international architects continue to unleash their fantasies here.

Architecture is just one manifestation of Catalan creativity. The heady mix of Gothic monuments and contemporary skyscrapers is accompanied by a bevy of world-class museums that take you from the wonders of giant Romanesque frescos to the playfulness of Joan Miró, from pre-Columbian South American gold to early Picasso.

***Barcelonins* are passionate about their cooking.** Thousands of restaurants offer an incredible palette for the palate, from traditional Catalan cuisine to the last word in 21st-century *nueva cocina española*. A plethora of tippling establishments and dance clubs also spreads in a hedonistic arc across the city – drop into century-old taverns or glam it up in bright seaside bars.

Shoppers, meanwhile, may never make it to a museum. L'Eixample is filled with avenues lined with top boutiques and shopping galleries, while the meandering streets of the Ciutat Vella hide all manner of unique finds from vintage boutiques and record stores to wine sellers and handicraft shops.

> This is a city of medieval lanes, elegant boulevards and sun-kissed beaches

Park Güell (p178)

PHOTOGRAPHER: PABLO CUSINE / IMAGEBROKER ©

25

Top Experiences

25 Barcelona's Top Experiences

La Sagrada Família (p130)

One of Barcelona's icons, this Modernista masterpiece remains a work in progress more than 80 years after the death of its creator, Antoni Gaudí. Fanciful, profound, inspired by nature and barely restrained by a Gothic style, Barcelona's quirky temple soars skyward with an almost playful majesty. Stepping through its sculpted portals is like walking into a fairy tale, where a forest of columns branch toward the ceiling and light shimmers through brilliant stained-glass windows. Rich with beautifully wrought detail and packed with symbols, the basilica invites hours of contemplation.

2

La Rambla (p52)

Sure, it's the most touristy spot in town. But you can't come to Barcelona and not stroll down this famous pedestrian boulevard. It's sensory overload – with a parade of people amid open-air cafes, fragrant flower stands, a much-overlooked mosaic by Joan Miró and rather surreal human sculptures. Key venues line both sides of the street, including the elegant Gran Teatre del Liceu (p57), the sprawling La Boqueria market (p82) and several intriguing galleries.

BARCELONA'S TOP 25 EXPERIENCES

Museu Picasso (p92)

For a portrait of the artist as a young man, head to Museu Picasso, which showcases perhaps the world's best collection of the master's early work. Picasso lived in Barcelona between the ages of 15 and 23, and elements of the city undoubtedly influenced his work, from the dramatic, wide-eyed frescoes hanging in the Museu Nacional d'Art de Catalunya to the imaginative *trencadís*-style mosaics (pre-Cubist some say) of Gaudí. The museum's setting inside five contiguous medieval mansions adds to the appeal. Picasso's *Dona Maria Agustina Sarmiento*, No 3 from *Las Meninas*

The Best...
Museums

MUSEU PICASSO
Finest collection of early works by the legendary Spanish artist. (p92)

MACBA
Proof of Barcelona's place at the cutting edge of contemporary art. (p81)

FUNDACIÓ JOAN MIRÓ
World's biggest Miró collection, in the city of his birth. (p170)

MUSEU NACIONAL D'ART DE CATALUNYA
Fine Romanesque art collection in a striking neo-baroque palace. (p160)

The Best...
Modernista Buildings

LA PEDRERA
Gaudí's famous head-turner on busy Passeig de Gràcia. (p142)

LA SAGRADA FAMÍLIA
Spain's most popular visitor attraction – come and see why. (p130)

PALAU DE LA MÚSICA CATALANA
Music turned to glass and stone. (p99)

CASA AMATLLER
The dark horse of the Manzana de la Discordia. (p134)

La Catedral (p54)

La Catedral is a masterpiece of Catalan Gothic architecture. Wander wide-eyed through the shadow-filled interior, which houses a dozen well-concealed chapels, an eerie crypt and a curious garden-style cloister, which has 13 geese connected to Barcelona's co-patron saint, Santa Eulàlia. Outside, there's always entertainment afoot, from *sardana* dancing on weekends to periodic processions and open-air markets.

La Pedrera (p142)

Astonishing architectural works dominate L'Eixample. The area was a blank canvas for some of Spain's finest buildings, erected in the late 19th and early 20th centuries. At La Pedrera, one of Gaudí's masterpieces, you'll find classic Gaudí flourishes: an undulating cliff-like facade, wildly sculpted wrought-iron balconies and cavern-like parabolic arches. On the rooftop, you can clamber beneath much-photographed chimney pots.

Església de Santa Maria del Mar (p102)

Blessed in 1384, this church is one of the purest examples of Catalan Gothic. It was raised in record time with stones painstakingly carried down from a quarry on Montjuïc. The church is remarkable for its architectural harmony and managed to survive a devastating 11-day fire during the civil war. Live concerts and recitals are regularly staged inside.

Mercat de la Boqueria (p82)

This temple of temptation is one of Europe's greatest permanent produce fairs. Restaurant chefs, homemakers, office workers and tourists all stroll amid the seemingly endless bounty of glistening fruits and vegetables, gleaming fish counters, dangling rolls of smoked meats, pyramids of pungent cheeses, barrels full of olives and marinated peppers, and chocolate truffles and other sweets. A handful of popular tapas bars serve up delectable morsels so you won't have to walk away empty-handed. There's always a line, but it's well worth the wait.

Museu Nacional d'Art de Catalunya (p160)

For many Catalans, Catalonia is not Spain but a country unto its own, with a unique and proud history. The Museu Nacional d'Art de Catalunya proves the point with an impressive collection that delves into the riches of 1000 years of Catalan art. Its Romanesque frescoes, altarpieces and wood carvings, rescued from decaying churches in the Pyrenees, are truly staggering, and its collection of Gothic art gives a meaningful context to the Barri Gòtic down below.

The Best... Live-Music Spots

HARLEM JAZZ CLUB
Small, atmospheric spot in the old town that's great for hearing jazz. (p66)

JAZZ SÍ CLUB
Intimate space in El Raval that hosts a wide range of sounds, including flamenco. (p84)

SALA APOLO
Photogenic old theatre where you can catch top local bands followed by DJs working a dance-loving crowd. (p171)

SIDECAR FACTORY CLUB
Young festive space on Plaça Reial that's known for its indie bands. (p68)

Camp Nou (p183)

For the sports-minded, little can compete with the spectacle of a match at FC Barcelona's massive football stadium. With a loyal fan base and an incredibly gifted team led by the likes of Lionel Messi, Camp Nou always hosts a good show. If you can't make it to a game, it's still worth visiting. The 'Camp Nou Experience' is an interactive museum and stadium tour that takes you through the locker rooms and out onto the pitch, which is hallowed ground for many Catalans.

The Best...
Parks

PARC DE LA CIUTADELLA
The manicured gardens make a serene setting for a stroll after spending time in the narrow lanes of the Ciutat Vella. (p95)

PARC DE COLLSEROLA
Find your own private space in Europe's largest municipal park. (p187)

MONTJUÏC
Parks and gardens lace the lofty vantage points around the Castell de Montjuïc. (p162)

PARK GÜELL
Here Gaudí turned his hand to landscape gardening. (p178)

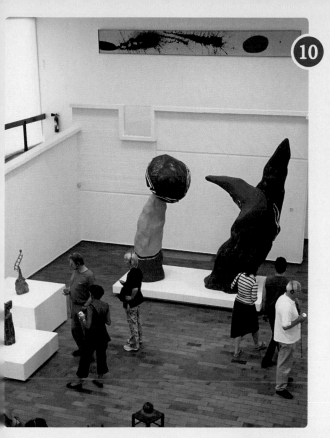

Fundació Joan Miró (p170)

10

Picasso was born in Málaga and Dalí hailed from Figueres, but surrealist visionary Joan Miró was a true dyed-in-the-wool *barcelonin*. As a revolutionary artist and proud Catalan, Miró etched much of his legacy on the city. The Fundació Joan Miró contains a treasure trove of his work, spanning a long and illustrious career. Footage of Miró and works by contemporaries provide an illuminating portrait of the artist and his time. The spacious gallery is set up on Montjuïc and is flanked by sculpture gardens.

Park Güell (p178)

What a fine flop! It started in 1900 as the dream of *barcelonin* magnate Eusebi Güell for an English-style 'garden city' for the hoity-toity and ended up as an enchanting park for the hoi polloi designed by Antoni Gaudi. Dazzling mosaic-covered architectural details, curious Hansel-and-Gretel-style gatehouses and a museum packed with Gaudían intrigue are but a few of the park's many captivating features. Don't miss the splendid view over the city from the cross-topped Turó del Calvari.

11

GÜNTER GRAFENHAIN / HUBER / 4CORNERS ©

Casa Batlló (p139)

Yet another of Gaudí's stunning Modernista masterpieces, Casa Batlló has astonishing details. Shimmering blue and green tiles, wildly sculpted balconies and bone-like columns adorn its facade, while the roof undulates like the scaly backside of a dragon. Inside, you glimpse the artistry that left nothing to chance, from curved and sinuous walls to corridors of parabolic arches: the brilliant use of organic forms coupled with the masterful use of natural light and colour showcase Gaudí's talents at the height of his career.

Barceloneta Seafood (p116)

Barcelona's gastronomy combines regional cuisine, experimentalism and artistic chefs. Then there's the simplicity of Barceloneta restaurateurs who have been knocking out uncomplicated but magnificent seafood dishes for decades. Whether stopping by a tapas bar for anchovies and *cava* (Catalan sparkling wine), or lingering over an afternoon-long lunch of *suquet* (hearty seafood stew), seafood lovers should not miss Barceloneta.

Costa Brava–style seafood stew

Gardens of Montjuïc (p158)

After a few days of exploring the narrow lanes of the Ciutat Vella and the bustling boulevards of L'Eixample, you may need a dose of greenery and fresh air. The scenic gardens of Montjuïc provide the perfect antidote. Here you'll find elegant manicured gardens complete with fountains and sculptures, all overlooking the restless city below. You can take scenic walks through greenery, enjoy a picnic with views of the sea or delve into the world of Mediterranean flora at the Jardí Botànic (p167).

14

The Best...
Catalan Restaurants

CAN CULLERETES
An elegant, artwork-filled classic that's been serving up Catalan success since 1786. (p63)

PLA
Mouth-watering dishes that blend Catalan traditions with accents from the east. (p62)

CAN MAJÓ
Simple but brilliant seafood enjoyed al fresco while overlooking Barceloneta's beachfront. (p116)

CASA CALVET
Creative cooking in a Gaudí-designed interior. (p146)

The Best...
Gothic Masterpieces

LA CATEDRAL
Contemplate the incredible decoration on the northwest facade. (p54)

ESGLÉSIA DE SANTA MARIA DEL MAR
Catalan Gothic at its purest and most refined. (p102)

MUSEU MARÍTIM
One of the largest shipyards in Europe once lay under these Gothic arches. (p115)

ESGLÉSIA DE SANTS JUST I PASTOR
Often neglected example of early Gothic ecclesial architecture. (p60)

15

ROBERT BIRD- ALAMY ©

DIRK RENCKHOFF / ALAMY ©

Museu Marítim (p115)

Venice had its Arsenal and Barcelona the Reials Drassanes (Royal Shipyards), from which Don Juan of Austria's flagship galley was launched to lead a joint Spanish-Venetian fleet into the momentous Battle of Lepanto against the Turks in 1571. This site has been a museum since the 1940s and it's a fascinating place to explore Barcelona's tabled maritime legacy. On display are vessels and models of all types, representing all epochs from sail to steam. The highlight is a life-sized replica of Don Juan of Austria's 16th-century galley.

Tibidabo (p187)

Come to the mountain. The trip to the city's highest peak, Tibidabo, is an old-style family outing that bursts with nostalgia. The panoramic vistas are themselves a fine reward and the amusement-park rides are a retro trip to fun parks of yore. One of the best parts of the experience is getting here. Take the old tram that rattles along an avenue lined with Modernista mansions. Then hop aboard the funicular for a speedy ascent to the top, where the city and sea spread out beneath you.

Stone apostle at Temple del Sagrat Cor (p187)

Palau de la Música Catalana (p99)

Finished in 1908, this Modernista gem remain an enchanting concert setting. The exterior and foyer are opulent, but these are nothing compared with the auditorium interior. Stepping inside is like entering a nether world, with a magnificent stained glass skylight and wonderfully baroqu carvings adorning the stage area.

LONELY PLANET / GETTY IMAGES ©

Cafe Culture in Gràcia (p189)

Gràcia bubbles with life. A separate town until 1897, its warren of straight, narrow streets and lanes opens here and there onto a series of peaceful squares, each dotted with outdoor cafes and bars that invite lingering. Spend the day window-shopping amid cutting-edge boutiques, vintage shops and tiny food markets, then join the bohemian crowd over a few drinks. For something a little different, pull up a chair at picture-perfect La Nena (p183), famed for its thick rich hot chocolate.

The Best...
Viewpoints

TIBIDABO
Ascend the old church or the new tower for an even better view. (p187)

CASTELL DE MONTJUÏC
Strategically positioned fortress atop Montjuïc. (p162)

LA SAGRADA FAMÍLIA
Head up one of the towers for bird's-eye rooftop views. (p130)

TRANSBORDADOR AERI
Grab the cable car over the restored Port Vell up to Montjuïc. (p113)

18

Bars in El Raval (p83)

Of the old town districts, El Raval is the grittiest and perhaps the sexiest. Long a slum and still edgy in parts, it's perfect for a night of bar-crawling. You'll find a mix of 19th-century drinking dens, jazz-filled absinthe bars, tiny DJ clubs and sleek modern lounges all vying for attention. The crowd is no less diverse: bohemians and out-of-towners, tourists and touts, artists and characters who might have just stepped from the pages of a Carlos Ruiz Zafón novel are all here.

The Best...
Bars with a View

MIRABLAU
Gaze out over the city from this magnificently sited bar in Tibidabo. (p190)

OPIUM MAR
Popular bar and dance club perched right on the waterfront. (p121)

LA CASETA DEL MIGDIA
Gaze through the pine-scented surrounds to the sea beyond at this well-hidden Montjuïc gem. (p171)

LOOK DIE BILDAGENTUR DER FOTOGRAFEN GMBH / ALAMY ©

LOWER EAST SIDE

20

Shopping in El Born (p104)

As reinventions go, once-decrepit El Born is up there with New York's Lower East Side as the ghetto that made good. A time traveller from the 1980s would have trouble recognising this compact pocket of La Ribera, with its cool bars, trendy restaurants and – for haters of modern chain stores – chic indie boutiques. In addition to hip little fashion boutiques, these medieval lanes hide a fascinating collection of shops, from magic stores and early 20th-century coffee roasters to hallowed wine cellars and picture-perfect patisseries.

DIEGO LEZAMA / GETTY IMAGES ©

Municipal Beaches (p114)

An afterthought until the 1980s, Barcelona's beaches are now one of the city's finest selling points, luring recreationists who might otherwise have headed to the Costa del Sol or the Caribbean. In summer, crowds pack the sands for volleyball, football and frolicking in the waves. *Chiringuitos* (beachside bars) dole out snacks and cold drinks. During the weekends, the beach party continues long after sundown. Platja de Bogatell

Gran Teatre del Liceu (p57)

The splendiferous Gran Teatre del Liceu has been knocking out Puccini arias longer than – well – Puccini. If you can't make a performance, come for a guided tour, where you'll get a peak at the grand foyer, with its thick pillars and sumptuous chandeliers. Head up the marble staircase to the fresco-filled Saló dels Miralls (Hall of Mirrors) before heading into the gilded theatre itself.

MACBA (p81)

The ever-expanding contemporary art collection of the restlessly dynamic MACBA starts in the Gothic chapel of the Convent dels Àngels and continues into the main gleaming-white building across the square. It's a stage for the best of Catalan, Spanish and international contemporary art. Artists frequently on show include Antoni Tàpies, Miquel Barceló and a host of very-now installation artists. The ultramodern white building, designed by North American architect Richard Meier, was one of a series of art and cultural institutions that helped revitalise El Raval. MACBA; architect: Richard Meier & Partners

23

The Best...
Outdoor
Activities

BEACH PROMENADE
Go for a walk, a bike ride or a jog along the lovely 4.6km-long seaside path. (p110)

BOAT TOURS
Go for a sunset cruise for a picturesque view of Barcelona and its sparkling waterfront. (p236)

PICNIC ON MONTJUÏC
Buy goodies at Mercat de la Boqueria, then head up to Montjuïc for a picnic with fantastic views. (p162)

PARC D'ATTRACIONS
Take in hyperfast rides, 3D movies and 19th-century puppetry at this lively amusement park. (p187)

The Best...
Unexpected
Spots

OBSERVATORI FABRA
Book for dinner under
the stars in this Zona Alta
observatory. (p181)

COSMOCAIXA
Wander through a lush
piece of the Amazon
rainforest without leaving
Europe. (p180)

EL REY DE LA MAGIA
Century-old magic shop
that materialises like
something out of a Carlos
Ruiz Zafón novel. (p105)

SINAGOGA MAJOR
Inspect Roman and medi-
eval ruins in a synagogue
reclaimed for posterity in
the 1990s. (p61)

Museu-Monestir de Pedralbes (p181)

Founded in the 14th century by Queen Elisenda of Montcada
for the Poor Clares, this peaceful convent feels like a world
removed from the bustling 21st-century city beyond its gates.
The three-storey cloister is an exquisite work of Catalan
Gothic architecture. Enter the medieval building and wander
through the refectory, kitchens, stables, stores and reconstructed infirmary – all of which give a good idea of convent
life. Upstairs, a small collection of monastery art completes
the time travel with works by Catalan artists dating back to
the Middle Ages.

(25)

Waterfront Promenade (p110)

Barcelona's waterfront is abuzz these days, not just with fit *barcelonins* jogging, biking, blading and bantering their way through the afternoon siesta, but also with a slew of ambitious architectural projects that have created a new Barcelona apart from the Gothic city of lore. The best way to see it all is to hire a bike and cycle up the promenade (safely separated from traffic) from Barceloneta to the supermodern El Fòrum. You'll pass lovely beaches, intriguing public art and plenty of places to refuel along the way.

Top Days in Barcelona

Barcelona's Must-Sees

On your first day in Barcelona, visit the city's major highlights: stroll La Rambla, explore the atmospheric lanes of the Barri Gòtic and linger over the stunning artistry of La Sagrada Família. History, great architecture and a celebrated food market are all part of this sensory-rich experience.

❶ La Rambla (p52)

Start with La Rambla. Don't miss the human statues, the Miró mosaic and key buildings facing La Rambla, including the 18th-century Palau de la Virreina.

LA RAMBLA ➲ MERCAT DE LA BOQUERIA
🏃 Find the market's entrance on La Rambla's west side.

❷ Mercat de la Boqueria (p82)

Packed with culinary riches, this staggering market is a stomping ground for chefs and conjurers, weekend cooks and hungry-looking tourists. Don't leave without having a few snacks – perhaps from one of the delectable tapas bars in the back.

MERCAT DE LA BOQUERIA ➲ BARRI GÒTIC
🏃 Turn left into Plaça Reial after passing Carrer de Ferran.

❸ Barri Gòtic (p47)

Delve into Barcelona's old city. Cross the picturesque Plaça Reial (p57) before wandering narrow lanes that date back to at least the Middle Ages. Make your way to the magnificent Catedral (p54), then visit the Temple Romà d'August (p61).

Plaça Reial (p57)
PHOTOGRAPHER: PIETRO CANALI / SIME / 4CORNERS ©

BARRI GÒTIC ➲ CAFÈ DE L'ACADÈMIA
🏃 Cross Plaça de Sant Jaume, walk along Carrer de la Ciutat and take the first left.

❹ Lunch at Cafè de l'Acadèmia (p63)

Arrive early to get a seat at this small atmospheric restaurant serving excellent Catalan cuisine. The multicourse lunch special is fantastic value.

CAFÈ DE L'ACADÈMIA ➲ LA SAGRADA FAMÍLIA
Ⓜ Take Line 4 north from Jaume I; transfer at Passeig de Gràcia for Line 2 to Sagrada Família.

❺ La Sagrada Família (p130)

Roll the drums, turn on the stage lights and get ready for Spain's most visited church. This one-of-a-kind religious monument is as unique as the Giza pyramids and as beautiful as the Taj Mahal.

LA SAGRADA FAMÍLIA ➲ ALKIMIA
🏃 Walk three blocks northwest along Carrer de Sardenya and turn left on Carrer de l'Indústria.

❻ Dinner at Alkimia (p143)

This much-lauded restaurant serves daring new Catalan cuisine. For pure decadence, opt for the 10-course tasting menu, a great chance to see the culinary magic worked by head chef Jordi Vilà.

Mar i Muntanya (Sea & Mountain)

This itinerary takes you along the promenade that skirts the Mediterranean, then into the old fishing quarter of Barceloneta before whisking you up to the heights of Montjuïc for fine views, fragrant gardens and superb art galleries – including two of the city's top museums.

❶ Barceloneta Beach (p114)

Start the morning with a stroll along the waterfront. Take in the scenic views of this once derelict area that experienced a dramatic makeover in days before and after the 1992 Olympics. Look north and you'll see Frank Gehry's shimmering fish sculpture while to the south rises the spinnaker-shaped tower of the W Hotel.

BARCELONETA BEACH ❍ CAN MAJÓ

🏃 Look for the restaurant just north of the rectangular beach sculpture, off Carrer del Almirall Aixada.

❷ Lunch at Can Majó (p116)

You'll find more great views at Can Majó, a seafood restaurant with outdoor tables overlooking the seaside. Top picks include the hearty seafood platter or the *suquets* (fish stews).

CAN MAJÓ ❍ TRANSBORDADOR AERI

🏃 Walk to the southern end of Barceloneta and you'll see the cable car to your right.

❸ Transbordador Aeri (p113)

After lunch take a scenic ride on this aerial cable car, which affords fantastic views over the port and the dazzling city beyond. At the top, you'll arrive in Montjuïc, a mini-mountain that's packed with gardens – both sculptural and floral – as well as a few first-rate museums.

TRANSBORDADOR AERI ❍ FUNDACIÓ JOAN MIRÓ

🚡 Take the cable car up to Montjuïc, disembark and follow the main road 800m west.

❹ Fundació Joan Miró (p170)

You can see a full range of works by one of the giants of the art world at this impressive museum. Paintings, sculptures and drawings by the prolific Catalan artist are displayed along with photos and other media elucidating Miró's life. Outside is a peaceful sculpture garden with views over Poble Sec.

FUNDACIÓ JOAN MIRÓ ❍ MUSEU NACIONAL D'ART DE CATALUNYA

🏃 Follow the path through the sculpture gardens east, take the steps up to main road and continue east to the museum.

❺ Museu Nacional d'Art de Catalunya (p160)

Not to be missed is the incomparable collection of artwork inside the enormous Museu Nacional d'Art de Catalunya. The highlight is the impressive Romanesque collection – rescued from 900-year-old churches in the Pyrenees. Other halls showcase Catalan works from the Middle Ages up to the early 20th century. Out front, you can take in the view over Plaça d'Espanya to the distant peak of Tibidabo.

MUSEU NACIONAL D'ART DE CATALUNYA ❍ TICKETS

🏃 Descend toward Plaça d'Espanya. Turn right before the fountain, left on Carrer de Leida and right on Avinguda del Paral·lel.

❻ Tickets (p167)

You'll need to book weeks in advance, but it's well worth the effort if you can score a table at Tickets, one of Barcelona's best restaurants. Ferran Adrià, the culinary mastermind behind molecular gastronomy, serves up dazzling bites of creativity at this highly imaginative restaurant.

Museu Nacional d'Art de Catalunya (p160)
PHOTOGRAPHER: FOTOGRAFEN GMBH / ALAMY ©

La Ribera

Like Barri Gòtic to the west, La Ribera has narrow cobblestone streets and medieval architecture galore. Yet it is also home to high-end shopping, a brilliant Modernista concert hall and a treasure trove of artwork by Picasso. Great restaurants and a fanciful green space complete the Ribera ramble.

DAY 3

① Museu Picasso (p92)

Picasso spent his formative years in Barcelona and you can see his early masterpieces inside this inspiring museum, which contains some 3500 of his works. Perhaps just as impressive as the artwork are the galleries themselves – set in a series of merchant houses dating back to the 1300s.

MUSEU PICASSO ➲ EL BORN
🏃 Stroll southeast along Carrer de Montcada.

② Window Shopping in El Born (p104)

The medieval streets of El Born hide an abundance of shopping intrigue, from magic shops to purveyors of fine wines to eye-catching fashion boutiques. For unique, beautifully made men's and women's designs, stop in the Barcelona-born boutique Custo Barcelona (p105).

EL BORN ➲ CAL PEP
🏃 Walk across Plaça de les Olles.

③ Lunch at Cal Pep (p101)

For lunch, belly up to the bar at this bustling eatery for some of the city's tastiest seafood tapas. Set on a tiny square, this place is always packed – and for good reason.

CAL PEP ➲ ESGLÉSIA DE SANTA MARIA DEL MAR
🏃 Walk northwest along Carrer de la Vidriería and turn left on Carrer de Santa Maria.

④ Església de Santa Maria del Mar (p102)

A few blocks away is one of the most captivating Catalan Gothic churches. The 14th-century masterpiece soars above the medina-like streets surrounding it.

ESGLÉSIA DE SANTA MARIA DEL MAR ➲ PARC DE LA CIUTADELLA
🏃 Walk northeast on Carrer de Santa Maria and continue around the former Mercat del Born site to the park.

⑤ Parc de la Ciutadella (p95)

Just east of the compact streets of La Ribera, you can catch your breath strolling through the open green expanse of this manicured park. You'll find sculptures, a small zoo, the Parlament de Catalunya and the centerpiece, a dramatic if utterly artificial waterfall dating from the 19th century.

PARC DE LA CIUTADELLA ➲ PALAU DE LA MÚSICA CATALANA
🏃 Take Carrer de la Princesa back into El Born and turn right after 200m, making your way northwest.

⑥ Palau de la Música Catalana (p99)

Designed by Domènech i Montaner in the early 1900s, this intimate concert hall is a Modernista masterpiece, with luminescent stained glass and elaborately sculpted details throughout. Come for a concert, but it's also worth returning by day for a guided tour.

PALAU DE LA MÚSICA CATALANA ➲ EL XAMPANYET
🏃 Make your way back (southeast) to Carrer de Montcada.

⑦ El Xampanyet (p104)

Just up the road, El Xampanyet is a festive spot to end the night. You can sample mouth-watering bites and let your cup runneth over with ever-flowing *cava* (Catalan sparkling wine). It's usually crowded but friendly, just politely elbow your way in for a bit of refreshment.

Parc de la Ciutadella (p95)
PHOTOGRAPHER: JOSE FUSTE RAGA / CORBIS ©

DAY 4

Art & Architecture

This tour takes you up to the enchanting (if accidental) park Gaudí designed overlooking the city, down the elegant architectural showpiece avenue of Passeig de Gràcia and into El Raval. There you'll find the city's top contemporary art museum anchoring Barcelona's most bohemian neighbourhood.

① Park Güell (p178)

Go early to Park Güell to beat the crowds and see the early morning rays over Barcelona and the Mediterranean beyond. Stroll the expanse of the park, taking in the mosaic-covered Banc de Trencadís, the fairy-tale-like columns of Sala Hipóstila and the view from Turó del Calvari. End your visit at Casa Museu Gaudí, where you can learn more about the life and work of the great Catalan architect.

PARK GÜELL ➲ GRÀCIA
Ⓜ Take Line 3 from Vallcarca to Fontana.

② Gràcia (p191)

The village-like feel of Gràcia makes for some great exploring. Stroll from plaza to plaza along the narrow shop-lined lanes, stopping perhaps at open-air cafes along the way. Good streets for browsing include Carre de Verdi, Travessera de Gràcia and Carrer de Torrijos.

GRÀCIA ➲ BOTAFUMEIRO
🏃 Walk southwest along Travessera de Gràcia and turn right on Carrer Gran de Gràcia.

③ Lunch at Botafumeiro (p183)

One of Barcelona's best seafood restaurants serves up delectable fare from the Galician coast. Finding a table even at lunchtime can sometimes be a challenge, though you can usually get a spot at the bar.

BOTAFUMEIRO ➲ PASSEIG DE GRÀCIA
🏃 Walk southeast along Carrer Gran de Gràcia, which leads into Passeig de Gràcia after 400m.

④ Passeig de Gràcia (p125)

After taking in the bohemian charm of Gràcia, head over to L'Eixample for a look at high-concept architecture. Passeig de Gràcia is a busy but elegant boulevard lined with exquisite Modernista buildings and fanciful boutiques. You'll see incredible designs by Gaudí, including La Pedrera (p142) and Casa Batlló (p139).

PASSEIG DE GRÀCIA ➲ MACBA
🏃 Continue along Passeig de Gràcia, cross Plaça de Catalunya to La Rambla and turn right on Carrer del Bonsuccés.

⑤ MACBA (p81)

A few streets away from Placa d'Espanya you'll reach the city's top contemporary art gallery, MACBA. It houses an excellent range of Catalan and European works from WWII to the present.

MACBA ➲ EL RAVAL
🏃 Walk along Carrer dels Àngels and turn left on Carrer del Carme.

⑥ El Raval (p71)

Spend the early evening strolling the lively multicultural street scene of El Raval. You'll find record stores, vintage fashion and curious bric-a-brac throughout. Stop for a breather in the pretty courtyard of the Antic Hospital de la Santa Creu (p76) and check out another Gaudí masterpiece at the Palau Güell.

EL RAVAL ➲ KOY SHUNKA
Ⓜ Take Line 3 from Paral·lel to Catalunya.

⑦ Dinner at Koy Shunka (p63)

Top off your night with a multicourse feast at Koy Shunka. This zenlike den of haute cuisine features a magnificent marriage of Catalan creativity with Japanese tradition. The 11-course *menú degustacion gastronómico* is worth the hefty price tag.

Antic Hospital de la Santa Creu (p76)

Month by Month

 ## January

Festes dels Tres Tombs

In addition to live music and *gegants* (papier maché giants worn over the shoulders of processionists), the festival dedicated to Sant Antoni features a parade of horse-drawn carts in L'Eixample near the Mercat de Sant Antoni every 17 January.

February

Carnestoltes/ Carnaval

Celebrated in February or March, this festival involves several days of fancy-dress parades and merrymaking, ending on the Tuesday before Ash Wednesday. The *Gran Rua* (Grand Parade) takes place on the Saturday evening from 5.30pm.

Festes de Santa Eulàlia

Around 12 February, this big winter fest celebrates Barcelona's first patron saint with a week of cultural events, from concerts to *castellers* (human-castle builders). See www.bcn. cat/santaeulalia for more details.

 ## April

Día de Sant Jordi

Catalonia honours its patron saint, Sant Jordi (St George), on 23 April. Traditionally, men give women a rose and women give men a book – and La Rambla and Plaça de Sant Jaume fill with book and flower stalls.

Feria de Abril de Catalunya

Andalucía comes to the Parc del Fòrum with this week-long southern festival featuring flamenco, a funfair and plenty of food and drink stalls. It kicks off in late April.

 ## May

L'Ou Com Balla

On Corpus Christi (late May or June), L'Ou com Balla ('the Dancing Egg') bobs on top of flower-festooned fountains around the city. There's also an early evening procession from La Catedral and *sardanes* (traditional Catalan folk dance) is danced out front at 7pm.

Primavera Sound

For three days in late May (or early June), the Auditori Fòrum and other locations around town welcome a host of international DJs and musicians (www. primaverasound.com).

Festival de Flamenco de Ciutat Vella

One of the best occasions to see great flamenco in

Barcelona, this concentrated festival is held over four days at the Centre de Cultura Contemporània de Barcelona (CCCB).

June

✪ Festival del Grec

This eclectic program of theatre, dance and music runs for most of the summer. Performances are held all over the city, including at the Teatre Grec (Map p164) amphitheatre on Montjuïc, from which the festival takes its name (www.barcelonafestival. com, in Catalan).

✪ La Revetlla de Sant Joan/Verbenas de Sant Joan

The night before the Día de San Juan Bautista (Feast of St John the Baptist, 24 June), the people of Barcelona hit the streets or hold parties at home to celebrate the Revetlla de Sant Joan (St John's Night), which involves drinking, dancing, bonfires and fireworks.

✪ Pride Barcelona

The Barcelona Gay Pride festival is a week of celebrations held towards the end of June with a crammed program of culture and concerts, along with the traditional Gay Pride march on the last Sunday of the month (www.pridebarcelona.org, in Catalan).

✪ Sónar

Usually in mid-June, Sónar is Barcelona's celebration of electronic music and is said to be Europe's biggest such event. Locations change each year (www. sonar.es).

August

✪ Festa Major de Gràcia

Locals compete for the most elaborately decorated street in this popular week-long Gràcia festival held around 15 August. People pour in to listen to bands in the streets and squares, fuel on snacks and drink at countless street stands (www. festamajordegracia.org, in Catalan).

✪ Festa Major de Sants

The district of Sants launches its own week-long version of decorated mayhem, held around 24 August, hot on the heels of Gràcia's (www.festamajor desants.net, in Catalan).

✪ Festes de Sant Roc

For four days in mid-August, Plaça Nova in the Barri Gòtic becomes the scene of parades, the *cor-* *refoc* (fire race), a market, traditional music and magic shows for kids.

September

✪ Festes de la Mercè

Barcelona's co-patron saint is celebrated with fervour in this massive four-day fest. The city stages sporting events, free concerts, human towers of *castellers,* folksy *sardanes*, parades of *gegants* and *capgrossos* (big heads), and a huge *correfoc* (www.bcn.cat/ merce).

✪ Festa Major de la Barceloneta

Barcelona's other big September celebration honours the local patron saint, Sant Miquel, on 29 September. It lasts about a week and involves plenty of dancing and drinking, especially on the beach.

December

🔒 Fira de Santa Llúcia

Held from early December to Christmas, this holiday market has hundreds of stalls selling all manner of Christmas decorations and gifts – including the infamous Catalan Nativity scene character, the *caganer* (the crapper).

What's New

For this new edition of Discover Barcelona, our authors have hunted down the fresh, the transformed, the hot and the happening. These are some of our favourites. For up-to-the-minute recommendations, see lonelyplanet.com/barcelona.

1 TICKETS – A NEW ADRIÀ ADVENTURE
If you didn't make it to El Bulli, despair not. The Adrià brothers have opened up Tickets, a new venture that promises to keep true to their innovative spirit and blow minds and tastebuds – if you can get a table, that is. Booking is strictly online, two months in advance, so get clicking and hope for the artiest bite in town. (p167)

2 PALAU GÜELL REOPENS
After nearly two decades under wraps, the restored Palau Güell opened in 2011 to spectacular effect. Gaudí's early project shows the extent of his innovative genius. (p76)

3 FILMOTECA DE CATALUNYA
Will this be the project that finally gentrifies El Raval? The Filmoteca de Catalunya opened in February 2012 and aims to act as a cultural convergence zone. (p84)

4 MEET THE LOCALS
Airbnb offers a fantastic new way of finding well-priced accommodation – and living as the locals do. You can rent a room in a *barcelonin's* house, or even occupy an entire apartment. (www.airbnb.com)

5 JAPANESE CUISINE BLOSSOMS
A number of excellent Japanese restaurants are popping up across town. Choose from sushi hotspot Koy Shunka, fantastic fusion *izakaya* Can Kenji and more. (p63, p143)

6 MUSEU MARÍTIM
The wonderful Museu Marítim plans to reopen fully in 2013 – don't miss its great galleys and other seafaring wonders, and interactive displays that fascinate kids and grownups alike. (p115)

7 MUSEU D'IDEES I INVENTS DE BARCELONA
This fun and educational museum opened in 2011 in the midst of Barri Gòtic, with original, quirky and hands-on displays. (p57)

8 DISSENY HUB
It's been a few years in the making, but the stunning new building of the Disseny Hub at Plaça de les Glòries is set to open in the summer of 2013. (p94)

9 MUSEU FREDERIC MARÈS
Following a two-year renovation completed in 2011, Museu Frederic Marès reopened, with even better displays and more extensive works on view in the staggering 'Collector's Cabinet'. (p62)

Get Inspired

Books

The Shadow of the Wind (Carlos Ruiz Zafón) With a twisting, turning plot that uses post-civil-war Barcelona as a vivid backdrop, Catalan-native Zafón's classic has sold millions.

Homage to Catalonia (George Orwell) Orwell's reportorial masterpiece provides on-the-spot commentary of the city at one of the most volatile moments of its history during the civil war.

Cathedral of the Sea (Ildefonso Falcones) Historical novel set in 14th-century Barcelona against a backdrop of the Inquisition and grand building projects.

Homage to Barcelona (Colm Tóibín) Easy-to-digest travelogue of the city by the noted Irish writer.

Films

All About My Mother One of Pedro Almodovar's best-loved films is full of plot twists and dark humour, complete with trans-sexual prostitutes and doe-eyed nuns.

L'Auberge Espagnol This warmly told coming-of-age story shows what happens when a mishmash of young students are thrown together on their first trip abroad.

Barcelona Whit Stillman's smart romantic comedy revolves around two American expats living in Barcelona in the late '80s.

♫ Music

Joan Manuel Serrat Acclaimed troubadour and king of Nueva Canción; key track 'Mediterráneo'.

The Pinker Tones Electronic alternative pop band; key track 'The Whistling Song'.

Sopa de Cabra Ultimate Catalan rock band; key track 'Si et Quedes amb Mi'.

Luís Llach Hugely popular Catalan-language singer; key song 'Laura'.

Websites

Barcelona Tourism (www.barcelonaturisme. cat) Official Barcelona tourism website.

Lonely Planet (www. lonelyplanet.com) Up-to-date hotel and restaurant reviews plus Thorn Tree travel forum.

What Barcelona (www. whatbarcelona.com) Easy-to-navigate travel site.

Short on time?

This list will give you an instant insight into the city.

Read Celebrated art critic Robert Hughes pays homage to a city of burgeoning creativity in *Barcelona, the Great Enchantress*.

Watch In *Vicky Cristina Barcelona*, Woody Allen gives Barcelona the Manhattan treatment, showing its mix of beauty and neuroticism.

Listen Ojo de Brujo's *Bari* is a superb album that blends flamenco with hip-hop and electronica.

Log on Le Cool (lecool.com) has a free weekly guide to what's happening in Barcelona (and other cities).

Casa Batlló (p139)

Need to Know

Currency
The euro (€)

Language
Spanish and Catalan

Visas
Not required for US, Canadian, Australian, New Zealand or South African visitors for up to 90 days. European Union nationals can stay indefinitely.

Money
ATMs widely available. Credit cards accepted in most hotels, shops and restaurants.

Mobile Phones
Local SIM cards can be used in unlocked European and Australian phones. Set other phones to roaming.

Time
Central European Time (GMT/UTC plus one hour)

Wi-Fi
Common in midrange and top-end hotels, hostels and some cafes. Usually free.

Tipping
A service charge is usually included. For top-end places, it's common to tip 5% to 10%.

For more information, see Survival Guide (p227).

When to Go

Barcelona

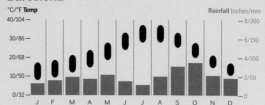

Spring (Mar–May) For pleasant weather, come in late spring.
Summer (Jun–Aug) Peak tourist season. Crowds swarm the city.
Autumn (Sep–Nov) Warm but pleasant. October can be rainy.
Winter (Dec–Feb) Expect cool blue skies. Snowfall is very rare.

Advance Planning

Two months before Reserve a table at a top restaurant. Buy tickets for important football matches.

One month before Check out reviews for theatre and live music and book tickets.

One week before Browse the latest nightlife listings, art exhibitions and other events to attend while in town. Reserve spa visits and organised tours.

A few days before Check the forecast on weather.com.

Your Daily Budget

Budget under €50
- Dorm beds €15–€25
- Set lunches from €9
- Free museums on Sundays

Midrange €50–€200
- Standard double room €80–€120
- Two-course dinner with wine for two €50
- Walking and guided tours €15–€25

Top end over €200
- Boutique and luxury hotels €200 and up
- Multi-course meal at top restaurants €80 per person
- Concert tickets to Palau de la Música Catalana around €50

Arriving in Barcelona

El Prat Airport Frequent Aerobuses make the 35-minute run into town (€5.65) from 6am to 1am. Taxis cost around €25. Train operator Renfe runs the R2 Nord line every half hour from the airport to Estació Sants and Passeig de Gràcia in central Barcelona.

Estació Sants Long-distance trains arrive at this big station near the centre of town, which is linked by metro to other parts of the city.

Estació del Nord The long-haul bus station is in L'Eixample, about 1.5km northeast of Plaça de Catalunya. It's a short walk from several metro stations.

Getting Around

Metro The most convenient way to get around. Runs from 5am to midnight Sunday through Thursday, to 2am on Friday and 24 hours on Saturday. Targeta T-10 (10-ride passes) are the best value at €9.25. Otherwise it's €2 per ride.

Bus The hop-on, hop-off Bus Turístic, which leaves from Plaça de Catalunya, is handy for those wanting to see the city's highlights in one or two days.

Walking For exploring the old town, all you need is a good pair of walking shoes.

Sleeping

Barcelona has a wide range of sleeping options from inexpensive hostels hidden in the old quarter to luxury hotels overlooking the waterfront. Good-value options include small-scale B&B-style apartment rentals scattered around the city. Typical prices for a midrange room for two people runs from about €80 to €120 per night. Wherever you stay it's wise to book well ahead. If you plan to travel around holidays like Christmas, New Year's Eve, Easter or in the summer months, reserve a room three or four months ahead of time.

Useful Websites

o **Airbnb** (www.airbnb.com) The global network has hundreds of rooms and apartments listed for Barcelona.

o **Oh-Barcelona** (www.oh-barcelona.com) Selection of good-value hotels, hostels and apartment rentals.

o **Barcelona 30** (www.barcelona30.com) Economical options for staying on a budget.

What to Bring

o **An appetite for fresh seafood and excellent, inexpensive wines**

o **A Catalan phrasebook** Although you can get by in Spanish (and English in many parts), Catalans really appreciate the effort.

o **A rain jacket** Especially if you come in early spring or in the autumn.

Be Forewarned

o **Theft** Petty theft is a major problem in the city centre. Be vigilant and keep a close guard on your possessions.

o **Areas to avoid** El Raval can be a little sketchy late at night, particularly in the southern part of the neighbourhood.

o **Seasons** Locals disappear in August, with many restaurants and shops closing or keeping limited hours.

o **Crowds** Prepare for heavy tourist crowds if coming in the summer.

La Rambla & Barri Gòtic

Packed with historic treasures, Barri Gòtic is one of Europe's most atmospheric neighbourhoods. Its tangle of narrow lanes and tranquil plazas lie amid Roman ruins, medieval churches and converted palaces, with history lurking around every lamplit corner. There are swarms of tourists afoot, but these cobbled streets have plenty of local character, with first-rate restaurants, creative boutiques and a vibrant nightlife keeping things buzzing until early in the morning.

Nearby, La Rambla is Spain's most talked-about boulevard. It certainly packs a lot of colour into a short walk, with flower stands, historic buildings, a sensory-rich food market, overpriced beers, tourist tat and a ceaselessly changing parade of people from all corners of the globe. Once a river and sewage ditch on the edge of medieval Barcelona, it still marks the southwest flank of Barri Gòtic.

Plaça Reial (p57)

La Rambla & Barri Gòtic Highlights

Strolling La Rambla (p52)

Snaking its way through the Ciutat Vella, this 1.2km-long boulevard is always awhirl with activity. There are street performers, food and drink stalls, souvenir stands and a pastiche of architectural intrigue lining both sides of the street. Come early in the morning to see La Rambla at its most serene, then return later to the people-packed lane to see it in all its carnivalesque glory.

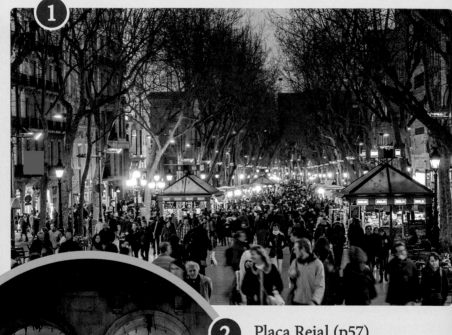

Plaça Reial (p57)

The elegant Plaça Reial is wonderfully recuperative after wandering the narrow, sometimes pungent streets of the medieval quarter. Outdoor cafes and restaurants set beneath the arcades draw a relaxed crowd by day, while after dark the plaza becomes a hidden hive of candlelit restaurants and clubs. A trickling fountain, intricately sculpted street lamps and occasional live music sets the scene.

Museu d'Història de Barcelona (p67) **3**

More subterranean adventure trail than stash of dusty exhibits, this museum takes visitors on a journey through time. Start in ancient Roman-era Barcino and stroll past fragments of old bathhouses, laundrettes and wine-making stores. Then wind your way up through the centuries past Visigothic ruins, picture-perfect Gothic halls and medieval chapels.

ANNA SERRANO / SIME / 4CORNERS ©

JUERGEN RICHTER / GETTY IMAGES ©

4 La Catedral (p54)

La Catedral de la Santa Creu i Santa Eulàlia is a riot of Gothic and gargoyles, high altars and murky crypts, Catalan legends and 13 resident geese. Like many Spanish churches, it is a hybrid – the 14th-century shell has been overlaid by a 19th-century neo-Gothic facade – a factor that makes it all the more fascinating and enigmatic. Don't miss the superb view from the rooftop.

5 Plaça de Sant Jaume (p56)

The epicentre of the historic Ciutat Vella (Old City), this plaza has been an essential part of civic life since the Romans erected a forum here 2000 years ago. Several key government buildings continue to play a role in political affairs, including the Ajuntament, where Barcelona's first ruling council met in the 1300s. By day, the buzzing plaza brings a mishmash of bureaucrats, protestors and gawking tourists.

Plaça de Sant Jaume during Festes de la Mercè (p41)

La Rambla & Barri Gòtic Walk

This scenic walk through the Barri Gòtic will take you back in time to the early days of Roman-era Barcino. Amid architectural treasures from previous centuries, you'll pass picturesque plazas, looming Gothic churches and an atmospheric quarter once the centre of a medieval Jewish quarter.

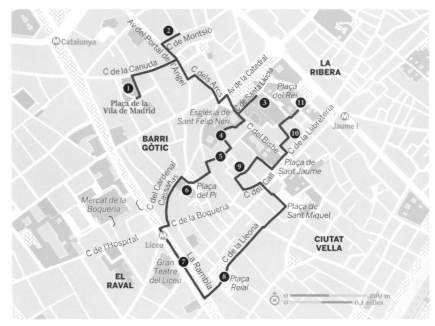

WALK FACTS

- **Start** Plaça de la Vila de Madrid
- **Finish** Plaça del Rei
- **Distance** 2.5km
- **Duration** Two hours

❶ Roman Tombs

On Plaça de la Vila de Madrid is a sunken garden with various **Roman tombs** (p61). It was customary to line highways leading out of cities with tombs and it's believed this road connected Roman Barcino with the Via Augusta, which linked Rome and Cádiz.

❷ Els Quatre Gats

Next, head over to one of the few Modernista buildings in the Gothic quarter. **'The Four Cats'** restaurant, started life as Casa Martí. From 1897 to 1903, it was the hang-out for bohemians and artists, including Picasso.

❸ La Catedral

Head down Avinguda del Portal de l'Angel to the magnificent **cathedral** (p54). Before entering, look at the three Picasso friezes on the building facing the square.

❹ Plaça de Sant Felip Neri

Enter the former gates of the ancient fortified city and turn right into **Plaça de Sant**

Felip Neri. Note the shrapnel-scarred walls of the **old church**, damaged by pro-Francist bombers in 1939.

⑤ Santa Eulàlia

Head out of the square and turn right. On this narrow lane, you'll spot a small **statue** of Santa Eulàlia (p205), one of Barcelona's patron saints. Martyred by the Romans, she allegedly suffered numerous tortures.

⑥ Església de Santa Maria del Pi

Make your way west to the 14th-century **Església de Santa Maria del Pi** (p57), which is famed for its magnificent rose window. Adjacent to the church are two serene plazas with outdoor cafes.

⑦ La Rambla

Continue west to Barcelona's liveliest **pedestrian boulevard** (p52). As you stroll south, you'll walk over a striking **Miró mural** and pass the **Gran Teatre del Liceu**, Barcelona's famous opera house.

⑧ Plaça Reial

Turn down the small lane leading into **Plaça Reial** (p57), one of Barcelona's prettiest squares.

⑨ Sinagoga Major

Make your way northeast to the atmospheric, narrow lanes of **El Call**, the medieval Jewish quarter until a bloody pogrom of 1391. The **Sinagoga Major** (p61), one of Europe's oldest, was discovered in 1996.

⑩ Roman Temple

Head across Plaça de Sant Jaume and turn left after Carrer del Bisbe. You'll soon pass the remnants of a **Roman temple**, with four columns hidden in a small courtyard.

⑪ Plaça del Rei

The final stop is **Plaça del Rei**. The former palace houses a superb **history museum** (p67), which boasts significant Roman ruins underground.

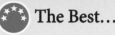 **The Best...**

PLACES TO EAT

Pla Mouth-watering fusion fare in a spacious medieval dining room. (p62)

La Vinateria dell Call An atmospheric setting for classic Catalan and Mediterranean cooking in El Call. (p63)

Koy Shunka Artfully prepared Japanese cuisine is worth a splurge – especially the 11-course *menú degustación*. (p63)

Can Culleretes Barcelona's oldest dining room is a mural-filled classic straight from the 18th century. (p63)

PLACES TO DRINK

Oviso Bohemian drinking den on Plaça de George Orwell. (p64)

Čaj Chai Charming cafe hidden away in El Call. (p65)

Marula Cafe A small soul-loving dance spot. (p65)

HISTORICAL TREASURES

Temple Romà d'August Mighty columns from a once great empire. (p61)

Via Sepulcral Romana Funereal markers from the days of Barcino. (p61)

Sinagoga Major A tiny medieval synagogue attests to a once flourishing Jewish quarter. (p61)

Els Quatre Gats
LONELY PLANET / GETTY IMAGES ©

Flanked by narrow traffic lanes and plane trees, the middle of La Rambla is a broad pedestrian boulevard, crowded every day until the wee hours with a cross-section of *barcelonins* (people of Barcelona) and out-of-towners. Dotted with cafes, restaurants, kiosks and news stands, and enlivened by buskers, pavement artists, mimes and living statues, La Rambla rarely allows a dull moment.

Map p58

M Catalunya, Liceu or Drassanes

La Rambla de Canaletes

The stretch from Plaça de Catalunya is La Rambla de Canaletes, named after an inconspicuous turn-of-the-20th-century **drinking fountain**, the water of which supposedly emerges from what were once known as the springs of Canaletes. It used to be said that *barcelonins* 'drank the waters of Les Canaletes'. People claim that anyone who drinks from the fountain will return to Barcelona. Delirious football fans gather here to celebrate whenever the main home side, FC Barcelona, wins a cup or the league premiership.

Església de Betlem

Just north of Carrer del Carme, this **church** was constructed in baroque style for the Jesuits in the late 17th and early 18th centuries to replace an earlier church destroyed by fire in 1671. Fire was a bit of a theme for this site: the church was once considered the most splendid of Barcelona's few baroque offerings, but leftist arsonists torched it in 1936.

Palau Moia

Looming over the eastern side of La Rambla, **Palau Moja** is a rare pure neo-classical pile. Its classical lines are best appreciated from across La Rambla.

Palau de la Virreina

The **Palau de la Virreina** is a grand 18th-century rococo mansion (with some neoclassical elements) that houses a municipal arts-and-entertainment information and ticket office. It's home to the **Centre de la Imatge**, which has rotating photography exhibits. Admission prices and opening hours vary.

Mosaïc de Miró

At Plaça de la Boqueria, where four side streets meet just north of Liceu Metro station, you can walk all over a Miró – the colourful **mosaic** in the pavement. Miró chose this site since it's near the house where he was born on the Passatge del Crèdit. The mosaic's bold colors and vivid swirling forms are instantly recognisable to Miró fans, but plenty of tourists stroll right over it without noticing it. Near the bottom of the work, there's one tile signed by the artist.

La Rambla dels Caputxins

Named after a now nonexistent monastery, this stretch of La Rambla runs from Plaça de la Boqueria to Carrer dels Escudellers. The latter street is named after the potters' guild, founded in the 13th century, whose members lived and worked here. On the western side of La Rambla is the Gran Teatre del Liceu (p57). Further south on the eastern side is the entrance to the palm-shaded Plaça Reial (p57).

La Rambla de Santa Mònica

The final stretch of La Rambla widens out to approach the Mirador de Colom overlooking Port Vell. La Rambla here is named after the Convent de Santa Mònica, which once stood on the western flank of the street. It has since been converted into an art gallery and cultural centre, the **Centre d'Art Santa Mònica**, which tends to exhibit modern, multimedia installations; admission is free.

Civil War & La Rambla

La Rambla saw action during the Civil War. Orwell vividly described the avenue gripped by revolutionary fervour in the early days of the war: 'Down the Ramblas, the wide central artery of the town where crowds of people streamed constantly to and fro, the loud-speakers were bellowing revolutionary songs all day and far into the night...There was much in it that I did not understand, in some ways I did not even like it, but I recognised it immediately as a state of affairs worth fighting for.' Later in the war, heavy street fighting took place on La Rambla. Anarchists even shot at Orwell while he was dashing across La Rambla.

Don't Miss
La Catedral

Approached from the broad Avinguda de la Catedral, Barcelona's central place of worship presents a magnificent image. The richly decorated main (northwest) facade, laced with gargoyles and the stone intricacies you would expect of northern European Gothic, sets it quite apart from other churches in Barcelona. The facade was actually added in 1870, but it's based on a 1408 design. The rest of the building was built between 1298 and 1460. The other facades are sparse in decoration, and the octagonal, flat-roofed towers are a clear reminder that, even here, Catalan Gothic architectural principles prevailed.

Map p58

☎ 93 342 82 60

www.website.es/catedralbcn

Plaça de la Seu

admission free, special visit €5, coro admission €2.20

🕐 8am-12.45pm & 5.15-8pm Mon-Sat, special visit 1-5pm Mon-Sat, 2-5pm Sun & holidays

Ⓜ Jaume I

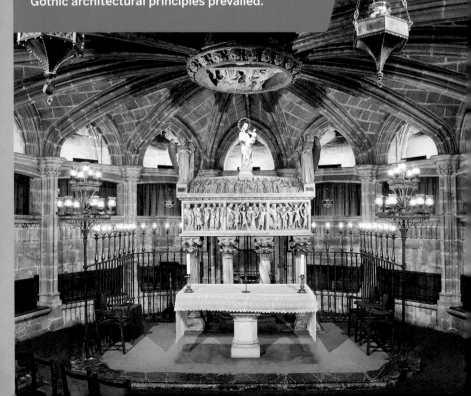

Choir

In the middle of the central nave is the late-14th-century exquisitely sculpted timber *coro* (choir stalls). The coats of arms on the stalls belong to members of the Barcelona chapter of the Order of the Golden Fleece. Emperor Carlos V presided over the order's meeting here in 1519. Take the time to look at the craft up close; the Virgin Mary and Child depicted on the pulpit are especially fine.

Rooftop View

With so much going on inside, it's easy to forget the outside. The roof is notable not just for the views of medieval Barcelona but also for the opportunity to evaluate the cathedral's huge footprint from above. Access to the higher echelons is gained via a lift from the Capella de les Animes del Purgatori near the northeast transept.

Geese

The Tower of London has ravens; Barcelona's Catedral has geese. The 13 birds in the leafy *claustre* (cloister) supposedly represent the age of Santa Eulàlia at the time of her martyrdom and have, generation after generation, been squawking here since medieval days. They make fine watchdogs!

Crypt

Here lies the hallowed tomb of Santa Eulàlia, one of Barcelona's two patron saints, more affectionately known as Laia. The reliefs on the alabaster sarcophagus, executed by Pisan artisans, recount some of her tortures and, along the top strip, the removal of her body to its present resting place.

Baptismal Font

Columbus purportedly kidnapped two dozen North American Indians from the Caribbean island of Hispaniola after his first voyage and brought them back to Spain. Only six survived the journey and, according to legend, they were bathed in holy water at this font just left from the main entrance.

Don't Miss List

BY GORKA REGIDOR, TOUR GUIDE AND FOUNDER OF RUNNER BEAN TOURS

1 CRYPT OF SANTA EULÀLIA
References to the patron saint of Barcelona can be found all over the cathedral but nowhere is as striking as in the crypt. In the centre, an Italian 15th-century alabaster sarcophagus stands where Eulàlia's remains supposedly still lie within. The crypt only opens on the 12 February, Saint Eulàlia's Day, but you can take a peek from the outside. Add 50 céntimos to the box and let the place light up for a more intimate experience.

2 MAIN NAVE
If there is an organ concert going on, sit down on one of the benches, relax and wonder at the magnificence of this Catalan Gothic stone masterpiece. The sounds from the 15th-century carved wooden organ surround the whole place with magic and mystery.

3 THE CHOIR
In 1519, the Order of the Golden Fleece, the elite of Europe's nobility, were invited to Barcelona by the king of Spain, Charles I. A visit to the cloister is a voyage to old times with the coat of arms of each participant painted on the back of the chairs. Try to find Henry VIII of England!

4 CLOISTER
A glimpse of Paradise where the 13 geese in honour of Saint Eulàlia live. While you walk around, look at the tombstones on the floor and find shoes, scissors and the different symbols of the medieval guilds (including shoemakers, tailors and carpenters). If you are here during the Corpus Christi, marvel at one of Barcelona's most popular traditions: the *Ou Com Balla* (dancing egg).

5 EXTERIOR GARGOYLES
There are 160 different gargoyles in the cathedral. Always a good excuse to lift your eyes to the sky and discover not only the obvious dragons and mythological beasts, but also elephants, unicorns and medieval warriors. Great for the young ones and for the not so young.

Discover La Rambla & Barri Gòtic

Getting There & Away

○ **Metro** Key stops near or on La Rambla include Catalunya, Liceu and Drassanes. For Barri Gòtic's east side, Jaume I and Urquinaona are handiest.

○ **Bus** Airport and night buses arrive and depart from Plaça Catalunya.

○ **Taxi** Easiest to catch on La Rambla or Plaça Catalunya.

St George's Door at Palau del Lloctinent; sculptor: Josep Maria Subirachs

◉ Sights

La Rambla   Street
See p52.

La Catedral   Church
See p54.

FREE **Palau del Lloctinent**   Historic Site
(Carrer dels Comtes; ⊙10am-7pm; Ⓜ Jaume I) This converted 16th-century palace has a peaceful courtyard worth wandering through. Have a look upwards from the main staircase to admire the extraordinary timber *artesonado,* a sculpted ceiling made to seem like the upturned hull of a boat. It was done in the 16th century by Antoni Carbonell. Exhibitions, usually related in some way to the archives, are sometimes staged.

Museu Diocesà   Museum
(Casa de la Pia Almoina; ☎93 315 22 13; www.arqbcn.org; Avinguda de la Catedral 4; adult/child €6/3; ⊙10am-2pm & 5-8pm Tue-Sat, 11am-2pm Sun; Ⓜ Jaume I) The city's main centre of charity was located here in the 11th century, although the much-crumbled remains of the present building date to the 15th century. Today it houses the Diocesan Museum, which has a small exhibit on Gaudí (including a fascinating documentary on his life and philosophy) on the top floor. There's also a sparse collection of medieval religious art usually supplemented by a temporary exhibition or two.

Plaça de Sant Jaume   Square
(Ⓜ Liceu or Jaume I) In the 2000 or so years since the Romans settled here, the area

around this square (often remodelled), which started life as the forum, has been the focus of Barcelona's civic life. Facing each other across it are the Palau de la Generalitat (seat of Catalonia's regional government) on the north side and the Ajuntament (town hall) to the south. Behind the Ajuntament rise the awful town hall offices built in the 1970s over Plaça de Sant Miquel. Opposite is a rare 15th-century gem, Casa Centelles, on the corner of Baixada de Sant Miquel. You can wander into the fine Gothic-Renaissance courtyard if the gates are open.

Ajuntament   Architecture
(📞93 402 70 00; www.bcn.cat; Plaça de Sant Jaune; 🕙10.30am-1.30pm Sun; Ⓜ️Liceu or Jaume I) The Ajuntament, otherwise known as the Casa de la Ciutat, has been the seat of power for centuries. The Consell de Cent (the city's ruling council) first sat here in the 14th century, but the building has lamentably undergone many changes since the days of Barcelona's Gothic-era splendour.

Palau de la Generalitat   Palace
(www.gencat.cat; Plaça de Sant Jaune; Ⓜ️Liceu or Jaume I) Founded in the early 15th century, the Palau de la Generalitat is open on limited occasions only (the second and fourth weekends of the month, plus open-door days). The most impressive of the ceremonial halls is the **Saló de Sant Jordi**, named after St George, the region's patron saint. At any time, however, you can admire the original Gothic main entrance on Carrer del Bisbe. To join weekend visits, book on the website.

Museu d'Idees i
Invents de Barcelona   Museum
(Museum of Ideas and Inventions; 📞93 332 79 30; www.mibamuseum.com; Carrer de la Ciutat 7; adult/child €7/5; 🕙10am-7pm Tue-Sat, to 2pm Sun; Ⓜ️Jaume I) New in 2011, this museum has a fascinating collection of curiosities from the world of both brilliant and bizarre inventions: mops with microphones on the handle (so you can sing while you work), a seat for inserting suppositories, mugs with biscuit storage, wristbands

that measure UV rays and eyeglasses adjustable to any prescription.

Plaça de Sant Josep Oriol   Square
(Ⓜ️Liceu) This small plaza is the prettiest in the Barri Gòtic. Its bars and cafes attract buskers and artists and make it a lively place to hang out. It is surrounded by quaint streets, many dotted with appealing cafes, restaurants and shops. Looming over the square is the flank of the **Església de Santa Maria del Pi** (🕙9.30am-1pm & 5-8.30pm; Ⓜ️Liceu), a Gothic church built in the 14th to 16th centuries. With its 10m diameter, the beautiful rose window above its entrance on Plaça del Pi is claimed by some to be the world's biggest.

Plaça Reial   Square
(Ⓜ️Liceu) One of Barcelona's most photogenic squares, Plaça Reial is a delightful retreat from the traffic and pedestrian mobs on La Rambla. Numerous eateries, bars and nightspots lie beneath the arcades of 19th-century neoclassical buildings, with a buzz of activity at all hours. The lamp posts by the fountain are Antoni Gaudí's first known works in the city.

Gran Teatre del Liceu   Architecture
(📞93 485 99 14; www.liceubarcelona.com; La Rambla dels Caputxins 51-59; 🕙guided tour 10am, unguided visits 11.30am, noon, 12.30pm & 1pm; Ⓜ️Liceu) If you can't catch a night at the opera, you can still have a look around one of Europe's greatest opera houses, known to locals as the Liceu. Built in 1847, the Liceu launched such Catalan stars as Josep (aka José) Carreras and Montserrat Caballé. Fire virtually destroyed it in 1994, but city authorities were quick to get it back into operation. Carefully reconstructing the 19th-century auditorium and installing the latest in theatre technology, technicians brought the Liceu back to life in October 1999. You can take a 20-minute quick turn around the main public areas of the theatre or join a one-hour guided tour.

Mirador de Colom   Viewpoint
(📞93 302 52 24; Plaça del Portal de la Pau; lift adult/child €4/3; 🕙8.30am-8.30pm;

58

La Rambla & Barri Gòtic

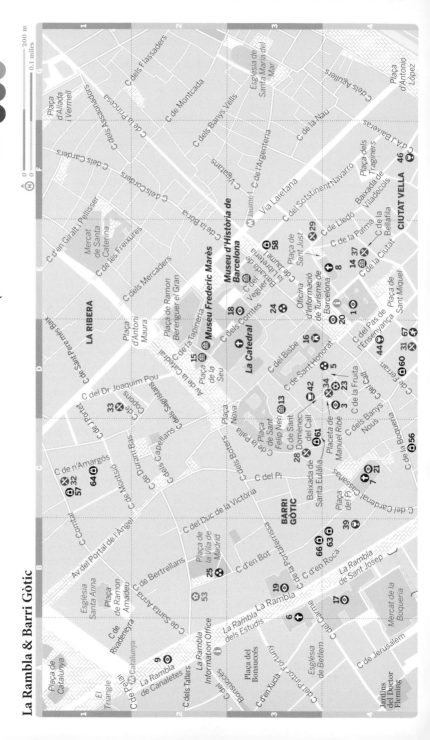

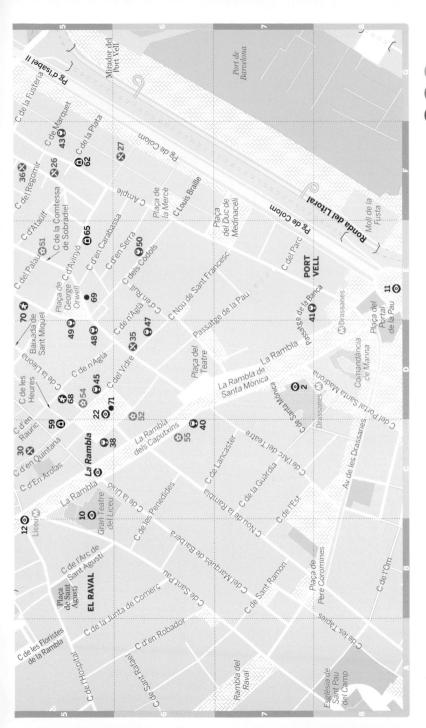

EL RAVAL

PORT
VELL

Port de
Barcelona

Ronda del Litoral

Pg de Colom

Moll de la
Fusta

Mirador del
Port Vell

Pg d'Isabel II

C de la Fusteria

C de Marquet

C de la Plata

Pg de Colom

Plaça de
la Mercè

C Louis Braille

Plaça del
Duc de
Medinaceli

C del Regomir

C d'Atauir

C de la Comtessa
de Sobradiel

C d'Avinyó

C d'en Carabassa

C d'en Serra

C dels Còdols

C Nou de Sant Francesc

Passatge de la Pau

C del Parc

Passatge de la Banca

Plaça del
Portal
de la Pau

C del Palau

Plaça de
George
Orwell

C del Rull

C d'en Agla

Baixada de
Sant Miquel

C de les
Heures

C de la Lleona

C de n'Agla

C del Vidre

Plaça del
Teatre

La Rambla

La Rambla de
Santa Mònica

C del Portal Santa Madrona

Comandància
de Marina

Drassanes

Av de les Drassanes

C d'en
Rauric

C d'en Quintana

C d'En Arolas

C de la Unió

Gran Teatre
del Liceu

C de les Penedides

C Nou de la Rambla

C de l'Arc del Teatre

C de la Guàrdia

C de l'Est

Plaça de
Pere Coromines

C de l'Om

La Rambla

La Rambla
dels Caputxins

C de Lancaster

Liceu

Plaça
de Sant
Agustí

C de l'Arc de
Sant Agustí

C de Sant Pau

C del Marquès de Barberà

C de Sant Ramon

C de les Floristes
de la Rambla

C de l'Hospital

C de la Junta de Comerç

C d'en Robador

C de Sant Rafael

Rambla del
Raval

C de les Tàpies

Església de
Sant Pau
del Camp

La Rambla & Barri Gòtic

Ⓜ Drassanes) High above the swirl of traffic on the roundabout below, Columbus keeps permanent watch, pointing vaguely out to the Mediterranean. Built for the Universal Exhibition in 1888, the monument allows you to zip up 60m in the lift for bird's-eye views back up La Rambla and across the ports of Barcelona.

Església de Sants Just i Pastor
Church

(☏ 93 301 74 33; www.basilicasantjust.cat; Plaça de Sant Just 5; ⊙ 11am-2pm & 5.30-8pm

Mon-Sat, 10am-1pm Sun; Ⓜ Liceu or Jaume I)
This somewhat neglected, single-nave
church, with chapels on either side of the
buttressing, was built in 1342 in Catalan
Gothic style on what is reputedly the site
of the oldest parish church in Barcelona.
Inside, you can admire some fine stained-
glass windows.

FREE Centre d'Interpretació
del Call   Historic Site
(☑ 93 256 21 22; www.museuhistoria.bcn.cat;
Placeta de Manuel Ribé; ☺ 11am-2pm Tue-Fri,
to 7pm Sat & Sun; Ⓜ Jaume I or Liceu) Once a
14th-century house of the Jewish weaver
Jucef Bonhiac, this small visitors centre
is dedicated to the history of Barcelona's
Jewish quarter, the Call.

Sinagoga Major   Synagogue
(☑ 93 317 07 90; www.calldebarcelona.org;
Carrer de Marlet 5; admission by suggested
donation €2.50 ; ☺ 10.30am-6.30pm Mon-Fri, to
2.30pm Sat & Sun; Ⓜ Liceu) In the heart of El
Call – Barcelona's medieval Jewish quarter
– this was one of four synagogues in the
medieval city. Fragments of medieval
and Roman-era walls remain in the small
vaulted space that you enter from the
street. Also remaining are tanners' wells
installed in the 15th century. The second
chamber has been spruced up for use as
a synagogue. A remnant of late-Roman-
era wall here, given its orientation facing
Jerusalem, has led some to speculate
that there was a synagogue here even in
Roman times.

FREE Temple Romà d'August   Ruin
(Carrer del Paradis; ☺ 10am-8pm Tue-Sun;
Ⓜ Jaume I) Opposite the southeast end of
La Catedral, narrow Carrer del Paradis
leads towards Plaça de Sant Jaume. Inside
No 10, itself an intriguing building with
Gothic and baroque touches, are four
columns and the architrave of Barcelona's
main Roman temple, dedicated to Caesar
Augustus and built to worship his imperial

highness in the 1st century AD. You are
now standing on the highest point of Roman Barcino, Mont Tàber (a grand total of
16.9m, unlikely to induce altitude sickness).

Via Sepulcral
Romana   Archaeological Site
(☑ 93 256 21 00; www.museuhistoria.bcn.cat;
Plaça de la Vila de Madrid; admission €2; ☺ 11am-
2pm Tue-Fri, to 7pm Sat & Sun; Ⓜ Catalunya)
Along Carrer de la Canuda, a block east
of the top end of La Rambla, is a sunken
garden where a series of Roman tombs
lies exposed. The burial ground stretches
along either side of the road that led
northwest out of Barcelona's Roman
predecessor, Barcino. Roman law forbade
burial within city limits and so everyone,
the great and humble, were generally
buried along roads leading out of cities.

Domus Romana   Archaeological Site
(☑ 93 256 21 00; www.museuhistoria.bcn.cat;
Carrer de la Fruita 2; admission €2; ☺ 10am-
2pm Sat & Sun; Ⓜ Liceu) The remains of a
Roman *domus* (town house) have been
unearthed and opened to the public. The
house lay close to the Roman forum and
the owners were clearly well off. Apart
from getting something of an idea of daily
Roman life through these remains, the
location also contains six medieval grain
silos installed when the Jewish quarter,
the Call, was located in this area.

Museu del Calçat   Museum
(Footwear Museum; ☑ 93 301 45 33; Plaça de
Sant Felip Neri 5; admission €2.50; ☺ 11am-2pm
Tue-Sun; Ⓜ Jaume I) This obscure museum is
home to everything from Egyptian sandals
to dainty ladies' shoes of the 18th century.
The museum and cobblers' guild, which
has its roots in the city's medieval past,
were moved here shortly after the civil war.

BARBARA BOENSCH / IMAGEBROKER ©

 Don't Miss
Museu Frederic Marès

One of the wildest collections of historical curios lies inside this vast medieval complex, once part of the royal palace of the counts of Barcelona. Frederic Marès i Deulovol (1893-1991) was a rich sculptor, traveller and obsessive collector. He specialised in medieval Spanish sculpture, huge quantities of which are displayed in the basement and on the ground and 1st floors – including some lovely polychrome wooden sculptures of the Crucifixion and the Virgin.

The top two floors comprise 'the collector's cabinet', a mind-boggling array of knick-knacks: medieval weaponry, finely carved pipes, delicate ladies fans, intricate 'floral' displays made of seashells and 19th-century daguerreotypes and photographs. A room that once served as Marès' study and library is now crammed with sculpture. The shady courtyard houses a pleasant summer cafe (Cafè de l'Estiu) worth a visit after browsing the collections.

NEED TO KNOW

📞 93 256 35 00; www.museumares.bcn.es; Plaça de Sant Iu 5; admission €4.20, after 3pm Sun & 1st Sun of month free; ⏰10am-7pm Tue-Sat, 11am-8pm Sun; Ⓜ Jaume I

Eating

La Rambla is fine for people-watching, but no great shakes for the palate. Instead venture off into the streets that wind into the Barri Gòtic and your belly (and wallet)

will be eternally grateful. Inside the medieval labyrinth, choices abound.

Pla   Fusion €€
(📞 93 412 65 52; www.elpla.cat; Carrer de la Bellafila 5; mains €18-24; ⏰dinner; 🖊; Ⓜ Jaume I)
One of Gòtic's long-standing favourites, Pla is a stylish, romantically lit medieval

den (with a huge stone arch) where the cooks churn out such temptations as oxtail braised in red wine, seared tuna with roasted aubergine, and 'Thai-style' monkfish with prawns, lemongrass and apple foam. It has a tasting menu for €36 Sunday to Thursday.

La Vinateria dell Call   Spanish €€

(☎ 93 302 60 92; http://lavinateriadelcall.com; Carrer de Sant Domènec del Call 9; small plates €7-11; ⏱ dinner; Ⓜ Jaume I) In a magical setting in the former Jewish quarter, this tiny jewelbox of a restaurant serves up tasty Iberian dishes including Galician octopus, cider-cooked chorizo and the Catalan *escalivada* (roasted peppers, aubergine and onions) with anchovies. Portions are small and made for sharing, and there's a good and affordable selection of wines.

Koy Shunka   Japanese €€€

(☎ 93 412 79 39; www.koyshunka.com; Carrer de Copons 7; multicourse menus €72-108; ⏱ lunch Tue-Sun, dinner Tue-Sat; Ⓜ Urquinaona) Down a narrow lane north of the Cathedral, Koy Shunka opens a portal to exquisite dishes from the East – mouth-watering sushi, sashimi, seared Wagyu beef and flavour-rich seaweed salads are served alongside inventive cooked fushion dishes like *almejas finas al vapor con sake* (steamed clams with sake) or *tempura de vieira y langostino con setas de japonesas* (tempura of scallops and king prawns with Japanese mushrooms). Don't miss the house specialty of *toro* (tender tuna belly).

Can Culleretes   Catalan €€

(☎ 93 317 30 22; Carrer Quintana 5; mains €8-14; ⏱ lunch & dinner Tue-Sat, lunch Sun; Ⓜ Liceu) Founded in 1786, Barcelona's oldest restaurant is still going strong, with tourists and locals flocking to enjoy its rambling interior, old-fashioned tile-filled decor, and enormous helpings of traditional Catalan food. The multicourse lunch specials (€12.80) are good value.

Cafè de l'Acadèmia   Catalan €€

(☎ 93 319 82 53; Carrer de Lledó 1; mains €13-17; ⏱ Mon-Fri; Ⓜ Jaume I) Expect a mix of traditional dishes with creative twists. At lunchtime, Ajuntament (town hall) office workers pounce on the *menú del día* (€14, or €10 at the bar). Later, it is more romantic, as low lighting emphasises the intimacy of the timber ceiling and wooden decor. Offerings range from *chuletón* (huge T-bone steak) for two to *guatlla farcida de foie d'ànec i botifarra amb salsa de ceps* (quail stuffed with duck foie gras and sausage with a mushroom sauce).

Cererìa   Vegetarian €€

(☎ 93 301 85 10; Baixada de Sant Miquel 3; mains €9-16; ⏱ dinner Mon-Sat; 🛜 🚭; Ⓜ Jaume I) Black-and-white marble floors, a smattering of old wooden tables and ramshackle displays of instruments (most made on-site) lend a certain bohemian charm to this small vegetarian restaurant. The pizzas are delicious here, and feature organic ingredients – as do the flavourful galettes, dessert crêpes and bountiful salads.

Cervecería Taller de Tapas   Spanish €€

(☎ 93 481 62 33; Carrer Comtal 28; mains €8-15; ⏱ 10am-midnight Mon-Sat, from noon Sun; Ⓜ Urquinaona) Amid white stone walls and a beamed ceiling, this buzzing, easygoing place serves a broad selection of tapas as well as changing daily specials like *cochinillo* (roast suckling pig). A smattering of beers from across the globe – Leffe Blond, Guinness, Brahma (Brazil) and Sol (Mexico) – add to the appeal.

Agut   Catalan €€

(www.restaurantagut.com; Carrer d'en Gignàs 16; mains €16-25; ⏱ lunch & dinner Tue-Sat, lunch Sun; Ⓜ Drassanes) Deep in the Gothic labyrinth lies this classic eatery. A series of cosy dining areas is connected by broad arches while, high up, the walls are tightly lined by artworks. There's art in what the kitchen serves up too, from the oak-grilled meat to a succulent variety of seafood offerings, like the *cassoleta de rap a l'all cremat amb cloïsses* (monkfish with browned garlic and clams).

Los Caracoles   Spanish €€

(☎ 93 301 20 41; www.los-caracoles.es; Carrer dels Escudellers 14; mains €13-32; Ⓜ Drassanes) Run by the fifth generation of the Bofarull family, 'The Snails' started life as a tavern

in 1835 and is one of Barcelona's best-known restaurants. Several interlocking rooms (consider asking for the small medieval-looking banquet room), with centuries of history seemingly greased into the tables and garlic-clad walls, may distract you from the house specialities: rotisserie chickens and snails.

Bar Celta
Galician €€

(Carrer de la Mercè 16; tapas €3-6; ⌚noon-midnight Tue-Sun; **M**Drassanes) This bright, rambunctious tapas bar specialises in *pulpo* (octopus) and other sea critters like *navajas* (razor clams). Even the most demanding of Galician natives give this spot the thumbs up. Sit at the bar, order a bottle of Ribeiro and the traditional Galician *tazas* (little white cups) and tuck into your *raciones* (larger portions of tapas dishes).

Caelum
Cafe €

(☎93 302 69 93; Carrer de la Palla 8; snacks €2-4; ⌚10.30am-8.30pm Mon-Thu, 10.30am-11.30pm Fri & Sat, 11.30am-9pm Sun; **M**Liceu) Centuries of heavenly gastronomic tradi-

tion from across Spain are concentrated in this exquisite medieval space in the heart of the city. There's also an atmospheric underground chamber where you can secret yourself for tea and pastries from 3.30pm to closing time.

Milk
Brunch €

(www.milkbarcelona.com; Carrer d'en Gignàs 21; mains €9-10; ⌚10am-4pm & 6.30-11.30pm; **M**Jaume I) Also known to many as a cool cocktail spot, the Irish-run Milk's key role for Barcelona night owls is providing morning-after brunches (served till 4pm). Avoid direct sunlight and tuck into pancakes, eggs Benedict and other hangover dishes in a small but cosy setting.

♀ Drinking & Nightlife

Oviso
Bar

(Carrer d'Arai 5; ⌚10am-2am; **M**Liceu) Oviso is a popular budget-friendly restaurant

with outdoor tables on the plaza, but shows its true bohemian colours by night, with a wildly mixed crowd, a rock-and-roll vibe and a two-room fin de siècle interior plastered with curious murals – geese taking flight, leaping dolphins and blue peacocks framing a bright red wall.

La Cerveteca
Bar

(Carrer de Gignàs 25; ⏱4-10pm Mon-Thu, 1-11pm Fri & Sat, 1-10pm Sun; ⓜJaume I) An unmissable stop for beer lovers, La Cerveteca serves an impressive variety of global craft brews. In addition to scores of bottled brews, there's a frequent rotation of what's on draught.

Čaj Chai
Cafe

(☎93 301 95 92; Carrer de Sant Domènec del Call 12; ⏱3-10pm Mon, 10.30am-10pm Tue-Sun; ⓜJaume I) Inspired by Prague's bohemian tearooms, this bright and buzzing cafe in the heart of the old Jewish quarter is a tea connoisseur's paradise. Čaj Chai stocks over 100 teas from China, India, Korea,

Japan, Nepal, Morocco and beyond. It's a much-loved local haunt.

Marula Cafè
Bar

(www.marulacafe.com; Carrer dels Escudellers 49; ⏱11pm-5am; ⓜLiceu) A fantastic funk find in the heart of the Barri Gòtic, Marula will transport you to the 1970s and the best in funk and soul. James Brown fans will think they've died and gone to heaven. It's not, however, a monothematic place and occasionally the DJs slip in other tunes, from breakbeat to house.

Polaroid
Bar

(Carrer dels Còdols 29; ⏱7pm-2.30am; ⓜDrassanes) True to name, Polaroid is a blast from the past with its VHS tapes mounted on the walls, old film posters, comic-book-covered tables, action-figure displays and other kitschy decor. Not surprisingly, it draws a fun, unpretentious crowd who come for cheap *cañas*

65

(draught beer, €2), good mojitos and free popcorn.

Dusk
Lounge

(Carrer de la Mercè 23; ⌚6pm-2.30am; **M**Drassanes) Tucked away on an atmospheric lane in the Gothic quarter, Dusk teeters between rowdy bar and intimate cocktail lounge. It has various rooms with low lighting, age-old brick walls and comfy couches framed by red curtains but also shows sports on a big-screen TV. It's a mostly foreign crowd swilling cocktails and nibbling on tapas.

Bosc de les Fades
Lounge

(Passatage de la Banca 5; ⌚10am-1am; **M**Drassanes) True to name, the 'Forest of the Faeries' offers a whimsical retreat from the busy Ramblas nearby. Lounge chairs and lamplit tables are scattered beneath an indoor forest complete with trickling fountain and grotto.

Barcelona Pipa Club
Bar

(☎93 302 47 32; www.bpipaclub.com; Plaça Reial 3; ⌚10pm-4am; **M**Liceu) This pipe smokers' club is like an apartment, with all sorts of interconnecting rooms and knick-knacks – notably the pipes after which the place is named. Buzz at the door and head two floors up.

Blondie
Bar

(www.blondie-bcn.com; Carrer d'en Roca 14; ⌚8pm-2am; **M**Liceu) This Italian-run bar has subtle, multicoloured lighting, black-and-white tile walls, Estrella Galicia beer (the country's crispest lager) and something of a conspiratorial air.

El Paraigua
Bar

(☎93 302 11 31; www.elparaigua.com; Carrer del Pas de l'Ensenyança 2; ⌚10am-midnight Mon-Wed, 11am-2am Thu-Sat; **M**Liceu) A tiny chocolate box of dark tinted Modernisme, the 'Umbrella' has been serving up drinks since the 1960s. The turn-of-the-20th-century decor was transferred here from a shop knocked down elsewhere in the district and cobbled back together to create this cosy locale. In the basement bar area, DJs spin on Thursdays (from 10pm)

and live bands – funk, soul, rock, blues – hold court on Fridays and Saturdays (from 11.30pm).

Blvd
Club

(☎93 301 62 89; www.boulevardcultureclub.com; La Rambla 27; ⌚midnight-6am Wed-Sat; **M**Drassanes) Flanked by striptease bars (in the true spirit of the lower Rambla's old days), this place has undergone countless reincarnations. The culture in this club is what a long line-up of DJs brings to the (turn)table. With three different dance spaces, one of them upstairs, it has a deliciously tacky feel, pumping out anything from 1980s hits to house music (especially on Saturdays in the main room).

Karma
Club

(☎93 302 56 80; www.karmadisco.com; Plaça Reial 10; ⌚midnight-5.30am Tue-Sun; **M**Liceu) During the week Karma plays good, mainstream indie music, while on weekends the DJs spin anything from rock to disco.

La Macarena
Club

(☎637 416647; www.macarenaclub.com; Carrer Nou de Sant Francesc 5; ⌚midnight-5am; **M**Drassanes) You simply won't believe this was once a tile-lined Andalucian flamenco musos' bar. Now it is a dark dance space, of the kind where it is possible to sit at the bar, meet people around you and then stand up for a bit of a shake to the DJ's electro and house offerings, all within a couple of square metres.

ⓧ Entertainment

Harlem Jazz Club
Live Music

(☎93 310 07 55; www.harlemjazzclub.es; Carrer de la Comtessa de Sobradiel 8; admission €6-15; ⌚8pm-4am Tue-Thu & Sun, to 5am Fri & Sat; **M**Drassanes) This narrow, old-town dive is one of the best spots in town for jazz. Usually there are two sessions with different musos each night. Get in early if you want a seat in front of the stage.

LONELY PLANET / GETTY IMAGES ©

Don't Miss
Museu d'Història de Barcelona

One of Barcelona's most fascinating museums takes you back through the centuries to the very foundations of Roman Barcino. You'll stroll amid extensive ruins of the town that flourished here following its founding by Emperor Augustus around 10 BC. Equally impressive is the setting inside the former Palau Reial Major (Grand Royal Palace) on Plaça del Rei (King's Sq, the former palace's courtyard), among the key locations of medieval princely power in Barcelona.

Below ground is a remarkable walk through about 4 sq km of excavated Roman and Visigothic Barcelona. After the display on the typical Roman domus (villa), you reach a public laundry; outside in the street were containers for people to urinate into, as the urine was used as disinfectant. You pass dyeing shops, a public cold-water bath and shops dedicated to the making of *garum* (a fish sauce enjoyed across the Roman Empire), a 6th-century church and winemaking stores.

Ramparts then wind upward, past remains of the gated patio of a Roman house, the medieval Palau Episcopal (Bishops' Palace) and into two broad vaulted halls with displays on medieval Barcelona. The finale is the Saló del Tinell, the royal palace banqueting hall and a fine example of Catalan Gothic (built 1359-70). It was here that Fernando and Isabel heard Columbus' first reports of the New World.

NEED TO KNOW

☎ 93 256 21 00; www.museuhistoria.bcn.cat; Plaça del Rei; adult/child €7/free, from 4pm 1st Sat of month and from 3pm Sun free; ⊙10am-7pm Tue-Sat, 10am-8pm Sun; M Jaume I

Jamboree — Live Music

(📞 93 319 17 89; www.masimas.com/jamboree; Plaça Reial 17; admission €8-13; 🕐 8pm-6am; Ⓜ Liceu) Since long before Franco bit the dust, Jamboree had been bringing joy to the jivers of Barcelona, with headline jazz and blues acts of the calibre of Chet Baker and Ella Fitzgerald. Nowadays two concerts are held most nights (at 8pm and 10pm), after which Jamboree morphs into a DJ-spinning club at midnight.

Sidecar Factory Club — Live Music

(📞 93 302 15 86; www.sidecarfactoryclub.com; Plaça Reial 7; admission €8-18; 🕐 10pm-5am Mon-Sat; Ⓜ Liceu) With its entrance on Plaça Reial, you can come here for a meal before midnight or a few drinks at ground level (which closes by 3am at the latest), or descend into the red-tinged, brick-vaulted bowels for live music most nights. Just about anything goes here, from UK indie through to country punk, but rock and pop lead the way.

L'Ateneu — Classical Music

(📞 93 343 21 61; www.masimas.com/fundacio; Carrer de la Canuda 6; admission €12-15; Ⓜ Catalunya) For intense 30-minute sessions of chamber music, pay a visit to this hallowed academic institution-cum-club. Concerts are typically held Fridays, Saturdays and Sundays at 6pm, 7pm and 8pm.

Gran Teatre Del Liceu — Theatre, Live Music

(📞 93 485 99 00; www.liceubarcelona.com; La Rambla dels Caputxins 51-59; 🕐 box office 1.30-8pm Mon-Fri & 1hr before show Sat & Sun; Ⓜ Liceu) Barcelona's grand old opera house, restored after fire in 1994, is one of the most technologically advanced theatres in the world. To take up a seat in the grand auditorium, returned to all its 19th-century glory but with the very latest in acoustic accoutrements, is to be transported to another age.

Tablao Cordobés — Flamenco

(📞 93 317 57 11; www.tablaocordobes.com; La Rambla 35; show €39, with dinner €62-70; 🕐 shows 8.15pm, 10pm & 11.30pm; Ⓜ Liceu) This *tablao* (restaurant where flamenco is performed) is typical of its genre and has been in business since 1970. Artists perform on a tiny hardwood stage with a vaulted backdrop that is supposed to make us think of Granada's El Alhambra.

Herboristeria Del Rei

🔒 Shopping

A handful of interesting shops dot La Rambla, but the real fun starts inside the labyrinth. Young fashion on Carrer d'Avinyó, a mixed bag on Avinguda del Portal de l'Àngel, some cute old shops on Carrer de la Dagueria and lots of exploring in tight old lanes awaits.

L'Arca de l'Àvia   Vintage, Clothing
(✏ 93 302 15 98; Carrer dels Banys Nous 20; Ⓜ Liceu) Grandma's chest is indeed full of extraordinary remembrances from the past, including 18th-century embroidered silk vests, elaborate silk kimonos and wedding dresses and shawls from the 1920s.

Taller de Marionetas Travi   Specialty
(✏ 93 412 66 92; Carrer de n'Amargós 4; 🕐 noon-9pm Mon-Sat; Ⓜ Urquinaona) Opened in the 1970s, this atmospheric shop sells handcrafted marionettes. Don Quixote, Sancho and other iconic Spanish figures are on hand, as well as unusual works from other parts of the world – including rare Sicilian puppets, pieces from Myanmar (Burma), Indonesia and other parts. Best of all, you can have a puppet made in your own likeness (prices from €300). Bring a photo and stop in for details.

Sala Parés   Arts & Crafts
(✏ 93 318 70 20; www.salapares.com; Carrer del Petritxol 5; 🕐 4-8pm Mon, 10.30am-2pm & 4.30-8pm Tue-Sat; Ⓜ Liceu) Picasso had works on sale here a century ago in what is one of the city's most venerable and still-dynamic private galleries.

Papabubble   Food
(✏ 93 268 86 25; www.papabubble.com; Carrer Ample 28; Ⓜ Liceu) It feels like a step into another era in this candy store, where they make up pots of rainbow-coloured boiled lollies, just like some of us remember from corner-store days as kids.

Xocoa   Food
(✏ 93 301 11 97; www.xocoa-bcn.com; Carrer del Petritxol 11-13; Ⓜ Liceu) Tucked along cafe- and boutique-lined Carrer de Petritxol, this den of dental devilry displays ranks and ranks of original chocolate bars, chocolates stuffed with sweet stuff, gooey pastries and more.

Espacio De Creadores   Fashion
(✏ 93 318 03 31; Carrer Comtal 22; Ⓜ Catalunya) For a broad selection of cut-price women's fashion and accessories by a long list of Spanish and some international designers, this outlet store claims to slash original prices by up to 70%.

Urbana   Fashion
(✏ 93 269 09 20; Carrer d'Avinyó 46; 🕐 11am-9pm Mon-Sat; Ⓜ Liceu) Colourful, fun city clothes, shoes and accessories await boys and girls in this easygoing store with Basque Country origins. It offers a variety of eye-catching apparel, like graphic T-shirts for men by Supremebeing, floral dresses by Yumi and stylish hats by Atlantis.

Herboristeria Del Rei   Specialty
(✏ 93 318 05 12; www.herboristeriadelrei.blog spot.com; Carrer del Vidre 1; 🕐 4-8pm Tue-Fri, 10am-8pm Sat; Ⓜ Liceu) Once patronised by Queen Isabel II, this timeless corner store flogs all sorts of weird and wonderful herbs, spices and medicinal plants. It's been doing so since 1823 and the decor has barely changed since the 1860s. Film director Tom Tykwer shot scenes of *Perfume: The Story of a Murderer* here.

El Ingenio   Specialty
(✏ 93 317 71 38; www.el-ingenio.com; Carrer d'en Rauric 6; Ⓜ Liceu) In this whimsical fantasy store you will discover giant Carnaval masks, costumes, theatrical accessories and other fun things. You can pick up some elegant Venetian masks, flamenco costumes, gorilla heads, yo-yos, kazoos, unicycles and other novelty items.

La Manual Alpargatera   Shoes
(✏ 93 301 01 72; http://homepage.mac.com/ manualp; Carrer d'Avinyó 7; Ⓜ Liceu) Everyone from Salvador Dalí to Jean Paul Gaultier has ordered a pair of *espadrilles* (rope-soled canvas shoes or sandals) from this famous store, which is the birthplace of the iconic footwear.

El Raval

Long one of the most rough-and-tumble parts of Barcelona, El Raval is now hip in a grungy, inner-city way. *Barcelonins* have even invented a verb for rambling around El Raval: *ravalejar*.

The northern half of El Raval is the best place to start your ramble – this part of the *barri* has an almost respectable air about it. Spend a day wandering along the art-shop filled Carrer del Pintor Fortuny, lunching in the colourful Mercat de la Boqueria and dedicating a few hours to the fascinating MACBA. Join the youthful set of hedonists on La Rambla del Raval and check out the strip's assortment of bars. Don't miss the striking cylindrical designer hotel Barceló Raval and its fashionable restaurant.

Night time is El Raval's forte. This is where you will find some of the more eccentric, trendy and downright ancient bars and clubs.

El Raval Highlights

MACBA (p81)

Usually referred to by its acronym MACBA, the Museu d'Art Contemporani de Barcelona, set on Plaça de Ángels (a hangout for local skateboarders), is stuffed with over seven decades' worth of modern art. This is the place to view the cutting edge of the contemporary scene in rooms flooded with natural light, courtesy of huge south-facing windows. Catalan and Spanish paintings form the backbone of the collection. MACBA, architect: Richard Meier & Partners

Mercat de la Boqueria (p82)

Plump and seductive fruits and vegetables, gleaming seafood counters, the earthy scent of artisanal cheeses. Mercat de la Boqueria is all this and much more. It's the city's oldest and most atmospheric market, a noisy melange of history, heritage and street theatre Not surprisingly, it's also one of the biggest tourist magnets – particularly the enticing row of tapas counters in the back.

MARCO CRISTOFORI / CORBIS ©

Palau Güell (p76) ③

Mega-rich industrialist Eusebi Güell and Modernista architect Gaudí are as synonymous with Barcelona as they are with each other. This gilded mansion, with its toadstool chimneys and gabled frontage, captures Gaudí in a youthful, less flamboyant incarnation. Art fiends flock here to gain an insight into a genius in the making.

④ Bars (p83)

Long infamous for its seedy nightlife and louche drinking holes, El Raval's abundant bars have been sanitised in recent years, replicating what happened in La Ribera's El Born district in the 1990s. Nonetheless, the neighbourhood still retains 'edge', along with enough grungy, open-all-night places to keep any Hemingway-emulating barfly happy for weeks. London Bar (p84)

⑤ Neighbourhood Eateries (p77)

Sitting in one of the most exciting parts of town, El Raval's ever-evolving restaurant scene is characterised by a diverse ethnic make-up and a hungry army of students. To meet the local need, the district's traditional eating houses have been complemented in recent years by vegetarian self-service joints, juice bars and the odd classy candlelit nook.

El Raval Walk

Edgy street art, hedonistic nightspots and colourful characters are part of the urban backdrop of ever-evolving El Raval. This journey takes in some of its diverse highlights with stops at bohemian drinking dens, architectural masterpieces and one magnificent food market (bring an appetite).

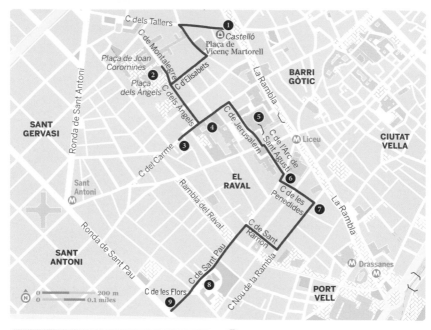

WALK FACTS

- **Start** La Rambla de Canaletes
- **Finish** La Confitería
- **Distance** 2.8km
- **Duration** Two hours

❶ Carrer des Tallers

Just off La Rambla, this narrow **pedestrian lane** has rhythm in its soul, with a smattering of CD and record stores as well as guitar shops. For a broad collection of sounds from Spain and beyond, stop in **Castelló** (p85).

❷ MACBA

Stroll past **Plaça de Vincenç Martorell**, a pleasant slice of local life, and make your way over to the **MACBA** (p81), which was a major catalyst to the cultural rebirth of El Raval. The ultra-modern all-white design by American architect Richard Meier was controversial for its dramatic contrast to the surrounding historic buildings.

❸ Bar Muy Buenas

For a refreshment, stop in **Bar Muy Buenas** (p83) on Carrer del Carme. Opened as a milk bar in the late 19th century, it retains much of its original Modernista decor. It's a welcoming spot for a tipple and snacks.

④ Antic Hospital de la Santa Creu

Up the road, have a wander through the peaceful courtyard of the **Antic Hospital de la Santa Creu** (p76), the city's main hospital in the 15th century. The impressive Gothic buildings now house cultural institutions, including a large library.

⑤ La Boqueria

Just east is the **Mercat de la Boqueria** (p82), the massive food market that brings gourmands to their knees. Fruits, cheeses, bakery items, wines, antipasti and other goodies make for a first-rate picnic. Or head to the tapas bars in the back.

⑥ Hotel España

After a few nibbles at La Boqueria, stroll over to **Hotel España** for classic Catalan fare. The famous dining rooms are part of the 1903 design by Domènech i Montaner and there is a magnificent alabaster fireplace designed by Eusebi Arnau.

⑦ Palau Güell

Make your way down Carrer de les Pen edides to one of El Raval's star attractions, the recently restored **Palau Güell** (p76), one of Gaudí's first major commissions. The classic Gaudí elements are at play, including colourful mosaic-covered chimney pots.

⑧ Església de Sant Pau del Camp

Next, stroll over to Barcelona's oldest church. Along the way, you'll pass the pedestrian-filled **La Rambla del Raval**, which has a fraction of the crowds of its cousin to the east. **Església de Sant Pau del Camp** has some wonderful Visigothic sculptural decoration on its doorway and a serene air. The cloister is the best example of Romanesque architecture in the city.

⑨ La Confitería

End your stroll at **La Confitería** (p83), one of El Raval's charming watering holes. Once a barber shop and then confectioner's, it was converted to a bar in 1998. Most of the elements are the real deal.

 ## The Best…

PLACES TO EAT

Bar Pinotxo One of the best tapas bars in La Boqueria. (p77)

Ca L'Isidre Classic Catalan cooking in an old-world setting. (p77)

Granja Viader Rich cups of hot chocolate are served up in this delightful Catalan-style milk bar. (p77)

Casa Leopoldo A seafood-loving 1929 gem that's a favourite of writer Manuel Vázquez Montalbán. (p77)

Elisabets A neighbourhood charmer that always packs a lunchtime crowd. (p77)

PLACES TO DRINK

Bar La Concha A raucous good time, particularly when drag shows are on. (p83)

La Confitería Mural-filled bar with 19th-century decor and excellent house-made vermouth. (p83)

33|45 Trendy cocktail bar that draws a fashionista crowd. (p83)

LIVE MUSIC

Jazz Sí Club This tiny spot has eclectic programming, including authentic Flamenco. (p84)

Robadors 23 Small jazz-loving joint. (p84)

Discover El Raval

76

Getting There & Away

- **Metro** El Raval is encircled by three Metro lines. Línies 1, 2 and 3 stop at strategic points around the district, so nothing is far from a Metro stop. The Línia 3 stop at Liceu is a convenient exit point.

Sights

Palau Güell Palace

(93 317 39 74; www.palauguell.cat; Carrer Nou de la Rambla 3-5; adult/reduced €10/8; 10am-8pm Apr-Sep, 10am-5.30pm Oct-Mar; M Drassanes) Finally reopened in its entirety in 2010 after nearly 20 years under refurbishment, this is a magnificent example of the early days of Gaudí's fevered architectural imagination – the extraordinary Modernista mansion, one of the few major buildings of that era raised in Ciutat Vella, gives an insight into its maker's prodigious genius.

Gaudí built the palace just off La Rambla in the late 1880s for his wealthy and faithful patron, the industrialist Eusebi Güell. Although a little sombre compared with some of his later whims, it is still a characteristic riot of styles (Gothic, Islamic, art nouveau) and materials. The hall is a parabolic pyramid – each wall an arch stretching up three floors and coming together to form a dome. The roof is a mad tumult of tiled mosaics and fanciful design in the building's chimney pots. Picasso – who, incidentally, hated Gaudí's work – began his Blue Period in 1902 in a studio across the street at Carrer Nou de la Rambla 10.

FREE **Antic Hospital de la Santa Creu** Historic Building

(93 270 23 00; www.bnc.cat; Carrer de l'Hospital 56; 9am-8pm Mon-Fri, to 2pm Sat; M Liceu) Behind the Mercat de la Boqueria (p82) stands what was, in the 15th century, the city's main hospital. The restored Antic Hospital de la Santa Creu (Former Holy Cross Hospital) today houses the **Biblioteca de Catalunya** (Library of Catalo-

Palau Güell
ALEKSANDAR TODOROVIC / SHUTTERSTOCK ©

nia; admission free; ⊘9am-8pm Mon-Fri, 9am-2pm Sat), as well as the **Institut d'Estudis Catalans** (Institute for Catalan Studies). The former hospital's Gothic chapel, **La Capella** (☎93 442 71 71; www.bcn.cat/lacapella; admission free; ⊘noon-2pm & 4-8pm Tue-Sat, 11am-2pm Sun & holidays), is worth poking your nose into for the frequent temporary exhibitions.

Entering from Carrer de l'Hospital, you find yourself in a delightfully bedraggled courtyard garden that is home to bums, earnest students on a break and a cheerful bar-cafe. Off the garden lies the entrance to the prestigious Massana conservatorium and, up a sweep of stairs, the library. The library is the single most complete collection of documents (estimated at around three million) tracing the region's long history. You can freely visit the most impressive part, the grand reading rooms beneath broad Gothic stone arches, where you can also see temporary displays of anything from old records to medieval monastic hymnals.

Centre de Cultura Contemporània de Barcelona   Cultural Building
(CCCB; ☎93 306 41 00; www.cccb.org; Carrer de Montalegre 5; 2 exhibitions adult/child under 16yr/senior & student €6/free/4.50, 1 exhibition €5/free/3, free on Wednesdays, 8-10pm Thu, 3-8pm Sun; ⊘11am-8pm Tue, Wed & Fri-Sun, 11am-10pm Thu; ⓂUniversitat) A complex of auditoriums, exhibition spaces and conference halls opened here in 1994 in an old 18th-century hospice, the Casa de la Caritat. The spectacular courtyard has a vast glass wall on one side. With 4500 sq metres of exhibition space, the centre hosts a constantly changing program of exhibitions, film cycles and other events.

✖ Eating

El Raval is possibly the most interesting part of the old town. Timeless classics of Barcelona dining are scattered across what was long the old city's poorest *barri*, and since the late 1990s, battalions of hip new eateries and artsy restaurants can be found in the area around MACBA.

Bar Pinotxo   Tapas €€
(Mercat de la Boqueria; meals €20; ⊘6am-5pm Mon-Sat Sep-Jul; ⓂLiceu) Bar Pinotxo is arguably La Boqueria's, and even Barcelona's, best tapas bar. It sits among the half-dozen informal eateries within the market, and the popular owner, Juanito, might serve up chickpeas with a sweet sauce of pine nuts and raisins, a fantastically soft mix of potato and spinach sprinkled with coarse salt, or a quivering cube of caramel sweet pork belly.

Ca L'Isidre   Catalan €€€
(☎93 441 11 39; www.calisidre.com; Carrer de les Flors 12; mains €20-70; ⊘Mon-Sat, closed Easter & 3 weeks in Aug; ⓂParal·lel) Lurking in an unappealing backstreet off El Raval, Ca L'Isidre is an old-world gem. Immaculately kept dining areas stretch away from the entrance, dominated by warm timber and tiles. The menu is a work of art in itself – try artichoke hearts stuffed with mushrooms and foie gras, tuna steak with a tomato coulis or lamb's brains with black butter.

Granja Viader   Cafe €
(☎93 318 34 86; www.granjaviader.cat; Carrer d'en Xuclà 4; ⊘9am-1.45pm & 5-8.45pm Tue-Sat, 5-8.45pm Mon; ⓂLiceu) For more than a century, people have flocked down this alley to get to the cups of homemade hot chocolate and whipped cream (ask for a *suís*) ladled out in this classic Catalan-style milk bar-cum-deli.

Casa Leopoldo   Catalan €€
(☎93 441 30 14; www.casaleopoldo.com; Carrer de Sant Rafael 24; meals around €50; ⊘lunch & dinner Tue-Sat, lunch Sun Sep-Jul; ⓂLiceu) Long hidden in the slum alleys of El Raval, this was writer Manuel Vázquez Montalbán's favourite restaurant. Several rambling dining areas in this 1929 classic have magnificent tiled walls and exposed beam ceilings. The mostly seafood menu is extensive and the wine list strong.

Elisabets   Catalan €
(☎93 317 58 26; Carrer d'Elisabets 2-4; mains €7-9; ⊘Mon-Sat Sep-Jul; ⓂCatalunya) This

El Raval

0 200 m
0 0.1 miles

CIUTAT VELLA

BARRI GÒTIC

MACBA

Plaça de la Universitat
Plaça de Castella
Plaça de Goya
Plaça del Pes de la Palla
Plaça de Joan Coromines
Plaça dels Àngels
Plaça de Vicenç Martorell
Plaça del Bonsuccés
Plaça de Ramon Amadeu
Plaça de la Vila de Madrid
Plaça Nova
Plaça de Sant Felip Neri
Plaça de St. Josep Oriol

Universitat
Catalunya
Liceu

C de Montsió
C de Pelai
C de les Ramelleres
C dels Tallers
C de Jovellanos
C de Gravina
Ronda de Sant Antoni
C de Valldonzella
C del Tigre
C del Lleó
C de Ferlandina
C de Sant Vicenç
C de la Lluna
C de Joaquín Costa
C del Peu de la Creu
C de Montalegre
C dels Àngels
C del Doctor Dou
C de les Egipcíaques
C del Carme
C de Jerusalem
C d'en Xuclà
C del Pintor Fortuny
C del Notariat
C d'Elisabets
C del Bonsuccès
C de la Cannuda
Av del Portal de l'Àngel
C de Duran i Bas
C de Bertrellans
C de Santa Anna
C dels Boters
C de la Palla
C del Pi
C de la Portaferrissa
C del Petritxol
C d'en Bot
C d'en Roca
C d'En Arolas
C de la Boqueria
C de Ferran
C de les Floristes de la Rambla
C de les Egipcíaques

La Rambla de Canaletes
La Rambla dels Estudis
La Rambla de Sant Josep
La Rambla
Pla de la Boqueria

Jardins del Doctor Fleming

1
2
3
4
6
7
12
13
14
15
16
19
21
23
28
34
35
36
37
39
40

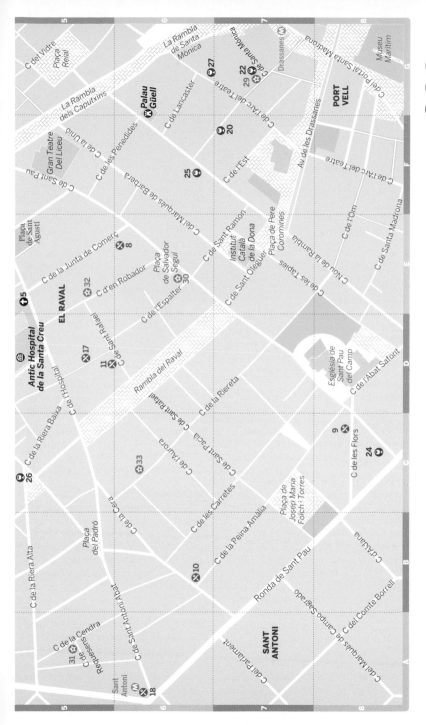

DISCOVER EL RAVAL

79

El Raval

unassuming restaurant is popular for no-nonsense local fare. The walls are lined with old radio sets and the *menú del día* (set menu, €10.75) varies daily.

Pla dels Àngels
Mediterranean €

(🕾93 329 40 47; www.semproniana.net; Carrer Ferlandina 23; set lunch €10, set dinner €15; meals €20; ☺1.30-4pm & 9-11.30pm daily; ⓂUniversitat) Just next door to MACBA, this is a suitably colourful and lively little bistro with brightly painted walls and tightly-squeezed tables in the back room. The cooking is Catalan-French and Italian, and can be quite quirky, with salads like mango, tofu, mint and oregano, and pear, chestnut and pine nut soup.

Sesamo
Vegetarian €

(🕾93 441 64 11; www.sesamo-bcn.com; Carrer de Sant Antoni Abat 52; ☺lunch & dinner Mon-Tue & Thu-Sat, lunch Sun; 🖋; ⓂSant Antoni) For 'food without beasts', this relaxed corner eatery attracts all sorts. Drop by for juices and pastries at breakfast, a three-course set lunch (around €7) or dinner.

Restaurant el Cafetí
Catalan €€

(🕾93 329 24 19; www.elcafeti.com; Passatge de Bernardí; mains €8-15, menú del dia €12; ☺lunch & dinner Tue-Sat, lunch Sun; ⓂLiceu) This diminutive eatery is filled with antique furniture and offers traditional local cooking, with one or two unorthodox variations. Paella and other rice dishes dominate.

Biblioteca
Mediterranean €€

(🕾93 412 62 21; www.bibliotecarestaurant.cat; Carrer de la Junta de Comerç 28; meals €35-40; ☺dinner Mon-Fri, lunch & dinner Sat; ⓂLiceu) Exposed-brick and creamy-white decor dominate in the 'Library', where the food represents much of Spain, with careful creative touches and a good wine list.

ART ON FILE/CORBIS ©. ARCHITECT: RICHARD MEIER & PARTNERS

 Don't Miss
MACBA

Designed by Richard Meier and opened in 1995, MACBA (Museu d'Art Contemporani de Barcelona) has become the city's foremost contemporary art centre, with captivating exhibitions for the serious art lover. The permanent collection is on the ground floor and dedicates itself to Spanish and Catalan art from the second half of the 20th century, with works by Antoni Tàpies, Joan Brossa and Miquel Barceló, among others, though international artists, such as Paul Klee, Bruce Nauman and John Cage are also represented.

The gallery, across two floors, is dedicated to temporary visiting exhibitions that are almost always challenging and intriguing. Across the main skateboard-infested square, the renovated 400-year-old Convent dels Àngels houses the **Capella Macba** (Plaça dels Àngels; **M**Universitat), where the MACBA regularly rotates selections from its permanent collection. The Gothic framework of the one-time convent church remains intact.

The library and auditorium stage regular concerts, talks and events, all of which are either reasonably priced or free. The extensive art bookshop is fantastic for both stocking up on art and art theory books, as well as quirky gifts and small design objects.

NEED TO KNOW

Museu d'Art Contemporani de Barcelona; 📞93 412 08 10; www.macba.cat; Plaça dels Àngels 1; adult/concession €7.50/6; 🕙11am-8pm Mon & Wed, to midnight Thu-Fri, 10am-8pm Sat, 10am-3pm Sun & holidays; **M**Universitat

Can Lluís   Catalan €€€
(Carrer de la Cera 49; meals €30-35; 🕙Mon-Sat Sep-Jul; **M**Sant Antoni) Three generations have kept this spick and span old-time classic in business since 1929. Expect fresh fish and seafood. The *llenguado* (sole) is oven cooked in whisky and raisins.

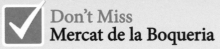

Don't Miss
Mercat de la Boqueria

One of the greatest sound, smell and colour sensations in Europe is Barcelona's most central produce market, the Mercat de la Boqueria. It spills over with all the rich and varied colour of plentiful fruit and vegetable stands, seemingly limitless varieties of sea critters, sausages, cheeses, meat (including the finest Jabugo ham) and sweets.

According to some chronicles, there has been a market in this place since 1217. As much as it has become a modern-day attraction, this has always been the place where locals have come to shop. Many of Barcelona's top restaurateurs buy their produce here, which vouches for the quality of the market's offer.

La Boqueria is dotted with half a dozen or so unassuming places to eat, and eat well, with stallholders opening up at lunchtime. Whether you eat here or if you're self-catering, it's worth trying some of Catalonia's gastronomical specialities, such as *bacallà salat* (dried salted cod) that usually comes in an *esqueixada*, a tomato, onion and black olive salad, topped with the dried cod; *calçots* (a cross between a leek and an onion), which are grilled and eaten as a messy whole; *cargols* (snails), a Catalan staple that is best eaten baked as *cargols a la llauna*; *peus de porc* (pork trotters) that are often stewed with snails; or *percebes*, a kind of shell that looks like witch fingers, that are much loved across Spain and eaten with a garlic and parsley sauce.

NEED TO KNOW
📞 93 412 13 15; www.boqueria.info; La Rambla 91; 🕐 8am-8.30pm Mon-Sat, closed Sun; Ⓜ Liceu

Mama I Teca Catalan €

(☎93 441 33 35; Carrer de la Lluna 4; mains €8-10; ⏰lunch & dinner Sun-Mon & Wed-Fri, dinner Sat; Ⓜ Sant Antoni) A tiny place with a half dozen tables, Mama i Teca is more a lifestyle than a restaurant. The setting is a multicultural and often rowdy street deep in El Raval. Locals drop in and hang about for a drink, and diners are treated to Catalan treats served without rush.

Olivia Cafe €

(☎93 318 63 80; Carrer Pintor Fortuny 22; ⏰9am-9pm Mon-Sat, 10am-9pm Sun Oct-May, 9am-9pm Mon-Sat June-Sept; 📶; Ⓜ Catalunya) A relaxed little cafe on a quiet Raval street, Olivia makes excellent cake (carrot, pineapple, you name it) and good coffee.

Drinking & Nightlife

Bars and clubs have been opening up along the long, slummy alleys of El Raval for the last two decades, making this one of the edgiest areas of town to go out. You'll find supertrendy places alongside some great old harbour-style taverns that still thrive – there are joints that have been the hangouts of the city's bohemia since Picasso's times.

The lower end of El Raval has a long history of dodginess and the area around Carrer de Sant Pau retains its edgy feel: drug dealers, pickpockets and prostitutes mingle with the streams of nocturnal hedonists. Keep your wits about you if walking around here late at night.

Bar la Concha Bar

(Carrer de la Guàrdia 14; ⏰5pm-3am; Ⓜ Drassanes) La Concha used to be a largely gay and transvestite haunt, but anyone is welcome and bound to have fun – especially when the drag queens come out to play. The music ranges from *paso dobles* (a kind of lively ballroom dance music) to Spanish retro pop.

La Confitería Bar

(Carrer de Sant Pau 128; ⏰11am-2am; Ⓜ Paral·lel) This is a trip into the 19th century. Until the 1980s it was a confectioner's shop, and although the original cabinets are now lined with booze, the look of the place has barely changed in its conversion into a laid-back bar.

33|45 Bar

(Carrer Joaquín Costa 4; ⏰10am-1:30am Mon-Thu, 10am-3am Fri & Sat, 10am-midnight Sun; Ⓜ Universitat) A super trendy cocktail bar on the nightlife-laden Joaquín Costa street, this place has excellent mojitos – even pink, strawberry ones! – and a fashionable crowd. The main area has DJ music and lots of excited noise making, while the back room is scattered with sofas and armchairs for a post-dancing slump.

Negroni Cocktail Bar

(Carrer de Joaquín Costa 46; ⏰7pm-2am Mon-Thu, 7pm-3am Fri & Sat; Ⓜ Liceu) The black and beige decor lures in a largely student set to try out the bar's cocktails, among them the flagship Negroni, a Florentine invention with one part Campari, one part gin and one part sweet vermouth.

Bar Muy Buenas Bar

(Carrer del Carme 63; ⏰9am-2am Mon-Thu, 9am-3am Fri & Sat, 7pm-2am Sun; Ⓜ Liceu) This bar started life as a late-19th-century corner store. The Modernista decor and relaxed company make this a great spot for a quiet mojito. You may catch a little live music or even a poetry reading, and can nibble on a limited menu of Middle Eastern titbits.

Bar Pastís Bar

(☎93 318 79 80; www.barpastis.com; Carrer de Santa Mònica 4; ⏰7.30pm-2am Sun-Fri, 7.30pm-3am Sat; Ⓜ Drassanes) A French cabaret theme (with lots of Piaf in the background) dominates this tiny, cluttered classic. It's been going, on and off, since the end of WWII. You'll need to be in here before 9pm to have a hope of sitting, getting near the bar or anything much else. On some nights it features live acts, usually performing French chansons.

London Bar
Bar

(Carrer Nou de la Rambla 34-36; ◷7.30pm-4am Tue-Sun; MLiceu) Open since 1909, this Modernista bar started as a hang-out for circus hands and was later frequented by the likes of Picasso, Miró and Hemingway. Today, it fills to the brim with punters at the long front bar and rickety old tables.

Marmalade
Bar

(www.marmaladebarcelona.com; Carrer de la Riera Alta 4-6; ◷7pm-3am; MSant Antoni) From the street you can see the golden hues of the backlit bar way down the end of a long lounge-lined passageway. To the left of the bar by a bare brick wall is a pool table, popular but somehow out of place in this chic, ill-lit chill den (with attached restaurant).

Casa Almirall
Bar

(Carrer de Joaquín Costa 33; ◷5.30pm-2.30am Sun-Thu, 7pm-3am Fri & Sat; MUniversitat) In business since the 1860s, this unchanged corner bar is dark and intriguing, with Modernista decor and a mixed clientele.

Moog
Club

(www.masimas.com/moog; Carrer de l'Arc del Teatre 3; admission €10; ◷midnight-5am; MDrassanes) This fun and minuscule club is a standing favourite with the down-town crowd. In the main dance area, DJs dish out house, techno and electro, while upstairs you can groove to a nice blend of indie and occasional classic-pop throwbacks.

⊛ Entertainment

Filmoteca de Catalunya
Cinema

(☏93 567 10 70; www.filmoteca.cat; Plaça Salvador Seguí 1-9 ; tickets from €2-4; ◷8am-10pm; MLiceu) After almost a decade in planning, the Filmoteca de Catalunya moved into this modern 6,000-sq-metre building in March 2012. In addition to two cinema screens totaling 555 seats, the new Filmoteca comprises a film library, a bookshop, a cafe, offices and a dedicated space for exhibitions.

Jazz Sí Club
Live Music

(☏93 329 00 20; www.tallerdemusics.com; Carrer de Requesens 2; admission €8, drink included; ◷6-11pm; MSant Antoni) A cramped little bar run by the Taller de Músics (Musicians' Workshop) serves as the stage for a varied program of jazz through to some good flamenco (Friday nights). Concerts start around 9pm but the jam sessions can get going as early as 6.30pm.

Robadors 23
Live Music

(Carrer d'en Robador 23; admission €2-3; ◷8pm-2am; MLiceu) On what remains a classic dodgy El Raval street, where a hardy band of streetwalkers, junkies and other misfits hang out in spite of all the work being carried out to gentrify the area, a narrow little bar has made a name for itself with its Wednesday night gigs.

Cangrejo
Gay Club

(☏93 301 29 78; Carrer de Montserrat 9; ◷9.30pm-1am Sun, Wed & Thu, 9.30pm-3am Fri & Sat; MDrassanes) This altar to kitsch, a dingy dance hall that has transgressed since the 1920s, is run by the tumescent underground cabaret figure of Carmen Mairena and exudes a gorgeously tacky feel, especially with the midnight drag shows on Friday and Saturday. Due to its popularity with tourists, getting in is all but impossible unless you turn up early.

Teatre Llantiol
Theatre

(☏93 329 90 09; www.llantiol.com; Carrer de la Riereta 7; admission €6-10; MSant Antoni) At this curious place in El Raval all sorts of odd stuff, from concerts and ballads to magic shows, is staged.

ⓑ Shopping

The area boasts a handful of art galleries around MACBA, along with a burgeoning secondhand and vintage clothes scene on Carrer de la Riera Baixa. Carrer dels Tallers is one of the city's main music strips.

HELEN CATHCART / ALAMY ©

Fantastik
Arts & Crafts

(www.fantastik.es; Carrer de Joaquín Costa 62; ⏰ 11am-2pm & 4-9pm Mon-Thu, 11am-9pm Fri & Sat, closed Sun; Ⓜ Universitat) Over four hundred products, including a Mexican skull rattle, robot moon explorer from China and recycled plastic zebras from South Africa, are to be found in this bright shop that sources its items from Mexico, India, Bulgaria, Russia, Senegal and 20 other countries.

La Portorriqueña
Coffee

(Carrer d'en Xuclà 25; Ⓜ Catalunya) Coffee beans from around the world, freshly ground before your eyes, has been the winning formula in this store since 1902. The street is good for little old-fashioned food boutiques.

Holala! Plaza
Fashion

(Plaça de Castella 2; Ⓜ Universitat) Vintage clothes are the name of the game, along with an eclectic programme of exhibitions and activities.

Castelló
Music

(Carrer dels Tallers 3 & 7; Ⓜ Catalunya) These two stores are part of a large family business that has been going since 1935 and which is said to account for a fifth of the retail record business in Catalonia.

Teranyina
Arts & Crafts

(Carrer del Notariat 10; Ⓜ Catalunya) Artist Teresa Rosa Aguayo runs this textile workshop in the heart of the artsy bit of El Raval. You can join courses at the loom, admire some of the rugs and other works that Teresa has created and, of course, buy them.

La Ribera

La Ribera is a fascinating blend of history and cutting edge. It has a warren of medieval buildings inhabited by celebrated museums, award-winning restaurants and eye-catching boutiques. The south part of the district, known as El Born, should be your first port of call. Here you'll find the magnificent Gothic Església de Santa Maria del Mar and the atmospheric Carrer de Montcada, a street lined with Gothic and baroque mansions as well as the city's major museums.

Passeig del Born was Barcelona's main square from the 13th to the 18th centuries and still has an air of excitement around it – dozens of bars, cafes and some good restaurants line it, and the streets that cross this short drag are packed with some impressive (quite high-end) shopping. It's a popular night-time area for locals, especially in the summer when terraces get full and bars throw open their doors.

Passeig del Born (p91)

La Ribera Highlights

El Born Reborn (p100)

Barcelona rarely stands still, especially in El Born, the tight grid of streets south of Carrer de la Princesa that has been transformed into its most à la mode neighbourhood. Passeig del Born and the Plaça de Santa María del Mar are the hottest strips: trendy boutiques merge with hip bars, specialist shops and experimental cuisine. The renaissance began in the 1990s but shows no signs of abating. Plaça de Santa María del Mar

1

2

Palau de la Música Catalan (p99)

Give a Modernista architect (Lluís Domènech i Montaner) carte blanche in a music theatre and this is what you get: a splendiferous quasi-palace. Dripping in intricate details, the 1908 palace is music recreated in stone and stained glass with fine acoustics to match. For the most intimate picture, take a guided tour and for a full music explosion, attend a performance.

Església de Santa Maria del Mar (p102) **3**

The Barri Gòtic might be Barcelona's quintessential medieval quarter, but you have to roam a few blocks east to view its greatest Gothic monument. This 14th-century church exhibits the purest manifestation of the Gothic genre. The exterior is rather monastic, but inside, soaring columns, a light-filled apse and magnificent stained-glass windows create a sense of solemn beauty.

LOOK DIE BILDAGENTUR DER FOTOGRAFEN GMBH / ALAMY ©

4

Parc de la Ciutadella (p95)

For a long time, La Ciutadella was the city's only green space and it still serves as a vital setting for a bit fresh air for residents living in the narrow lanes of the Ciutat Vella. Aside from offering the standard diversions of walking, jogging and lounging on the grass for an afternoon siesta, the park has a zoo, a Gaudíesque fountain, curious sculptures and the Catalan parliament. Parlament de Catalunya

5

Museu Picasso (p92)

Set in five adjacent Gothic-baroque mansions, this art museum showcases Picasso's early career. Works that predate the painter's Cubist reinvention in Paris offer insight into his youthful development. They also emphasise the role that Barcelona has played in influencing him. For late-career fans, a trio of rooms is dedicated to Picasso's reevaluation of Velázquez's *Las Meninas*.

La Ribera Walk

The star of the Ciutat Vella, La Ribera is packed with great monuments that span the centuries. Former jousting grounds, medieval merchant houses, one magnificent Gothic church and a celebrated music hall from the 20th century are all part of La Ribera's enchanting mix.

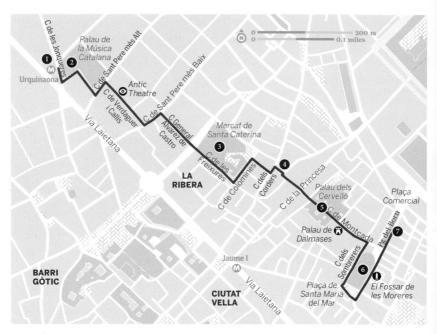

WALK FACTS
- **Start** Via Laietana
- **Finish** Passeig del Born
- **Distance** 1.8km
- **Duration** One hour

❶ La Caixa

An outstanding example of Modernista architecture, **La Caixa** savings bank pays homage to Barcelona's Gothic past, with its faux bell tower, arched windows, stained glass and sculpture. Note the statue of a woman holding a (savings) box in the corner. The logo of La Caixa – a blue star with a yellow circle above a red circle – was designed by Joan Miró and symbolizes a person dropping a coin into a piggy bank.

❷ Palau de la Música Catalana

Around the corner you'll find the extravagant **Palau de la Música Catalana** (p99), designed by Domènech i Montaner in the early 1900s. Sculptures of mythic figures (like flag-holding St George, a patron saint of Catalonia) and famous composers as well as ordinary Catalan citizens adorn the facade. To see the theatre, come back for a guided tour or an evening concert.

❸ Mercat de Santa Caterina

Make your way through the narrow lanes of La Ribera, passing by the **Antic Theatre**

(Carrer de Verdaguer i Callís 12) with its pleasant courtyard cafe. The next stop is the **Mercat de Santa Caterina** (p95), a modern version of a 19th-century market. In addition to a bounty of meats, fish, cheeses, olives and eateries, the market holds the remains of a 15th-century monastery.

④ Capella d'en Marcús

At the corner of Carrer dels Corders and the northern end of the street, just beyond the 19th-century Carrer de la Princesa, stands a Romanesque **chapel**, originally built in the 12th century. The Capella d'en Marcús once served as a wayfarers' stop on the road northeast out of medieval Barcelona.

⑤ Carrer de Montacada

During the Middle Ages **Carrer de Monta-cada** was the city's most stylish address for the merchant classes. The bulk of the great mansions remaining today date to the 14th and 15th centuries, and several have been converted into major museums, like the **Museu Picasso** (p92). By night, the baroque courtyard of the medieval Palau de Dalmases at number 20 hosts live music.

⑥ Església de Santa Maria del Mar

Barcelona's most stirring **Gothic structure** (p102) looms majestically above the compact cobblestone lanes of El Born. Inside, a real sense of light and space pervades the entire sanctuary of the church. Opposite the church's southern flank at El Fossar de les Moreres, an eternal flame commemorates the Catalan resistance fighters, buried here after the siege of Barcelona ended in defeat in September 1714 during the War of the Spanish Succession.

⑦ Passeig del Born

One of Barcelona's prettiest **pedestrian lanes** has a graceful setting amid outdoor cafes and bars. Still a favourite with prom-enading residents, the Passeig del Born was Barcelona's main square from the 13th to 18th centuries. Jousting tournaments, executions and other public entertainments took place here in the Middle Ages.

 The Best...

PLACES TO EAT

Casa Delfin First-rate Catalan cuisine on a lovely pedestrian boulevard. (p101)

Le Cucine Mandarosso Hearty Italian dishes, cooked to perfection. (p101)

El Passadís Del Pep A much-loved local seafood haunt. (p101)

Cal Pep Mouth-watering tapas. (p101)

PLACES TO DRINK

La Vinya del Senyor Great wine list and outdoor seating. (p104)

Gimlet Magical place serving up vintage cocktails. (p104)

El Xampanyet One of Barcelona's most famous (and jovial) *cava* bars. (p104)

Miramelindo Stylish spot on buzzing Passeig del Born. (p104)

ARTFUL SPACES

Església de Santa Maria del Mar Sublime Gothic cathedral. (p102)

Palau de la Musica Catalana A fairy-tale-like music hall. (p99)

Parc de la Ciutadella Pleasant green space with a dramatic cascade. (p95)

Cal Pep (p101)
FERRAN NADEU ©

Don't Miss
Museu Picasso

The setting alone, in five contiguous medieval stone mansions, makes the Museu Picasso unique (and worth the probable queues). The pretty courtyards, galleries and staircases preserved in the first three of these buildings are as delightful as the collection inside. The exhibitions showcase Picasso's early career. Works that predate the painter's Cubist reinvention in Paris offer insight into his youthful development. They also emphasise the role that Barcelona has played in influencing one of the giants of the art world.

Map p96

📞 93 256 30 00

www.museupicasso.bcn.es

Carrer de Montcada 15-23

adult/senior & child under 16yr/student €11/free/6, temporary exhibitions €6/free/2.90, 3-8pm Sun & 1st Sun of month free

🕐 10am-8pm Tue-Sun & holidays

Ⓜ Jaume I

The Collection

While the collection concentrates on Picasso's formative years, there is enough material from subsequent periods to give you a thorough impression of his versatility and genius. Above all, you come away feeling that Picasso was the true original, always one step ahead of himself (let alone anyone else), in his search for new forms of expression.

Early Work

A visit starts with sketches and oils from Picasso's earliest years in Málaga and La Coruña – around 1893–95. Some of his self-portraits and the portraits of his father, which date from 1896, are evidence enough of his precocious talent. *Retrato de la Tía Pepa* (*Portrait of Aunt Pepa*), done in Málaga in 1896, shows the incredible maturity of his brushstrokes and his ability to portray character – at the tender age of 15. Picasso painted the enormous *Ciència i Caritat* (*Science and Charity*) the same year, showcasing his masterful academic techniques of portraiture. His ingeniousness extends to his models too. His father stands in for the doctor, and the sick woman and child are modelled by a beggar whom he hired off the street along with her offspring.

Blue Period

Other highlights include paintings from Picasso's Blue Period. *Woman with Bonnet* is an important work from this time, depicting a captive from the Saint-Lazare women's prison and veneral disease hospital which Picasso visited when in Paris. This visit started Picasso's fascination with people in the down-and-out layers of society. His nocturnal blue-tinted views of *Terrats de Barcelona* (*Roofs of Barcelona*) and *El Foll* (*The Madman*) are cold and cheerless, yet somehow alive. During this period he frequently painted the city rooftops from different perspectives. He also did many drawings of beggars, the blind and the impoverished elderly throughout 1903 and 1904 – *El Foll* is one of the most impressive from those series.

Local Knowledge

Don't Miss List

BY MALÉN GUAL, CURATOR AT MUSEU PICASSO

1 **SCIENCE AND CHARITY**
In 1897, Picasso started work on a canvas that would strengthen his position in the Spanish art world: *Science and Charity*. Following the guidelines of social realism and in an absolutely academic style, the work is the postscript to that first period of his youth. It was painted when he was only 15 years old.

2 **DWARF-DANCER (LA NANA)**
When Picasso painted this in 1901, his work was influenced by Toulouse-Lautrec. However, unlike Lautrec's work, there is very little drawing in his oils. The application of the brushstroke is harsh, the colours are warm and vehement, and the paint is often applied in medium and light brushstrokes. He searched for subjects for his paintings in dancehalls and cabarets, like Le Moulin Rouge.

3 **EL PASEO DEL COLOM**
In 1917, Picasso came to Barcelona with the Russian Ballets in pursuit of one of the Russian ballerinas, Olga Kokhlova. In *El Paseo del Colom*, Passeig de Colon is seen from the Ranzini guest house where Olga was staying. The painting combines Cubism with Divisionism.

4 **HARLEQUIN**
Here Picasso opts for a return to Classicism, not only in the execution but also in the softness and subtlety of the tonalities, which is reminiscent of the harlequins of 1905. Picasso presented the work at the art exhibition of 1919.

5 **LAS MENINAS SUITE**
Between August and December 1957, Picasso carried out an exhaustive analysis of Velázquez's *Las Meninas*. This suite of 58 works is a comprehensive study of rhythm, colour and movement. It is also a constant play of imagination in metamorphosing the personalities of a number of the components of the work. However, his faithfulness and respect towards the atmosphere of Velázquez's work are evident through all the compositions.

Discover La Ribera

Getting There & Away

○ Metro Línia 4 coasts down the southwest flank of La Ribera, stopping at Urquinaona, Jaume I and Barceloneta. Línia 1 also stops nearby, at Urquinaona and Arc de Triomf (the nearest stop for the Parc de la Ciutadella).

◉ Sights

Museu Picasso   Museum
See p92.

Disseny Hub   Museum
(☏ 93 256 23 00; www.dhub-bcn.cat; Carrer de Montcada 12; adult/child under 16yr/senior & student €5/free/3, 3-8pm Sun free; ⏱ 11am-7pm Tue-Sat, to 8pm Sun, to 3pm holidays; Ⓜ Jaume I) The 13th-century Palau dels Marquesos de Llió (which underwent repeated alterations into the 18th century) is temporary home to part of the city's Disseny (Design) Hub collection of applied arts – this is where it has its temporary exhibitions, study galleries and activities.

Often the exhibition on the ground floor is free, while the more extensive 1st-floor exhibition is what you pay for (admission includes entry to both locations). The permanent collections of Disseny are housed in the Palau Reial de Pedralbes and the new building, scheduled for completion in 2013, will be in Plaça de les Glòries. The building's courtyard, with its cafe-restaurant, makes a delightful stop.

Museu de la Xocolata
TRAVEL PICTURES / ALAMY ©

Mercat de Santa Caterina   Market

(☏93 319 17 40; www.mercatsantacaterina.net; Avinguda de Francesc Cambó 16; ⏱7.30am-2pm Mon, to 3.30pm Tue, Wed & Sat, to 8.30pm Thu & Fri; Ⓜ Jaume I) Finished in 2005, this excellent produce market is distinguished by its kaleidoscopic and weirdly wavy roof, held up above the bustling produce stands, restaurants, cafes and bars by twisting slender branches of what look like grey steel trees.

The multicoloured ceramic roof (with a ceiling made of warm, light timber) recalls the Modernista tradition of *trencadís* decoration (a type of mosaic, such as that in Park Güell). Indeed, its curvy design, like a series of Mediterranean rollers, seems to plunge back into an era when Barcelona's architects were limited only by their (vivid) imagination.

The market's 1848 predecessor had been built over the remains of the demolished 15th-century Gothic Monestir de Santa Caterina, a powerful Dominican monastery. A small section of the church foundations is glassed over in one corner as an archaeological reminder (with explanatory panels), the **Espai Santa Caterina** (admission free; ⏱8.30am-2pm Mon-Wed & Sat, to 8pm Thu & Fri).

Parc de la Ciutadella   Park

(Passeig de Picasso; ⏱8am-6pm Nov-Feb, to 8pm Oct & Mar, to 9pm Apr-Sep; Ⓜ Arc de Triomf) Come for a stroll, a picnic, a visit to the zoo or to inspect Catalonia's regional parliament, but don't miss a visit to this, the most central green lung in the city. Parc de la Ciutadella is perfect for winding down.

After the War of the Spanish Succession, Felipe V razed a swath of La Ribera to build a huge fortress (La Ciutadella), designed to keep watch over Barcelona. It became a loathed symbol of everything Catalans hated about Madrid and the Bourbon kings,

and was later used as a political prison. Only in 1869 did the central government allow its demolition, after which the site was turned into a park and used for the Universal Exhibition of 1888.

The monumental **cascada** (waterfall) near the Passeig de Pujades park entrance, created between 1875 and 1881 by Josep Fontserè with the help of an enthusiastic young Gaudí, is a dramatic combination of statuary, rugged rocks, greenery and thundering water. All of it perfectly artificial! Nearby, hire a rowing boat to paddle about the small lake.

To the southeast, in what might be seen as an exercise in black humour, the fort's former arsenal now houses the **Parlament de Catalunya** (www.parlament.cat; ⏱guided tours 10am-1pm Sat, Sun & holidays).

The Passeig de Picasso side of the park is lined by several buildings constructed for, or just before, the Universal Exhibition. The medieval-looking caprice at the top end is the most engaging. Known as the **Castell dels Tres Dragons** (Castle of the Three Dragons), it long housed the Museu de Zoologia, which is now closed.

Zoo de Barcelona   Zoo

(☏902 457545; www.zoobarcelona.com; Passeig de Picasso & Carrer de Wellington; adult/child under 3yr/senior/child 3-12yr €17/free/8.90/10.20; ⏱10am-7pm Jun-Sep, to 6pm mid-Mar–May & Oct, to 5pm Nov–mid-Mar; 🚻; Ⓜ Barceloneta) The zoo is a great day out for kids, with 7500 critters that range from geckos to gorillas – there are more than 400 species, plus picnic areas dotted all around.

Museu de la Xocolata   Museum

(☏93 268 78 78; www.museuxocolata.cat; Plaça de Pons i Clerch; adult/child under 7yr/senior & student €4.30/free/3.65; ⏱10am-7pm Mon-Sat, to 3pm Sun & holidays; 🚻; Ⓜ Jaume I) Chocoholics have a hard time containing themselves in this museum dedicated to

La Ribera

Arc de Triomf

C de Girona

C d'Ali Bei

Ronda de Sant Pere

Pg de Lluís Companys

C del Bruc

C de Méndez Núñez

C de Lluís el Piadós

⊗19

Plaça de Sant Pere

C Comtal

C d'en Cortines

C del Portal Nou

Plaça del Comerç

Passatge de Sert

C de Sant Pere més Alt

C d'en Mònec

C d'en Llàstics

Plaça de Sant Agustí Vell

C del Comerç

C d'Ortigosa

C de Sant Pere Mitjà

C de Sant Pere més Baix

C dels Metges

Plaça de Sant Agustí Vell

36 *Palau de la Música* ⊕◉ *Catalana*

C de Mare de Déu del Pilar

C de Jaume Giralt

Former Convent de Sant Agustí

26

C de Verdaguer i Callis

21 ⊗

C d'en Giralt i Pellisser

C del Fonollar

Plaça d'Allada i Vermell

9 ▦

23 ⊗

Mercat de Santa Caterina

C dels Carders

⊕**34**

⊗**25**

C General Alvarez de Castro

6 ◉ **14** ⊗

LA RIBERA

5 ◉

C dels Assaonadors

Av de Francesc Cambó

C de les Freixures

C de Colomines

C dels Corders

⊗**24**

C de la Princesa

C del Dr Joaquim Pou

Plaça d'Antoni Maura

C dels Mercaders

C de la Bòria

Museu Picasso

▦ Palau dels Cervelló

Av de la Catedral

C de la Tapineria

10▦

41 ⊕

C de Montcada

4 ▦

⊕**42**

Plaça de la Seu

Plaça de Santa Llúcia

C de Santa Llúcia

C dels Comtes

Plaça de Ramon Berenguer el Gran

Carrer dels Cotoners

44

⊗**22**

27 ⊕

C dels Mirallers

C del Bro soli

⊕**29**

37 ⊕

C del Bisbe

Plaça de l'Àngel

C de l'Argenteria

C Vigatans

45 ⊕

C de Manresa

C de Basea

Església de Santa Maria del Mar

40 ⊕

C de la Llibreteria

C de Jaume I

Via Laietana

C del Sotstinent Navarro

30 ⊕

15 ⊗

C de les Caputxes

BARRI GÒTIC

C del Call

Plaça de Sant Jaume

Plaça de Sant Just

C de Lledó

CIUTAT VELLA

C de la Nau

46 ⊕

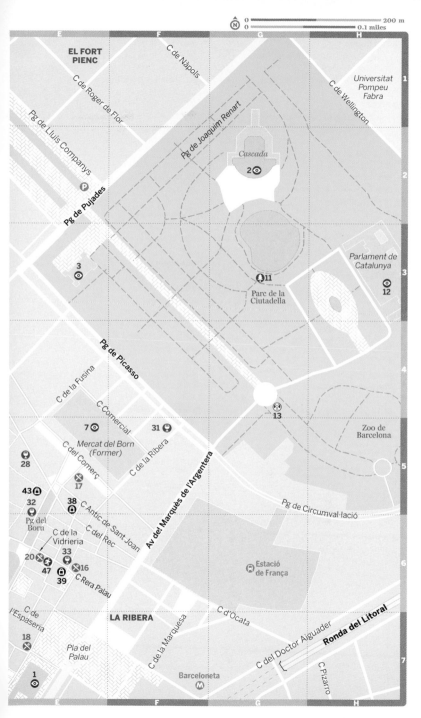

0   200 m
0   0.1 miles

EL FORT PIENC

C de Nàpols

C de Roger de Flor

C de Wellington

Universitat Pompeu Fabra

Pg de Lluís Companys

Pg de Joaquim Renart

Pg de Pujades

Cascada

2

3

Parlament de Catalunya

11

12

Parc de la Ciutadella

Pg de Picasso

C de la Fusina

C Comercial

7

31

Mercat del Born (Former)

C de la Ribera

C del Comerç

28

17

43

32

38

C Antic de Sant Joan

C del Rec

Av del Marquès de l'Argentera

13

Zoo de Barcelona

Pg de Circumval·lació

Pg del Born

C de la Vidrieria

20

33

47

16

39

C Rera Palau

Estació de França

LA RIBERA

C d'Ocata

C de l'Espaseria

18

Pla del Palau

C de la Marquesa

Ronda del Litoral

C del Doctor Aiguader

C Pizarro

Barceloneta

1

La Ribera

the fundamental foodstuff – especially when the entry ticket is a chocolate bar!

Under the Gothic arches of what remains of the convent's one-time cloister is a pleasant cafe-bar, the **Bar del Convent** (◷10am-9pm Mon-Thu, 11am-11pm Fri, 1pm-midnight Sat) – particularly good for families with children. Kids often play football in the cloister grounds. You enter at Carrer del Comerç 36.

Arxiu Fotogràfic
de Barcelona   Gallery
(☎93 256 34 20; www.bcn.cat/arxiu/fotografic; Plaça de Pons i Clerch; admission free; ◷10am-7pm Mon-Sat; Ⓜ Jaume I) On the 2nd floor of the former Convent de Sant Agustí is the modest exhibition space of this city photo archive. Photos on show are generally

related to the city, as the photo collection is principally devoted to that theme, from the late 19th century until the late 20th century.

Museu del Rei
de la Magia   Museum
(☎93 319 73 93; www.elreydelamagia.com; Carrer de l'Oli 6; with/without show €12/5; ◷6-8pm Thu, with show 6pm Sat & noon Sun; ✦; Ⓜ Jaume I) This museum is a timeless curio. It is the scene of magic shows, home (upstairs) to collections of material that hark back to the 19th-century origins of the shop (everything from old posters and books for learning tricks to magic wands and trick cards) and the place for budding magicians of all ages to enrol in courses. Seeing is believing.

NFII. SETCHFIELD / GETTY IMAGES ©

Don't Miss
Palau de la Música Catalana

This concert hall is a high point of Barcelona's Modernista architecture. It's not exactly a symphony, but more a series of crescendos in tile, brick, sculpted stone and stained glass. Built by Domènech i Montaner between 1905 and 1908 for the Orfeó Català musical society, it was conceived as a temple for the Catalan Renaixença (Renaissance). The *palau* (palace) was built with the help of some of the best Catalan artisans of the time, in the cloister of the former Convent de Sant Francesc, and since 1990 it has undergone several major changes.

The *palau*, like a peacock, shows off much of its splendour on the outside. Take in the principal facade with its mosaics, floral capitals and the sculpture cluster representing Catalan popular music.

Wander inside the foyer and restaurant areas to admire the spangled, tiled pillars. Best of all, however, is the richly colourful auditorium upstairs, with its ceiling of blue-and-gold stained glass and shimmering skylight that looks like a giant, crystalline, downward-thrusting nipple. Above a bust of Beethoven on the stage towers a wind-blown sculpture of Wagner's Valkyries (Wagner was top of the Barcelona charts at the time it was created). This can only be savoured on a guided tour or by attending a performance – either is highly recommended.

NEED TO KNOW

☎902 475485; www.palaumusica.org; Carrer de Sant Francesc de Paula 2; adult/child/student & EU senior €15/free/€7.50; ☺50min tours every 30 minutes 10am-6pm Easter week & Aug, 10am-3.30pm Sep-Jul; ⓂUrquinaona

99

Casa Llotja de Mar   Architecture

(La Llotja; ✆ 902 448448; www.casallotja.
com; Passeig d'Isabel II 1; M Barceloneta) The
centrepiece of the city's medieval stock
exchange (more affectionately known as
La Llotja) is the fine Gothic Saló de Con-
tractacions (Transaction Hall), built in the
14th century. Pablo Picasso and Joan Miró
attended the art school that was housed
in the Saló dels Cònsols from 1849. These
and five other halls were encased in a
neoclassical shell in the 18th century. The
stock exchange was in action until well
into the 20th century and the building
remains in the hands of the city's chamber of commerce. Occasionally it opens
the doors to the public but the rooms are
more generally hired out for events.

Mercat del Born   Market

(Plaça Comercial; M Barceloneta) Excavation
in 2001 at the former Mercat del Born,
a late-19th-century produce market
built of iron and glass, unearthed great
chunks of one of the districts flattened to
make way for the much-hated Ciutadella.

Historians found intact streets and the
remains of houses, dating as far back as
the 15th century. Excitement was such
that plans to locate a new city library in
the long-disused market were dropped.
Instead, the site will become a museum
and cultural centre – the projected date is
still unsure.

Eating

If you'd mentioned El Born (El Borne in
Spanish) in the early 1990s, you wouldn't
have raised much interest. Now the
area is peppered with bars, dance dives,
groovy designer stores and restaurants.
El Born is where Barcelona is truly
cooking – avant-garde chefs and fusion
masters have zeroed in on this southern
corner of La Ribera to conduct their
culinary experiments. If you don't want
to play such wild games, there's plenty of
the traditional stuff to choose from, too.

Left: El Xampanyet (p104); **Below:** Paella
(LEFT) BRENT WINEBRENNER / GETTY IMAGES ©; (BELOW) AUTHOR'S IMAGE LTD / ALAMY ©

Casa Delfín   Spanish €

(Passeig del Born 36; mains €4-12; ⊗noon-1am; MBarceloneta) One of Barcelona's culinary delights, Casa Delfín is everything you dream of when you think of Catalan (and Mediterranean) cooking. Start with the tangy and sweet *calçots* (a cross between a leek and an onion; January to March only) or salt-strewn *padron* peppers, and go on to grilled sardines specked with parsley, then tackle the meaty monkfish roasted in white wine and garlic.

Le Cucine Mandarosso   Italian €

(☎932 69 07 80; www.lecucinemandarosso.com; Carrer Verdaguer i Callis 4; mains €8, lunch menu €10; ⊗lunch & dinner; MUrquinaona) What a treat it is to discover the world of Mandarosso. This is comfort food done to perfection – the menu changes daily, with only six mains to choose from, five of which are pasta, and one vegetable, fish or meat. The antipasti can be vegetables, or fresh cheese, such as the wonderfully creamy *burrata* (fresh cheese made from mozzarella and cream), buffalo-milk mozzarella, or smoked scamorza and provola cheese.

El Passadís Del Pep   Seafood €€

(☎93 310 10 21; www.passadis.com; Pla del Palau 2; mains €15-20; ⊗lunch & dinner Tue-Sat, dinner Mon Sep-Jul; MBarceloneta) There's no sign, but locals know where to head for a seafood feast. They say the restaurant's raw materials are delivered daily from fishing ports along the Catalan coast. There is no menu – what's on offer depends on what the sea has surrendered on the day – but you can count on something along the lines of fresh seafood and/or fish, a bit of *jamón* (cured ham), tomato bread and grilled vegetables.

Cal Pep   Tapas €€

(☎93 310 79 61; www.calpep.com; Plaça de les Olles 8; mains €8-18; ⊗lunch Tue-Sat, dinner Mon-Fri Sep-Jul; MBarceloneta) It's getting a foot in the door here that's the

101

PIETRO CANALI / SIME / 4CORNERS ©

Don't Miss
Església de Santa Maria del Mar

At the southwest end of Passeig del Born stands the apse of Barcelona's finest Catalan Gothic church, Santa Maria del Mar (Our Lady of the Sea). Built in the 14th century with record-breaking alacrity for the time (it took just 54 years), the church is remarkable for its architectural harmony and simplicity. During construction the city's *bastaixos* (porters) spent a day each week carrying on their backs the stone required to build the church from royal quarries in Montjuïc. Their memory lives on in reliefs of them in the main doors and stone carvings elsewhere in the church.

The exterior gives an impression of sternness, and the narrow streets surrounding it are restrictive and claustrophobic. It may come as a (pleasant) surprise then, to find a spacious and light interior – the central nave and two flanking aisles separated by slender octagonal pillars give an enormous sense of lateral space.

The interior is almost devoid of imagery of the sort to be found in Barcelona's other large Gothic churches, but Santa Maria was lacking in superfluous decoration even before anarchists gutted it in 1909 and 1936. Keep an eye out for music recitals, often baroque and classical.

NEED TO KNOW
✆ 93 319 05 16; Plaça de Santa Maria del Mar; ⏱ 9am-1.30pm & 4.30-8pm; Ⓜ Jaume I

problem – there can be queues around the square with people trying to get in. And if you want one of the five tables out the back, you'll need to call ahead. Most people are happy elbowing their way to the bar for some of the tastiest gourmet seafood tapas in town. Pep recommends *cloïsses amb pernil* (clams and ham) or the *trifàsic* (combo of calamari, whitebait and prawns).

Pla de la Garsa
Catalan €€

(📞 933 15 24 13; www.pladelagarsa.com; Carrer dels Assaonadors 13; mains €10; 🕐dinner; Ⓜ Jaume I) This 17th-century house is the ideal location for a romantic candlelit dinner. Timber beams, anarchically scattered tables and soft ambient music combine to make an enchanting setting over two floors for traditional, hearty Catalan cooking, with dishes such as *timbal de botifarra negra* (a black pudding dish with mushrooms).

Tantarantana
Mediterranean €

(📞 93 268 24 10; Carrer d'en Tantarantana 24; mains €6-7; 🕐dinner Mon-Sat; Ⓜ Jaume I) Surrounded as it is by the furiously fashionable front-line nuclei of *nueva cocina española* – the new Spanish cuisine – this spot is a refreshing contrast. There is something comforting about the old-style marble-top tables, upon which you can sample simple but well-prepared dishes such as risotto or grilled tuna served with vegetables and ginger. It attracts a 30-something crowd who enjoy the outdoor seating in summer.

En Aparté
French €

(📞 932 69 13 36; www.enaparte.es; Carrer Lluis el Piados 2; mains €8-10; Ⓜ Arc de Triomph or Urquinaona) A great low-key place to eat good-quality French food, just off the quiet Plaça de Sant Pere. The restaurant is small but spacious, with sewing-machine tables and vintage details, and floor-to-ceiling windows that bring in some wonderful early-afternoon sunlight.

Mandarosso Pastis
Cafe, Pastelería €

(📞 933 19 05 02; www.lecucinemandarosso.com; Carrer General Alvarez de Castro 5-7; 🕐8am-9pm Tue-Sat, 9am-2pm Sun, closed Mon; Ⓜ Urquinaona) Little sister to Le Cucine Mandarosso (p101), this is its cake-focused cafe. The place is tiny, with two small tables and one wooden communal table, a little record player that blasts old hits, and the glowing cake counter. It also serves breakfast.

Bubó
Pastelería, Ristorante €

(📞 93 268 72 24; www.bubo.ws; Carrer de les Caputxes 6 & 10; 🕐4pm-midnight Mon, 10am-midnight Tue-Thu & Sun, 10am-2am Fri & Sat; Ⓜ Barceloneta) Carles Mampel is a sweet artist, literally. It is difficult to walk by his bar and pastry shop without taking a seat to try one of his fantasy-laden creations.

Lilipep
Cafe €

(📞 933 10 66 97; Carrer del Pou de la Cadena 8; 🕐10am-10pm Tue-Thu, to midnight Fri-Sun; 🛜🖨; Ⓜ Jaume I) If you're in need of a break from sightseeing or indeed a little drink with a *tapa* (included!), head for this German-Catalan concoction, hidden in a little side street off the Carrer de la Princesa. Help yourself to the books as you have your coffee and check out what the next live performance might be. There are vegetarian and meat-based dishes, and Lilipep also does hearty German breakfasts.

La Llavor dels Orígens
Catalan €

(www.lallavordelsorigens.com; Carrer de la Vidrieria 6-8; mains €8-10; 🕐12.30pm-12.30am; Ⓜ Jaume I) In this treasure chest of Catalan regional products, the shop shelves groan under the weight of bottles and packets of goodies. It also has a long menu of smallish dishes, such as *sopa de carbassa i castanyes* (pumpkin and chestnut soup) or *mandonguilles amb albergínies* (rissoles with aubergine), that you can mix and match over wine by the glass.

Bar Joan
Catalan €

(📞 93 310 61 50; Mercat de Santa Caterina; menú del día €11; 🕐lunch Mon-Sat; Ⓜ Jaume I) Along with the popular Cuines de Santa Caterina, there are a couple of bar-eateries in the Mercat de Santa Caterina. Bar Joan is known especially to locals for its *arròs negre* (cuttlefish-ink rice) on Tuesdays at lunchtime.

🍷 Drinking & Nightlife

Countless bars dot the elongated Passeig del Born and the web of streets winding off it and around the Església de Santa Maria del Mar – the area has an ebullient, party feel.

La Vinya del Senyor
Wine Bar

(Plaça de Santa Maria del Mar 5; ☺noon-1am Tue-Sun; Ⓜ Jaume I) Relax on the *terrassa*, which lies in the shadow of Església de Santa Maria del Mar, or crowd inside at the tiny bar. The wine list is long and there's a table for those who opt to sample by the bottle rather than the glass.

Gimlet
Cocktail Bar

(Carrer del Rec 24; cocktails €10; ☺10pm-3am; Ⓜ Jaume I) Transport yourself to a Humphrey Bogart movie. White-jacketed bar staff with all the appropriate aplomb will whip you up a gimlet or any other classic cocktail (around €10) your heart desires.

El Xampanyet
Wine Bar

(Carrer de Montcada 22; ☺noon-4pm & 7-11pm Tue-Sat, noon-4pm Sun; Ⓜ Jaume I) Nothing has changed for decades in this, a well-known *cava* bar. Plant yourself at the bar or seek out a table against the tiled walls for a glass or three of *cava* (Catalan sparkling wine) and an assortment of tapas, such as the tangy *boquerons en vinagre* (white anchovies in vinegar).

Miramelindo
Bar

(☎93 319 53 76; Passeig del Born 15; ☺8pm-2.30am; Ⓜ Jaume I) A spacious tavern in a Gothic building, this remains a classic on Passeig del Born for mixed drinks, while soft jazz and soul sounds float overhead. Try for a comfy seat at a table towards the back before it fills to bursting.

La Fianna
Bar

(www.lafianna.com; Carrer dels Banys Vells 15; ☺6pm-1.30am Sun-Wed, to 2.30am Thu-Sat; Ⓜ Jaume I) There is something medieval about this bar, with its bare stone walls, forged iron candelabra and cushion-covered lounges. This place heaves and, as the night wears on, it's elbow room only.

Mudanzas
Bar

(☎93 319 11 37; Carrer de la Vidrieria 15; ☺10am-2.30am; Ⓜ Jaume I) This was one of the first bars to get things into gear in El Born and it still attracts a faithful crowd.

It's a straightforward place for a beer, a chat and perhaps a sandwich.

Upiaywasi
Club

(☎93 268 01 54; Carrer d'Allada Vermell 11; ☺5pm-2am Mon-Thu, 5pm-3am Fri & Sat, 4pm-1am Sun; Ⓜ Barceloneta) Slide into this dimly lit cocktail bar, which crosses a chilled ambience with Latin American music. A mix of lounges and intimate table settings, chandeliers and muted decorative tones lends the place a pleasingly conspiratorial feel.

Magic
Club

(☎93 310 72 67; Passeig de Picasso 40; ☺11pm-6am Wed-Sun; Ⓜ Barceloneta) Although it sometimes hosts live acts in its sweaty, smoky basement, it's basically a straightforward, subterranean nightclub offering rock, mainstream dance faves and Spanish pop.

Entertainment

Palau de la Música Catalana
Live Music

(☎902 442882; www.palaumusica.org; Carrer de Sant Francesc de Paula 2; ☺box office 10am-9pm Mon-Sat; Ⓜ Urquinaona) A feast for the eyes, this Modernista pudding is also the city's traditional venue for classical and choral music. Just being here for a performance is an experience. Sip a preconcert tipple in the foyer, its tiled pillars all a-glitter. Head up the grand stairway to the main auditorium, a whirlpool of Modernista whimsy. The *palau* has a wide-ranging programme.

Shopping

The former commercial heart of medieval Barcelona is today still home to a cornucopia of old-style specialist food and drink shops, a veritable feast of aroma and atmosphere. They have been joined, since the late 1990s, by a raft of hip little fashion stores.

Casa Gispert
Food

(☎ 93 319 75 35; www.casagispert.com; Carrer dels Sombrerers 23; Ⓜ Jaume I) The wonderful, atmospheric and wood-fronted Casa Gispert has been toasting nuts and selling all manner of dried fruit since 1851.

Vila Viniteca
Drink

(☎ 902 327777; www.vilaviniteca.es; Carrer dels Agullers 7; ⏰ 8.30am-8.30pm Mon-Sat; Ⓜ Jaume I) One of the best wine stores in Barcelona (and Lord knows, there are a few), this place has been searching out the best in local and imported wines since 1932.

Galeria Maeght
Art

(☎ 93 310 42 45; www.maeght.com; Carrer de Montcada 25; ⏰ 11am-2pm & 3-7pm Tue-Fri, 11am-2pm Sat; Ⓜ Jaume I) This high-end gallery, housed in one of the fine medieval mansions for which this street is known, specialises in 20th-century masters. It is as enticing for the building as the art.

Coquette
Fashion

(☎ 93 295 42 85; www.coquettebcn.com; Carrer del Rec 65; Ⓜ Barceloneta) With its spare, cut-back and designer look, this fashion store is automatically attractive in its own right. Women will love to browse through casual, feminine wear by such designers as Tsunoda, Vanessa Bruno, Chloé Baño and Hoss Intropia.

El Magnífico
Coffee

(☎ 93 319 60 81; www.cafeselmagnifico.com; Carrer de l'Argenteria 64; Ⓜ Jaume I) All sorts of coffee has been roasted here since the early 20th century. The variety of coffee (and tea) available is remarkable – and the aromas hit you as you walk in. Across the road, the same people run the exquisite and much newer tea shop **Sans i Sans** (☎ 93 319 60 81; Carrer de l'Argenteria 59).

Hofmann Pastisseria
Food

(☎ 93 268 82 21; www.hofmann-bcn.com; Carrer dels Flassaders 44; Ⓜ Jaume I) With old timber cabinets, this bite-sized gourmet patisserie has an air of timelessness, although it is quite new. Choose between jars of delicious chocolates, the day's croissants and more dangerous pastries, or an array of cakes and other sweets.

El Rey de la Magia
Specialty

(☎ 93 319 39 20; www.elreydelamagia.com; Carrer de la Princesa 11; ⏰ 11am-2pm & 5-8pm Mon-Fri, 10am-2pm Sat; Ⓜ Jaume I) For more than 100 years, the people behind this box of tricks have been keeping locals both astounded and amused. Should you decide to stay in Barcelona and make a living as a magician, this is the place to buy levitation brooms, glasses of disappearing milk and decks of magic cards.

Nu Sabates
Shoes, Accessories

(☎ 93 268 03 83; www.nusabates.com; Carrer dels Cotoners 14; Ⓜ Jaume I) A couple of modern-day Catalan cobblers have put together some original handmade leather shoes (and a handful of bags and other leather items) in their stylish locale.

Custo Barcelona
Fashion

(☎ 93 268 78 93; www.custo-barcelona.com; Plaça de les Olles 7; Ⓜ Jaume I) The psychedelic decor and casual atmosphere lend this avant-garde Barcelona fashion store a youthful edge.The dazzling colours and cut of anything from dinner jackets to hot pants are for the uninhibited.

Barceloneta & the Waterfront

Barcelona's long, sundrenched waterfront provides a pleasant escape when you need a break from Gothic lanes and Modernista architecture. Heading northeast from the Ciutat Vella, you'll soon find yourself amid tempting seafood restaurants and waterfront bars, with a palm-lined promenade taking cyclists, joggers and strollers out to the beaches, which run some 4km up to Parc del Fòrum.

Abutting the waterfront is Barceloneta, an old fishing quarter laid out in the mid-18th century with narrow grid-like streets and an earthy feel. Countless seafood eateries and a handful of bohemian drinking dens lurk in this labyrinth.

On summer days, the area fills with sunseekers making their way to and from the people-packed sands nearby. There are beaches all the way north to El Fòrum. Along the sand, rustic summertime shacks called *chringuitos* (beach bars) dole out music and cocktails day and night.

Rambla de Mar (p110); designer: Viaplana & Piñon

Barceloneta & the Waterfront Highlights

Beaches (p114)

Other cities may have their diamond-dust beaches, but how often are they juxtaposed with 2000 rollercoaster years of history? Seven broad scimitars of sand lie within soccer-ball-lobbing distance of the Ciutat Vella and a slew of other heavyweight sights. In addition to frolicking in the sea, highlights include cycling the promenade, dining off Port Olímpic marina and having a sunset cocktail overlooking Barceloneta beach.

Seafood (p116)

In Barcelona, cooking is a form of alchemy, with the city exhibiting some of Spain's most daring and avant-garde cuisine. But down in the salty 18th-century grid of La Barceloneta, fresh seafood is served with less pretension. Roam the streets between tightly packed, family-run restaurants and look for local specialities such as *arròs negre* (squid-ink rice) and scallops in *cava* (Catalan sparkling wine).

L'Aquàrium (p112)

There are approximately 450 species of aquatic animals in this water-side aquarium, but it's the sharks that leave the biggest impression. An 80m-long underwater tunnel keeps the beasts at bay behind worryingly thin Plexiglas. After you've scared the wits out of the kids, calm them down in the museum's Mediterranean-themed interactive section. Afterwards, you can take a scenic stroll along Barcelona's revitalised Port Vell.

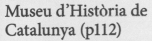

Museu d'Història de Catalunya (p112)

Catalan pride runs deep in Barcelona, a fiercely independent city with a history that often has more in common with Sardinia than Seville. To understand the complexities, head first to this multifarious museum, where you can learn about the unique story of Catalunya, from Stone Age peoples to the post-Franco years, with interactive displays on Roman rule, the Middle Ages, the Spanish Civil War and other pivotal epochs.

Museu Marítim (p115)

For a break from the art and architecture of the Ciutat Vella, dip into this fascinating museum set inside a massive Gothic shipyard. Barcelona is Europe's largest Mediterranean port, with a maritime legacy surpassed only by Venice's and the Museu Marítim is more than the usual stash of naval ephemera. Despite ongoing renovations the museum retains its prize exhibit: a replica of a 16th-century Spanish flagship.

Barceloneta & the Waterfront Walk

Once an industrial wasteland, Barcelona's waterfront was transformed for the 1992 Olympics, with artificial beaches, sculptures, marinas and a seaside promenade. This breezy ramble takes you through the former fishing village of La Barceloneta and past serene beaches out to Port Olímpic.

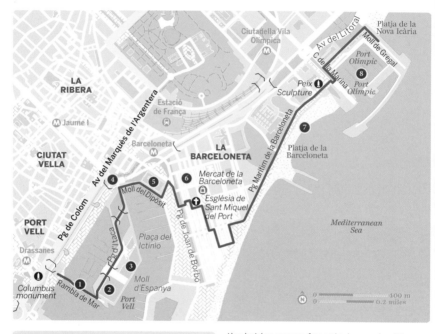

WALK FACTS

- **Start** Port Vell
- **Finish** Port Olímpic
- **Distance** 4.2km
- **Duration** Two hours

❶ Rambla de Mar

With your back to the Columbus monument, take a stroll out along the **Rambla de Mar**, a narrow pedestrian walkway out over the harbour. A natural continuation of La Rambla, this swing bridge provides a tranquil spot to take in the breezy views over Port Vell and Barcelona's much cleaned-up waterfront extension. Every hour or so, the bridge opens for entering and exiting sailboats.

❷ Maremàgnum

Anchoring the western side of the Rambla de Mar is **Maremàgnum**, a bubbling leisure centre with chirpy waterside restaurants, bars, shops and cinemas.

❸ L'Aquàrium

Next door you'll find one of Europe's largest aquariums, **L'Aquàrium** (p112), which is home to more than 11,000 different sea critters. The most spectacular is a varied collection of sharks, seen through a glass tunnel. Intrepid divers can even go for a swim with these massive predators.

4 Barcelona Head

As you make your way over to Barceloneta, you'll pass the colourful **Barcelona Head sculpture** by famous American pop artist Roy Lichtenstein. Unveiled in 1992, the sculpture pays homage to Gaudí and other Modernistas in its *trencadis* (use of broken tiles to form mosaics).

5 Museu d'Història de Catalunya

Housed in former warehouses, **Museu d'Història de Catalunya** (p112) provides a potted history of Catalonia. It also boasts a top-floor restaurant-bar with terrace. Downstairs, a series of upscale seafood eateries provide open-air dining facing the marina.

6 Barceloneta

Walk down Passeig de Joan de Borbó, a street that crackles with activity and draws a cross-section of society. Make your way into the compact lanes of **Barceloneta**, which still retains a bit of its salty character from when those crowded dwellings were mostly home to dockworkers and mariners. Stroll past the Baroque Església de Sant Miquel del Port and pass the lively Mercat de la Barceloneta.

7 Platja de la Barceloneta

The narrow streets of Barceloneta can feel claustrophobic after awhile, but luckily the expansive seafront is just steps away. Barcelona's inner-city beach **Platja de la Barceloneta** is packed with people and activity. A series of bars on the sand churn out meals, cocktails and music for the hordes of sun worshippers. Up in the northeast corner, a string of hip bar-restaurants get especially busy on languid summer nights.

8 Port Olímpic

A long promenade shadows the waterfront up to the marina of **Port Olímpic**, which was created for the 1992 Olympics and is jammed with seafood restaurants. An eye-catcher on the approach from Barceloneta is Frank Gehry's giant copper *Peix* (Fish) sculpture. Just to the north is the agreeable Platja de Nova Icària.

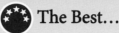 The Best...

PLACES TO EAT

Can Majó Open-air seafood feasts near the beachfront. (p116)

Maians Excellent cooking and unpretentious charm. (p117)

La Cova Fumada Hole-in-the-wall joint serving incredible food. (p117)

Els Pescadors One of Barcelona's best seafood restaurants. (p119)

Torre d'Alta Mar The great views match the top-notch cooking. (p118)

PLACES TO DRINK

Xampanyeria Can Paixano *Cava* bar that's perfect for an afternoon pick-me-up. (p121)

Absenta Kitsch-filled bar serving absinthe and housemade vermouth. (p121)

Opium Mar Ever popular seaside club and beachfront bar. (p121)

Razzmatazz Ibiza-stye clubbing is alive in El Poblenou. (p123)

SEASIDE ACTIVITIES

Orsom Take a sunset sail aboard a catamaran. (p123)

El Fòrum Bike to this post-millennial development along the waterfront. (p114)

Platja de la Mar Bella Take it all off on this clothing-optional beach. (p114)

Port Fòrum (p114)
JON MIKEL DURALDE / ALAMY ©

Discover Barceloneta & the Waterfront

🔄 Getting There & Away

○ **Walking** From the old city, La Rambla and Via Laietana are the main pedestrian access points across busy Ronda del Litoral.

○ **Metro** Go to Drassanes (Línia 3) to reach Port Vell; Barceloneta (Línia 4) has its own stop for the neighbourhood. Línia 4 continues out to Ciutadella Vila Olímpica (best stop for Port Olímpic) and El Maresme Fòrum near Parc del Fòrum.

L'Aquàrium
ANNA SERRANO / SIME / 4CORNERS ©

👁 Sights

Port Vell & La Barceloneta

L'Aquàrium Aquarium
(Map p116; ✆93 221 74 74; www.aquarium bcn.com; Moll d'Espanya; adult/child €18/13, dive €300; ☺9.30am-11pm Jul & Aug, to 9pm Sep-Jun, dive 9.30am-2pm Wed, Fri & Sat; ⓂDrassanes) It is hard not to shudder at the sight of a shark gliding above you, displaying its toothy, wide-mouthed grin. But this, the 80m shark tunnel, is the highlight of one of Europe's largest aquariums. It has the world's best Mediterranean collection and plenty of colourful fish from as far off as the Red Sea, the Caribbean and the Great Barrier Reef. All up, some 11,000 fish (including a dozen sharks) of 450 species reside here.

Back in the shark tunnel, which you reach after passing a series of themed fish tanks with everything from bream to sea horses, various species of shark (white tip, sand tiger, bonnethead, black tip, nurse and sandbar) flit around you, along with a host of other critters, from flapping rays to bloated sunfish. An interactive zone, Planeta Agua, is host to a family of Antarctic penguins and a tank of rays that you watch close up.

Divers with a valid dive certificate may dive in the main tank with the sharks.

Museu d'Història de Catalunya Museum
(Museum of Catalonian History; Map p116; ✆93 225 47 00; www.mhcat.net; Plaça de Pau Vila 3; adult/child permanent exhibition only €4/3, permanent & temporary exhibitions €5/4, 1st Sun of month free ; ☺10am-7pm Tue & Thu-Sat, to

8pm Wed, to 2.30pm Sun; Ⓜ Barceloneta) The Palau de Mar (Map p116) building facing the harbour once served as warehouses, but was transformed in the 1990s. Inside is the Museu d'Història De Catalunya, something of a local patriotic statement, but interesting nonetheless.

The permanent display covers the 2nd and 3rd floors, taking you from the Stone Age through to the early 1980s. It is a busy hotchpotch of dioramas, artefacts, videos, models, documents and interactive bits: all up, an entertaining exploration of 2000 years of Catalan history. See how the Romans lived, listen to Arab poetry from the time of the Muslim occupation of the city, peer into the dwelling of a Dark Ages family in the Pyrenees, try to mount a knight's horse or lift a suit of armour.

When you have had enough of all this, descend into a civil-war air-raid shelter, watch a video in Catalan on post-Franco Catalonia or head upstairs to the first-rate rooftop restaurant and cafe, 1881.

Outside the museum, you'll find a string of elegant open-air restaurants serving up classic seafood dishes.

Pailebot de Santa Eulàlia   Ship
(Map p116; Moll de la Fusta; adult/child incl Museu Marítim €4/free; ☺ noon-7.30pm Tue-Fri, 10am-7pm Sat & Sun; Ⓜ Drassanes) Along the palm-lined promenade Moll de la Fusta is moored a 1918 three-mast schooner restored by the Museu Marítim. You can see it perfectly well without going aboard, and there's not an awful lot to behold below decks. On occasion it sets sail for demonstration trips up and down the coast.

Transbordador Aeri   Cable Car
(Map p116; www.telefericodebarcelona.com; Passeig Escullera; 1 way/return €10/15; ☺ 11am-7pm, closed Jan-mid-Feb; Ⓜ Barceloneta, 🚌 17, 39 or 64) This cable car strung across the harbour to Montjuïc provides an eagle-eye view of the city. The cabins float between the Torre de Sant Sebastià (in La Barceloneta) and Miramar (Montjuïc), with a midway stop at the Torre de Jaume I in front of the World Trade Center. At the top of the Torre de Sant Sebastià is a spectacularly located restaurant, Torre d'Alta Mar.

Platjas
Beaches

(Map p120; 🚍 36 or 41, Ⓜ Ciutadella Vila Olímpic, Bogatell, Llacuna or Selva de Mar) A series of pleasant beaches stretches northeast from the Port Olímpic marina. They are largely artificial, but this doesn't stop an estimated seven million bathers from piling in every year!

The southernmost beach, **Platja de la Nova Icària**, is the busiest. Behind it, across the Avinguda del Litoral highway, is the Plaça dels Campions, site of the rusting three-tiered platform used to honour medallists in the sailing events of the 1992 games.

The next beach is **Platja de Bogatell**. Just in from the beach is the Cementiri de L'Est, created in 1773. It was positioned outside the then city limits for health reasons. Its central monument commemorates the victims of an 1821 yellow-fever epidemic.

Platja de la Mar Bella (with its brief nudist strip and sailing school) and **Platja de la Nova Mar Bella** follow, leading into the new residential and commercial waterfront strip, the Front Marítim, part of the Diagonal Mar project in the Fòrum district. It is fronted by the last of these artificial beaches to be created, **Platja del Llevant**.

Port Olímpic, El Poblenou & El Fòrum

Torre Agbar
Architecture

(Map p120; 📞 93 342 21 29; www.torreagbar.com; Avinguda Diagonal 225; Ⓜ Glòries) Barcelona's very own cucumber-shaped tower, Jean Nouvel's luminous Torre Agbar is one of the most daring additions to Barcelona's skyline since the first towers of La Sagrada Família. Completed in 2005, it shimmers at night in shades of midnight blue and lipstick red. Unfortunately, you can only enter the foyer on the ground floor, frequently used to host temporary exhibitions.

Parc del Centre del Poblenou
Park

(Map p120; Avinguda Diagonal; ⏰ 10am-sunset; Ⓜ Poblenou) Barcelona is sprinkled with parks whose principal element is cement, and Jean Nouvel's Parc del Centre del Poblenou, with its stylised metal seats and items of statuary, is no exception. However, the park's Gaudí-inspired cement walls are increasingly covered by sprawling bougainvillea and, inside, some 1000 trees of mostly Mediterranean species are complemented by thousands of smaller bushes and plants.

El Fòrum
Neighbourhood

(Map p120; Ⓜ El Maresme Fòrum) Before there was wasteland, half-abandoned factories and a huge sewage-treatment plant in the city's northeast corner. Now there are high-rise apartments, luxury hotels, a marina (Port Fòrum), a shopping mall and a conference centre.

The most striking element is the eerily blue, triangular *2001: A Space Odyssey*–style **Edifici Fòrum** building by Swiss architects Herzog & de Meuron.

A 300m stroll east from the Edifici Fòrum is the **Zona de Banys**, with kayaks and bikes available for rent, the option to learn diving, and other activities. This tranquil seawater swimming area was won from the sea by the creation of massive cement-block dykes. At its northern end, like a great rectangular sunflower, an enormous photovoltaic panel turns its face up to the sun to power the area with solar energy.

In summer, a weekend **amusement park** sets up with all the usual suspects: rides, shooting galleries, snack stands, inflatable castles and dodgem cars.

The **Parc de Diagonal Mar**, designed by Enric Miralles, contains pools, fountains, a didactic botanical walk (with more than 30 species of trees and other plants) and modern sculptures.

Museu Blau
Museum

(Blue Museum; Map p120; 📞 93 256 60 02; Parc del Fòrum; adult/child €6/2.70; ⏰ 10am-7pm Tue-Fri, to 8pm Sat & Sun; Ⓜ El Maresme Fòrum) Set inside the vaguely futuristic Edifici Fòrum, the Museu Blau, which opened in 2011, takes visitors on a journey all across the natural world. Multimedia and interactive exhibits explore topics like the history of evolution, earth's formation and the great scientists who have helped shape

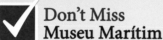

Don't Miss
Museu Marítim

These mighty Gothic shipyards are not as extensive as their Venetian counterparts but they're an extraordinary piece of civilian architecture nonetheless. Today the broad arches shelter the Museu Marítim, the city's seafaring-history museum and one of the most fascinating museums in town.

The shipyards were, in their heyday, among the greatest in Europe. Begun in the 13th century and completed by 1378, the long, arched bays (the highest arches reach 13m) once sloped off as slipways directly into the water, which lapped the seaward side of the Drassanes until at least the end of the 18th century. The centre of the shipyards is dominated by a full-sized replica (made in the 1970s) of Don Juan of Austria's flagship.

Fishing vessels, old navigation charts, models and dioramas of the Barcelona waterfront make up the rest of this engaging museum. The museum was being largely overhauled at the time of writing, and this should continue through 2013. When it reopens, visitors will encounter a greatly expanded collection with multimedia exhibits evoking more of Spain's epic history on the high seas. While this work continues, only a limited selection of the museum's objects can be seen.

The pleasant museum cafe offers courtyard seating and a small assortment of bites, as well as a decent *menú de mediodía* (set-price menu) at lunchtime.

NEED TO KNOW

Map p116; ☏ 93 342 99 20; www.mmb.cat; Avinguda de les Drassanes; adult/child under 7yr/senior & student €2.50/free/1.25, 3-8pm Sun free; ☉ 10am-8pm; Ⓜ Drassanes

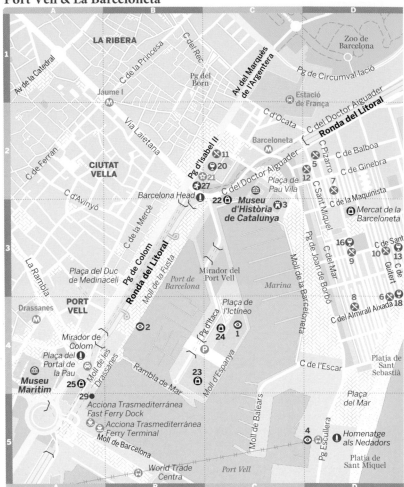

human knowledge. There are also specimens from the animal, plant and mineral kingdoms – plus dinosaur skeletons – all rather dramatically set amid the sprawling 9000 sq metres of exhibition space.

 Eating

Port Vell & La Barceloneta

For good food and atmosphere, head around to La Barceloneta, the lanes

of which fairly bristle with everything from good-natured, noisy tapas bars to upmarket seafood restaurants. Almost everything shuts on Sunday and Monday evenings.

Can Majó Seafood €€
(Map p116; ☏ 93 221 54 55; Carrer del Almirall Aixada 23; mains €18-24; ⊘ lunch & dinner Tue-Sat, lunch Sun; ⬚ 45, 57, 59, 64 or 157, Ⓜ Barceloneta) Virtually on the beach (with tables outside in summer), Can Majó has a long and steady reputation for fine seafood,

Port Vell & La Barceloneta

◎ Top Sights
Museu d'Història de Catalunya..........C2
Museu Marítim A4

◎ Sights
1 L'Aquàrium C4
2 Pailebot de Santa Eulàlia...................B4
3 Palau de Mar..........................C3
4 Transbordador Aeri......................D5

✖ Eating
5 Bitácora..............................D2
6 Can Majó D4
7 Can Maño D2
8 Can Ros D4
9 La Cova Fumada D3
10 Maians D3
11 Restaurant 7 Portes C2
Torre d'Alta Mar..................(see 4)
12 Vaso de Oro D2

◉ Drinking & Nightlife
13 Absenta D3
14 Catwalk..............................F1
15 CDLC F1
16 Ké? D3
17 Opium Mar F1
18 Santa Marta D3
19 Shôko F1
20 Xampanyeria Can Paixano C2

✪ Entertainment
21 Monasterio...........................B2

◉ Shopping
22 Feria de Artesanía del Palau
de Mar C3
23 Maremàgnum.........................B4
24 Mercado de Pintores...................C4
25 Port Antic A4

◉ Sports & Activities
26 Barcelona By Bike.....................F1
27 Barnabike...........................B2
28 Biciclot.............................F1
29 Orsom..............................A5

DISCOVER BARCELONETA & THE WATERFRONT EATING

particularly its rice dishes and bountiful *suquets* (fish stews). The *bollabessa de peix i marisc* (fish and seafood bouillabaisse) is succulent. Or try a big *graellada* (mixed seafood grill). Sit outside and admire the beach goers.

Maians
Tapas €
(Map p116; Carrer de Sant Carles 28; tapas €4-6; ☺Wed-Sun; Ⓜ Barceloneta) This tiny jovial bar and eatery in Maians serves excellent tapas to a hip, largely neighbourhood crowd. Highlights include the not-to-be-missed *cazón en adobo* (marinated fried dogfish) and *mejillones a la marinera* (mussels in a rich tomato broth) followed by hearty *arroz negra* (paella with cuttlefish).

La Cova Fumada
Tapas €
(Map p116; ✆93 221 40 61; Carrer de Baluard 56; tapas €3-6; ☺9am-3.20pm Mon-Wed,

9am-3.20pm & 6-8.20pm Thu & Fri, 9am-1.20pm Sat; **M**Barceloneta) There's no sign and few tourists in sight, but this tiny, buzzing family-run tapas spot always packs in a crowd. The secret? Mouth-watering *pulpo* (octopus), *calamar*, *sardinias* and 15 or so other small plates cooked up to perfection in the small open kitchen near the door.

Torre
d'Alta Mar   Mediterranean €€€
(Map p116; ☎ 93 221 00 07; www.torredealtamar. com; Torre de Sant Sebastià; mains around €30; ⏱lunch & dinner Tue-Sat, dinner Sun & Mon; 🚌17, 39, 57 or 64, **M**Barceloneta) Head 75m skyward to the top of the Torre de Sant Sebastià and take a ringside seat for magnificent city and waterfront views while dining on first-rate seafood. Menu hits include creamy rice with grilled prawns; scallops with artichoke, asparagus and ham; and roasted monkfish. Prices are steep (a multicourse lunch runs €48) and would seem poor value apart from the fine vistas.

Can Ros   Seafood €€
(Map p116; ☎ 93 221 45 79; Carrer del Almirall Aixada 7; mains €16-28; ⏱Tue-Sun; 🚌45, 57, 59, 64 or 157, **M**Barceloneta) The fifth generation is now at the controls in this immutable seafood favourite, which first opened in 1911. In a restaurant where the decor is a reminder of simpler times, there's a straightforward guiding principle: serve juicy fresh fish cooked with a light touch. Can Ros also does a rich *arròs a la marinera* (seafood rice), *fideuá* (similar to paella, but using vermicelli noodles as the base) with shrimp and clams and a mixed seafood platter for two.

Restaurant 7 Portes   Seafood €
(Map p116; ☎ 93 319 30 33; www.7portes.com; Passeig d'Isabel II 14; mains €14-28; ⏱1pm-1am; **M**Barceloneta) Founded in 1836 as a cafe and converted into a restaurant in 1929, this is a classic. It exudes an old-world atmosphere with its wood panelling, tiles, mirrors and plaques naming some of the famous – such as Orson Welles – who have passed through. Paella is the

Left: Xiringuito D'Escribà (p120); **Below:** Torre Agbar (p114); designer: Jean Nouvel

(LEFT) DIEGO LEZAMA / GETTY IMAGES ©; (BELOW) GIOVANNI GUARINO TRAVEL / ALAMY ©

speciality, or go for the surfeit of seafood in the *gran plat de marisc* (literally 'big plate of seafood'), big enough for two.

Vaso de Oro
Tapas €

(Map p116; Carrer de Balboa 6; tapas €5-9; ⏰10am-midnight; Ⓜ Barceloneta) Always packed, this narrow bar gathers a festive, beer-swilling crowd who come for fantastic tapas. Fast-talking, white-jacketed waiters will serve up a few quick quips with your plates of grilled *gambes* (prawns), *foie a la plancha* (grilled liver pâté) or *solomillo* (sirloin) chunks. Want something a little different to drink? Ask for a *flauta cincuenta* – half lager and half dark beer.

Can Maño
Spanish €

(Map p116; Carrer del Baluard 12; mains €8-12; ⏰Mon-Sat; Ⓜ Barceloneta) It may look like a dive, but you'll need to be prepared to wait before being squeezed in at a packed table for a raucous night of *raciones* (larger portions of tapa dishes; posted on

a board at the back) over a bottle of *turbio* – a cloudy white plonk. The seafood is abundant with first-rate squid, shrimp and fish served at rock-bottom prices.

Bitácora
Tapas €

(Map p116; Carrer de Balboa 1; tapas €4-8; ⏰10am-11pm Mon-Fri, to 5pm Sat; Ⓜ Barceloneta) This youthful little gem is a neighbourhood favourite for its simple but congenial ambience and well-priced tapas plates, which come in ample portions. Top picks: *calamares, boquerones* (anchovies), *gambas* (shrimp) and *vedella amb rulo de cabra* (veal with goat cheese).

Port Olímpic, El Poblenou & El Fòrum

Els Pescadors
Seafood €€

(Map p120; ☎93 225 20 18; www.elspescadors. com; Plaça de Prim 1; mains €16-28; ⏰daily; Ⓜ Poblenou) Set on a picturesque square lined with low houses and *bella ombre*

119

DISCOVER BARCELONETA & THE WATERFRONT EATING

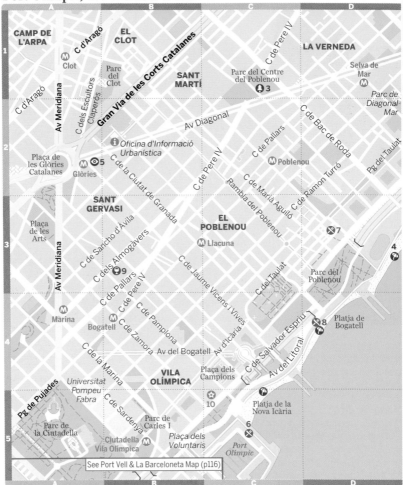

trees long ago imported from South America, this bustling family restaurant continues to serve some of the city's great seafood-and-rice dishes.

El Cangrejo Loco   Seafood €€

(Map p120; ✆93 221 05 33; www.elcangrejoloco. com; Moll de Gregal 29-30; mains €13-25, menú del día €25; ☉daily; Ⓜ Ciutadella Vila Olímpica) Of the hive of eating activity along the docks of Port Olímpic, the 'Mad Crab' is among the best. Fish standards, such as *bacallà* (cod) and *rap* (monkfish),

are served in various guises and melt in the mouth. The rich *paella de llamàntol* (lobster paella) is superb.

Xiringuito D'Escribà   Seafood €€

(Map p120; ✆93 221 07 29; www.escriba.es; Ronda Litoral 42; mains €18-22; ☉lunch daily year-round, dinner Thu-Sat Apr-Sep; Ⓜ Llacuna) The clan that brought you Escribà sweets and pastries also operates one of Barcelona's most popular waterfront seafood eateries.

Port Olímpic, El Poblenou & El Fòrum

Xampanyeria Can Paixano   Wine Bar

(Map p116; ☎93 310 08 39; Carrer de la Reina Cristina 7; tapas €3-6; ⊙9am-10.30pm Mon-Sat, to 1pm Sun; ☒Barceloneta) This lofty old champagne bar has a long run on a winning formula. The standard poison is bubbly rosé in elegant little glasses, combined with bite-sized *bocadillos* (filled rolls). This place is jammed to the rafters, and elbowing your way to the bar to ask harried staff for menu items can be a titanic struggle.

Absenta   Bar

(Map p116; Carrer de Sant Carles 36; ☒Barceloneta) Decorated with old paintings, vintage lamps and curious sculpture (including a dangling butterfly woman and face-painted TVs), this whimsical and creative drinking den takes its liquor seriously. Stop in for the house-made vermouth or for more bite try one of many absinthes on hand.

Opium Mar   Club

(Map p116; ☎902 267486; www.opiummar.com; Passeig Marítim de la Barceloneta 34; ⊙8pm-6am; ☒Ciutadella Vila Olímpica) This seaside dance place has a spacious dance floor that attracts a mostly foreign crowd. It only begins to fill from about 3am and is best in summer, when you can spill onto a terrace overlooking the beach. The

⊙ Drinking & Nightlife

The northeastern end of the beach on the Barceloneta waterfront near Port Olímpic is a pleasant corner of evening chic that takes on a balmy, almost Caribbean air in the warmer months. A selection of restaurant-lounges and trendy bar-clubs vies for your attention. Several other attractive options are scattered about away from this core of night-time entertainment.

beachside outdoor section works as a chilled restaurant-cafe by day.

CDLC
Lounge

(Map p116; www.cdlcbarcelona.com; Passeig Marítim de la Barceloneta 32; Ⓘnoon-3am; Ⓜ Ciutadella Vila Olímpica) Seize the night by the scruff at the Carpe Diem Lounge Club, where you can lounge in Asian-inspired surrounds. Ideal for a slow warm-up before heading to the nearby clubs. You can come for the food or wait until about midnight, when they roll up the tables and the DJs and dancers take full control.

Ké?
Bar

(Map p116; Carrer del Baluard 54; Ⓘ11am-2am; Ⓜ Barceloneta) An eclectic and happy crowd hangs about this hippie-ish little bar near La Barceloneta's market. Pull up a padded 'keg chair' or grab a seat on one of the worn lounges in back and join in the animated conversation wafting out over the street.

Santa Marta
Bar

(Map p116; Carrer de Guitert 60; Ⓘ10.30am-7pm Sun, Mon, Wed & Thu, to 10pm Fri & Sat; Ⓑ45, 57, 59 & 157, Ⓜ Barceloneta) This chilled bar just back from the beach attracts a garrulous mix of locals and expats, who come for light meals, beers and prime people-watching at one of the outdoor tables near the boardwalk.

Shôko
Lounge

(Map p116; www.shoko.biz; Passeig Marítim de la Barceloneta 36; Ⓘnoon-3am Tue-Sun; Ⓜ Ciutadella Vila Olímpica) This stylish restaurant, club and beachfront bar brings in a touch of the Far East via potted bamboo, Japanese electro and Asian-Med fusion cuisine. As the food is cleared away, Shôko transforms into a deep-grooving nightspot with international DJs like Groove Armada and Felix da Housecat spinning for the beautiful crowd. The open-sided beachfront lounge is a popular spot for a sundowner.

Catwalk
Club

(Map p116; Ⓙ93 224 07 40; www.clubcatwalk.net; Carrer de Ramon Trias Fargas 2-4; admission €15-18; Ⓘmidnight-6am Thu-Sun; Ⓜ Ciutadella Vila Olímpica) A well-dressed crowd piles in here for good house music, occasionally mellowed down with more body-hugging electro, R&B, hip hop and funk. Alternatively, you can sink into a fat lounge for a quiet tipple and whisper.

Transbordador Aeri (p113)

NICK SERVIAN / ROBERT HARDING WORLD IMAGERY / CORBIS ©

DISCOVER BARCELONETA & THE WATERFRONT DRINKING & NIGHTLIFE

Waterfront Markets

On weekends, Port Vell springs to life with a handful of markets selling a mix of antiques, contemporary art and crafts at key points along the waterfront.

At the base of La Rambla, the small **Port Antic** (Map p116; Plaça del Portal de la Pau; ☺10am-8pm Sat & Sun; Ⓜ Drassanes) market is a requisite stop for strollers and antique hunters.

Near the Palau de Mar, you'll find **Feria de Artesanía del Palau de Mar** (Map p116; Moll del Dipòsit; ☺10am-8pm Sat & Sun; Ⓜ Barceloneta), with artisans selling a range of crafty items, including jewellery, graphic T-shirts, handwoven hats, fragrant candles and soaps, scarves and decorative items.

Take a stroll along the pedestrian-only Rambla de Mar to reach the weekend art fair **Mercado de Pintores** (Map p116; Passeig d'Ítaca; ☺10am-8pm Sat & Sun; Ⓜ Drassanes), with a broad selection of paintings both collectable and rather forgettable.

Razzmatazz Club
(Map p120; ☎93 320 82 00; www.salarazzmatazz.com; Carrer de Pamplona 88; admission €15-30; ☺midnight-3.30am Thu, to 5.30am Fri & Sat; Ⓜ Marina or Bogatell) Bands from far and wide occasionally create scenes of near hysteria in this, one of the city's classic live-music and clubbing venues. On weekends the live music then gives way to club sounds. Five different clubs in one huge postindustrial space attract people of all dance persuasions and ages.

 Entertainment

Monasterio Live Music
(Map p116; ☎616 287197; Passeig d'Isabel II 4; ☺9pm-2.30am; Ⓜ Barceloneta) Wander downstairs to the brick vaults of this jamming basement music den. There's a little of everything, from jazz on Sunday night to blues jams on Thursdays, rock and roll on Tuesdays and up-and-coming singer-songwriters on Mondays.

Yelmo Cines Icària Cinema
(Map p120; ☎93 221 75 85; www.yelmocines.es; Carrer de Salvador Espriu 61; Ⓜ Ciutadella Vila Olímpica) This vast cinema complex screens movies in the original language on 15 screens, making for plenty of choice.

 **Shopping**

Maremàgnum Mall
(Map p116; www.maremagnum.es; Moll d'Espanya 5; ☺10am-10pm; Ⓜ Drassanes) Created out of largely abandoned docks, this buzzing shopping centre, with its bars, restaurants and cinemas, is pleasant enough for a stroll virtually in the middle of the old harbour. The usual labels are on hand, including the youthful Spanish chain Mango, mega-retailer H&M and eye-catching fashions from Barcelona-based Desigual.

 Sports & Activities

Orsom Cruise
(Map p116; ☎93 441 05 37; www.barcelona-orsom.com; Moll de les Drassanes; adult/child €14/11; ☺Apr-Oct; Ⓜ Drassanes) Aboard a large sailing catamaran, Orsom makes the 90-minute journey past Port Olímpic, the beaches and out to the Fòrum and back. There are three departures per day (four on weekends in July and August), and the last is a jazz cruise, scheduled around sunset. The same company also runs five daily, 50-minute speedboat tours (adult/child €12/8).

La Sagrada Família & L'Eixample

By far the most extensive of Barcelona's districts, this sprawling grid is full of subidentities. Almost all the city's Modernista buildings were raised in L'Eixample. The pick of them line Passeig de Gràcia, but hundreds adorn the area. Work on Gaudí's La Sagrada Família church continues.

As Barcelona's population exploded, the medieval walls were knocked down by 1856. In 1869, work began on L'Eixample (the Extension) to fill the open country that then lay between Barcelona and Gràcia. Building continued until well into the 20th century. Well-to-do families snapped up prime plots and raised fanciful buildings in the eclectic style of the Modernistas.

Shoppers converge on Passeig de Gràcia and La Rambla de Catalunya. At night, mainly from Thursday to Saturday, Carrer d'Aribau and nearby streets are home to a buzzing nightlife scene. The 'Gaixample', around Carrer del Consell de Cent and Carrer de Muntaner, is the centre of gay nightlife.

Casa Batlló (p139)

La Sagrada Família & L'Eixample Highlights

La Sagrada Família (p130)

Spain's biggest tourist attraction, La Sagrada Família, is a unique, extraordinary piece of architecture. Conceived as atonement for Barcelona's sins of modernity, this giant church became Gaudí's holy mission and, in medieval fashion, is still under construction 100 years after its inception. At once ancient and thoroughly modern, La Sagrada Família is packed with religious iconography and symbolism, and leaves no one unmoved.

Fundació Antoni Tàpies (p135)

Take a pioneering Modernista building by architect Luís Domènech i Montaner and stuff it with works by one of Spain's great painters, Antoni Tàpies. This collection showcases hundreds of pieces of the Catalan painter, sculptor and theorist, from surrealist works of the 1940s to imaginative sculpture-like pieces of 1970s Abstract Expression.

La Pedrera (p142)

One of Passeig de Gràcia's most captivating Modernista structures, La Pedrera is in the top tier of Gaudí's achievements. Officially called Casa Milà after its owners, it was nicknamed La Pedrera (The Stone Quarry) by bemused locals who watched Gaudí build it from 1905 to 1910. Conceived as an apartment block, it bears all the trademarks of Gaudí: swirling staircases, hallucinogenic curves and not a straight line in sight.

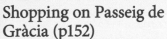

Shopping on Passeig de Gràcia (p152)

Once a lane that linked Barcelona to the village of Gràcia, the elegant, tree-lined Passeig de Gràcia has metamorphosed into the city's most opulent boulevard. Heaving with posh hotels and punctuated with architectural nods to Catalonia's Modernista movement, it is feted most for its shopping. Luxury labels share space with the odd indie fashion guerrilla.

Manzana de la Discordia (p128)

One block on Passeig de Gràcia is embellished with buildings by the three enfants terribles of early-20th-century Modernisme. Each building embodies a unique architectural style. Puig i Cadafalch's Casa Amatller (p134) is gabled and faintly Dutch, Domènech i Montaner's Casa Lleó Morera (p134) is whimsical with a regal quality and Gaudí's Casa Batlló (p139) is downright other-worldly.

La Sagrada Família & L'Eixample Walk

L'Eixample is packed with Modernista treasures. Start with the three unique buildings of the Manzana de la Discordia and end at La Sagrada Família.

WALK FACTS

- **Start** Passeig de Gràcia
- **Finish** La Sagrada Família
- **Distance** 3km
- **Duration** 1.5 hours

❶ Casa Lleó Morera

Near Carrer del Consell de Cent, have a look at the heavily ornamented facade of **Casa Lleó Morera** (p134), designed by Domènech i Montaner. Note the fine-featured sculptures of maidens holding the latest in early 20th-century technology: the telephone, the phonograph, the telegraph and the camera.

❷ Casa Amatller

A few doors up, you'll see Puig i Cadafalch's **Casa Amatller** (p134), which has a stepped Flemish Renaissance roof and a medi-evalesque facade adorned with whimsical statuary. Near the entrance portal, St George is impaling the dragon and there are more curious creatures on the second floor, including a monkey hammering on a forge.

❸ Casa Batlló

Casa Batlló (p139) shimmers in Gaudí-esque extravagance. Its symbolic meaning is open to interpretation but is undoubtedly connected with Catalan identity: a Carnaval celebration (the masklike balconies, the facade glittering like confetti), a fish (with scales and bonelike columns) and an abstract St George (the swordlike chimney) slaying the dragon (the scaly roof).

④ Fundació Antoni Tàpies

Just around the corner is another of Domènech i Montaner's fine works, which today houses the **Fundació Antoni Tàpies** (p135). The symmetrical brick exterior shows Muslim influences, while the wiry sculpture on the roof is a Tàpies creation and represents a chair jutting out of a cloud.

⑤ La Pedrera

Up the road is Casa Milà, better known as **La Pedrera** (p142) for its grey stone facade. The undulating walls and rippling wrought-iron balconies show organic influences. Up top stand the famous stone chimneys that resemble helmeted warriors, but you'll have to pay to see them.

⑥ Casa Thomas

Casa Thomas was one of Domènech i Montaner's earlier efforts. The ceramic details are a trademark and the massive ground-level wrought-iron decoration is magnificent. Wander inside to the Cubiña design store to admire his interior work.

⑦ Casa Llopis i Bofill

Casa Llopis i Bofill is an interesting block of flats designed by Antoni Gallissà. The graffiti-covered facade is particularly striking. The use of parabolic arches on the ground floor is a clear Modernista touch, as are the wrought-iron balconies.

⑧ La Sagrada Família

Strolling around **La Sagrada Família** (p130), you'll notice the wildly different styles of the Nativity Facade, completed during Gaudí's lifetime, and the Passion Facade, designed by Josep Maria Subirachs in the 1980s. Other key things to look for: the Risen Christ teetering halfway up the Passion Facade, eight completed belltowers with a different apostle seated at each and the image of Gaudí himself in the Passion Facade.

 The Best...

PLACES TO EAT

Tapaç 24 Innovative chef Carles Abellàn creates some of Barcelona's best tapas. (p143)

Can Kenji Mouth-watering dishes that blend Japanese tradition with Mediterranean verve. (p143)

Alkímia Magnificent Catalan cuisine by Michelin-starred Jordi Vila. (p143)

Cata 1.81 Lovely setting for gourmet tapas and wines by the glass. (p147)

PLACES TO DRINK

Monvínic Enchanting setting amid one of Spain's best wine bars. (p149)

La Fira Funhouse ambience and a staggering drinks selection. (p149)

Les Gens Que J'Aime Stylish but unpretentious gem in L'Eixample. (p151)

Dry Martini Classy bar serving Barcelona's best gin and tonics. (p150)

PLACES TO SHOP

Vinçon Beautifully designed furniture and housewares in a Modernista building. (p153)

Els Encants Vells Sprawling flea market that's full of treasures (and trash!) (p153)

El Bulevard dels Antiquaris Dozens of antique shops. (p153)

Casa Amatller (p134)
BETHUNE CARMICHAEL / GETTY IMAGES ©

Don't Miss
La Sagrada Família

If you have time for only one sightseeing outing, this should be it. La Sagrada Família inspires awe by its sheer verticality and magnificently elaborate design – inside and out. It may be unfinished, but it attracts around 2.8 million visitors a year and is the most visited monument in Spain. There's much to explore here – symbol-rich facades, an other-worldly interior and the on-site Museu Gaudí, which houses materials on the master's life and work.

Map p136

☏ 93 207 30 31

www.sagrada familia.org

Carrer de Mallorca 401

adult/child under 10yr/senior & student €13/free/11

🕑 9am-8pm Apr-Sep, to 6pm Oct-Mar

Ⓜ Sagrada Família

The Design

Gaudí devised a temple 95m long and 60m wide, able to seat 13,000 people. It was to have a central tower 170m high above the transept (representing Christ) and another 17 of 100m or more. The 12 towers along the three facades represent the Apostles, while the remaining five represent the Virgin Mary and the four Evangelists. With his characteristic dislike for straight lines (he said there were none in nature), Gaudí gave his towers swelling outlines inspired by the weird peaks of the holy mountain Montserrat outside Barcelona, and encrusted them with a tangle of sculpture that seems an outgrowth of the stone.

Guesses on when construction might be complete range from the 2020s to the 2040s. Already, some of the oldest parts of the church, especially the apse, have required restoration work.

The Interior

Inside, the roof is held up by a forest of extraordinary angled pillars. As the pillars soar towards the ceiling, they sprout a web of supporting branches, creating the effect of a forest canopy. The tree image is in no way accidental – Gaudí envisaged such an effect. Everything was thought through, including the shape and placement of windows to create the mottled effect of sunlight pouring through the branches of a thick forest.

Visiting La Sagrada Família

Although essentially a building site, the completed sections and the museum may be explored at leisure. Fifty-minute guided tours (€4) are offered. Alternatively, pick up an audio tour (€4). Enter from Carrer de Sardenya and Carrer de la Marina. Once inside, €2.50 will get you into lifts that rise up the towers of the Nativity and Passion facades. These two facades, each with four sky-scraping towers, are the sides of the church. The main Glory Facade, on which work is underway, closes off the southeast end on Carrer de Mallorca.

Don't Miss List

BY JORDI FAULÍ, DEPUTY ARCHITECTURAL DIRECTOR FOR LA SAGRADA FAMÍLIA

1 PASSION FACADE

Among the *Fachada de la Pasión*'s stand-out features are the angled columns, the dramatic scenes from Jesus' last hours, an extraordinary rendering of the Last Supper and a bronze door that reads like a sculptured book. But the most surprising view is from inside the door on the extreme right (especially in the afternoon with the sun in the west).

2 MAIN NAVE

The majestic *Nave Principal* showcases Gaudí's use of tree motifs for columns to support the domes. But it's the skylights that give the nave its luminous quality, with light flooding into the apse and main altar from the skylight 75m above the floor.

3 SIDE NAVE AND NATIVITY TRANSEPT

Although beautiful in its own right, this is the perfect place to view the sculpted treelike columns and get an overall perspective of the main nave. Turn around and you're confronted with the inside of the Nativity Facade, an alternative view that most visitors miss. The stained-glass windows are superb.

4 NATIVITY FACADE

The *Fachada del Nacimiento* is Gaudí's grand hymn to Creation. Begin by viewing it front-on, then draw close (but to one side) to make out the details of its sculpted figures. The complement to the finely wrought detail is the majesty of the four parabolic towers, which are topped by Venetian stained glass.

5 MODEL OF COLÒNIA GÜELL

The most interesting model in the Museu Gaudí is the church at Colònia Güell. It's upside down because that's how Gaudí worked to best study the building's form and structural balance.

La Sagrada Família

A Timeline

1882 Francesc del Villar is commissioned to construct a neo-Gothic church.

1883 Antoni Gaudí takes over as chief architect, and plans a far more ambitious church to hold 13,000 faithful.

1926 Death of Gaudí; work continues under Domènec Sugrañes. Much of the **apse** ❶ and **Nativity Facade** ❷ is complete.

1930 Bell towers ❸ of the Nativity Facade completed.

1936 Construction is interrupted by Spanish Civil War; anarchists destroy Gaudí's plans.

1939-40 Architect Francesc de Paula Quintana i Vidal restores the crypt and meticulously reassembles many of Gaudí's lost models, some of which can be seen in the **museum** ❹.

1976 Completion of **Passion Facade** ❺.

1986-2006 Sculptor Josep Subirachs adds sculptural details to the Passion Facade including the panels telling the story of Christ's last days, amid much criticism for employing a style far removed from what was thought typical of Gaudí.

2000 Central nave vault ❻ completed.

2010 Church completely roofed over; Pope Benedict XVI consecrates the church; work begins on a high-speed rail tunnel that will pass beneath the church's **Glory Facade** ❼.

2020-40 Projected completion date.

TOP TIPS

Light The best light through the stained-glass windows of the Passion Facade bursts through into the heart of the church in the late afternoon.

Time Visit at opening time on weekdays to avoid the worst of the crowds.

Views Head up the Nativity Facade bell towers for the views, as long queues generally await at the Passion Facade towers.

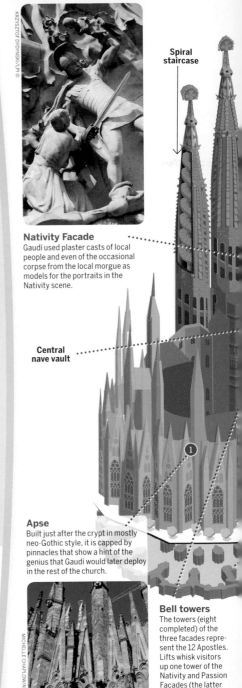

KRZYSZTOF DYDYNSKI/LP ©

Spiral staircase

Nativity Facade
Gaudí used plaster casts of local people and even of the occasional corpse from the local morgue as models for the portraits in the Nativity scene.

Central nave vault

Apse
Built just after the crypt in mostly neo-Gothic style, it is capped by pinnacles that show a hint of the genius that Gaudí would later deploy in the rest of the church.

MICHELLE CHAPLOW/ALAMY ©

Bell towers
The towers (eight completed) of the three facades represent the 12 Apostles. Lifts whisk visitors up one tower of the Nativity and Passion Facades (the latter gets longer queues) for fine views.

Passion Facade
See the story of Christ's last days from Last Supper to burial in an S-shaped sequence from bottom to top of the facade. Check out the cryptogram in which the numbers always add up to 33, Christ's age at his death.

STEPHEN SAKS/LPI ©

Completed church
Along with the Glory Facade and its four towers, six other towers remain to be completed. They will represent the four Evangelists, the Virgin Mary and, soaring above them all over the transept, a 170m colossus symbolising Christ.

Crypt
The first completed part of the church, the crypt is in largely neo-Gothic style and lies under the transept. Gaudí's burial place here can be seen from the Museu Gaudí.

Escoles de Gaudí

Museu Gaudí
Jammed with old photos, drawings and restored plaster models that bring Gaudí's ambitions to life, the museum also houses an extraordinarily complex plumb-line device he used to calculate his constructions.

DIANA BIER / ALAMY ©

Glory Facade
This will be the most fanciful facade of all, with a narthex boasting 16 hyperboloid lanterns topped by cones that will look something like an organ made of melting ice cream.

Discover La Sagrada Família & L'Eixample

🔄 Getting There & Away

○ **Metro** Four Metro lines criss-cross L'Eixample, three stopping at Passeig de Gràcia for the Manzana de la Discordia. Línia 3 stops at Diagonal for La Pedrera, while Línies 2 and 5 stop at Sagrada Família.

○ **Train** FGC lines from Plaça de Catalunya take you one stop to Provença, in the heart of L'Eixample.

◉ Sights

L'Esquerra de L'Eixample

FREE **Casa Amatller**   Architecture
(Map p144; 📞 93 487 72 17; www.amatller.org; Passeig de Gràcia 41; ⏱10am-8pm Mon-Sat, to 3pm Sun, guided tour in English noon Fri, in Catalan & Spanish noon Wed; Ⓜ Passeig de Gràcia) One of Puig i Cadafalch's most striking bits of Modernista fantasy, Casa Amatller combines Gothic window frames with a stepped gable borrowed from Northern European urban architecture. But the busts and reliefs of dragons, knights and other characters dripping off the main facade are pure caprice. The pillared foyer and staircase lit by stained glass are like the inside of some romantic castle.

The building was renovated in 1900 for the chocolate baron and philanthropist Antoni Amatller (1851–1910) and it will one day open partly to the public.

For now, you can wander into the foyer, admire the staircase and lift, and head through the shop to see the latest temporary exhibition out the back. Depending on the state of renovation, it is also possible to join a 1½-hour guided tour of the 1st floor, with its early-20th-century furniture and decor intact, and Amatller's photo studio.

Casa Lleó Morera   Architecture
(Map p144; Passeig de Gràcia 35; Ⓜ Passeig de Gràcia) Domènech i Montaner's 1905 contribution to the Manzana de la Discordia, with Modernista carving outside and a bright, tiled lobby in which floral motifs predominate, is perhaps the least odd-

Casa Amatller
ROBERT GEORGE YOUNG/ GETTY IMAGES ©

looking of the three main buildings on the block. If only you could get inside – they are private apartments. The 1st floor is giddy with swirling sculptures, rich mosaics and whimsical decor.

Fundació Antoni Tàpies Gallery

(Map p144; ☏ 93 487 03 15; www.fundaciotapies. org; Carrer d'Aragó 255; adult/child under 16yr €7/5.60; ☼10am-8pm Tue-Sun; Ⓜ Passeig de Gràcia) The Fundació Antoni Tàpies is both a pioneering Modernista building (completed in 1885) and the major collection of the leading 20th-century Catalan artist, Antoni Tàpies. A man known for his eso teric work, Tàpies died in February 2012, aged 88; he left behind a powerful range of paintings and a foundation intended to promote contemporary artists.

The building, designed by Domènech i Montaner for the publishing house Editorial Montaner i Simón (run by a cousin of the architect), combines a brick-covered iron frame with Islamic-inspired decoration. Tàpies crowned it with the meanderings of his own mind, a work called *Núvol i Cadira* (Cloud and Chair) that spirals above the building like a storm.

Although it's difficult to understand the art of Antoni Tàpies, it's worth seeing the one-hour documentary on his life, on the top floor, to understand his influences, method and the course of his interesting life. In his work, Tàpies expressed a number of themes, such as left-wing politics and humanitarianism; the practices of Zen meditation and its relationship between nature and insight; incarnation as seen in Christian faith; and art as an alchemy or magic.

The collection spans the arc of Tàpies' creations (with more than 800 works) and contributions from other contemporary artists.

Fundación Francisco Godia Gallery

(Map p144; ☏ 93 272 31 80; www.fundacionfgo dia.org; Carrer de la Diputació 250; adult/child under 5yr/student €6.50/free/3.50; ☼10am-8pm Mon & Wed-Sun; Ⓜ Passeig de Gràcia) Francisco Godia (1921–90), head of one of Barcelona's great establishment families, liked fast cars (he came sixth in the 1956 Grand Prix season driving Maseratis) and fine art. An intriguing mix of medieval art,

L'Eixample

Pàdua

GRÀCIA

Fontana (M)

C Gran de Gràcia

Travessera de Gràcia

Molina

Sant Gervasi

Via Augusta

Jardins de Moragas

Gràcia (M)

See Central L'Eixample Map on (p144)

C de Balmes

Via Augusta

Casa de les Punxes (Casa Terrades)

Plaça de Joan Carles I

C de Muntaner

Av Diagonal

C de Còrsega

(M) Diagonal

(M) Diagonal

P

L'ESQUERRA DE L'EIXAMPLE

10 ✗5

Plaça de Francesc Macià

8 ✗9

C de Buenos Aires

C de Londres

C de Casanova

C de París

6 ✗

Plaça del Doctor Ferrer Cajigal

C del Rosselló

C d'Enric Granados

(M) Provença

Passeig de Gràcia

Rambla de Catalunya

P

Av de Sarrià

C d'Aribau

C de Muntaner

C de València

Plaça del Doctor Letamendi

C d'Aragó

C de Balmes

Av de Josep Tarradellas

C de Casanova

Universitat Industrial

(M) Hospital Clínic

C de Mallorca

C d'Aragó

Universitat de Barcelona

C de Còrsega

C del Rosselló

C de Viladomat

C de Villarroel

Universitat

Plaça de la Universitat

(M)

Entença (M)

(M) Entença

C del Comte d'Urgell

Plaça de Castella

11 ❸

✗3

Plaça de Goya

Presó Model

Av de Roma

C de València

C de Calàbria

C de Viladomat

C de la Diputació

(M) Urgell

✗7

❸12

13 ✪

C d'Entença

C de Rocafort

C de Sepúlveda

C de Floridablanca

Sant Antoni

C de Llançà

Rocafort (M)

Gran Via de les Corts Catalanes

SANT ANTONI

Mercat de Sant Antoni

Tarragona (M)

Parc de Joan Miró

C de Tamarit

C de Mansó

Former Plaça de Braus Les Arenes

Av de Mistral

C del Parlament

Hostafrancs

(M) C de la Creu Coberta

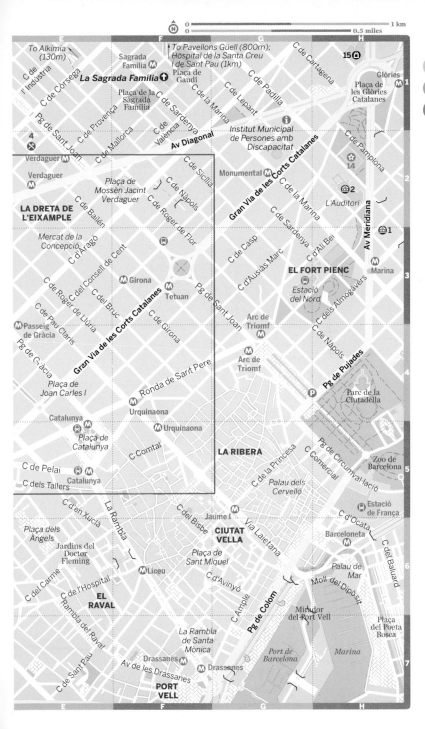

To Alkímia
(130m)

C de
l'Indústria

C de Còrsega

La Sagrada Família ⊕

Sagrada
Família Ⓜ

Plaça de
Gaudí

To Pavellons Güell (800m);
Hospital de la Santa Creu
i de Sant Pau (1km)

C de Padilla

C de Cartagena

15 🅐

Glòries Ⓜ

Plaça de
les Glòries
Catalanes

Plaça de la
Sagrada
Família

C de Sardenya

C de la Marina

C de Lepant

Pg de Sant Joan

4 ⊗

C de Provença

C de València

C de Mallorca

Av Diagonal

Institut Municipal
de Persones amb
Discapacitat

🛈

C de Pamplona

Verdaguer Ⓜ

Verdaguer
Ⓜ

**LA DRETA DE
L'EIXAMPLE**

Plaça de
Mossèn Jacint
Verdaguer

C de Sicília

C de Nàpols

C de Bailén

C de Roger de Flor

Monumental Ⓜ

Gran Via de les Corts Catalanes

C de la Marina

14 ✪

🏛 2
L'Auditori

Av Meridiana

🏛 1

Mercat de la
Concepció

C d'Aragó

C del Consell de Cent

C de Casp

C de Sardenya

C d'Ausiàs Marc

C d'Alí Bei

Marina Ⓜ

EL FORT PIENC

C de Roger de Llúria

C del Bruc

Ⓜ Girona

Tetuan Ⓜ

Pg de Sant Joan

C de Girona

C d'Ausiàs Marc

🄿
Estació
del Nord

C dels Almogàvers

C de Nàpols

C de Pau Claris

Ⓜ Passeig
de Gràcia

Pg de Gràcia

Gran Via de les Corts Catalanes

Arc de
Triomf Ⓜ

Arc de
Triomf Ⓜ

Pg de Pujades

Parc de la
Ciutadella

Plaça de
Joan Carles I

Ronda de Sant Pere

Urquinaona Ⓜ

Ⓜ Urquinaona

Pg de Circumval·lació

Pg de Pujades

Catalunya
🄡

Plaça de
Catalunya

C Comtal

LA RIBERA

Zoo de
Barcelona

C de Pelai
🄡 Ⓜ

Catalunya

C dels Tallers

C de la Princesa

C Comercial

Estació
de França

C d'Ocata

C d'en Xuclà

La Rambla

C del Bisbe

Jaume I Ⓜ

Via Laietana

Barceloneta Ⓜ

C del Baluard

Plaça dels
Àngels

Jardins del
Doctor
Fleming

**CIUTAT
VELLA**

Plaça de
Sant Miquel

Palau dels
Cervelló

Palau de
Mar

Moll del Dipòsit

C del Carme

C de l'Hospital

Ⓜ Liceu

C d'Avinyó

**EL
RAVAL**

Rambla del Raval

C Ample

Pg de Colom

Mirador
del Port Vell

Plaça
del Poeta
Bosca

La Rambla de
Santa
Mònica

Port de
Barcelona

Marina

C de Sant Pau

Drassanes Ⓜ

Av de les Drassanes

Ⓜ Drassanes

**PORT
VELL**

137

L'Eixample

ceramics and modern paintings make up this varied private collection.

Housed in Casa Garriga Nogués, this is a stunning, carefully restored Modernista residence originally built for a rich banking family by Enric Sagnier in 1902–05.

Museu del Perfum   Museum

(Map p144; ☑ 93 216 01 21; www.museudelperfum. com; Passeig de Gràcia 39; adult/student & senior €5/3; ☉ 10.30am-1.30pm & 4.30-8pm Mon-Fri, 11am-2pm Sat; Ⓜ Passeig de Gràcia) Housed in the back of the Regia (p153) perfume store, this museum contains everything from ancient Egyptian and Roman (the latter mostly from the 1st to 3rd centuries AD) scent receptacles to classic eau-de-cologne bottles – all in all, some 5000 bottles of infinite shapes, sizes and histories.

Museu del Modernisme Català   Museum

(Map p144; ☑ 93 272 28 96; www.mmcat.cat; Carrer de Balmes 48; adult/child under 5yr/child 5-16yr/student €10/free/5/7; ☉ 10am-8pm Mon-Sat, to 3pm Sun; Ⓜ Passeig de Gràcia) Housed in a Modernista building, the ground floor seems like a big Modernista furniture showroom. Several items by Antoni Gaudí, including chairs from Casa Batlló and a mirror from Casa Calvet, are supplemented by a host of items by his lesser-known contemporaries, including some typically whimsical, mock medieval pieces by Puig i Cadafalch.

The basement, showing off Modernista traits like mosaic-coated pillars, bare brick vaults and metal columns, is lined with Modernista art, including paintings by Ramon Casas and Santiago Rusiñol, and statues by Josep Llimona and Eusebi Arnau.

Universitat de Barcelona   Architecture

(Map p144; ☑ 93 402 11 00; www.ub.edu; Gran Via de les Corts Catalanes 585; ☉ 9am-9pm Mon-Fri; Ⓜ Universitat) Although a university was first set up on what is now La Rambla in the 16th century, the present, glorious mix of (neo) Romanesque, Gothic, Islamic and Mudéjar architecture is a caprice of the 19th century (built 1863–82). Wander into the main hall, up the grand staircase and around the various leafy cloister, or take a stroll in the rear gardens. On the 1st floor, the main hall for big occasions is the Mudéjar-style Paranimfo.

La Dreta de L'Eixample

La Sagrada Família   Church

See p130.

Hospital de la Santa Creu i de Sant Pau   Architecture

(☑ 93 317 76 52; www.rutadelmodernisme.com; Carrer de Cartagena 167; guided tour adult/ senior & student €10/5; ☉ tours 10am, 11am, noon & 1pm in English, others in Catalan, French & Spanish; Ⓜ Hospital de Sant Pau) Domènech i Montaner outdid himself with this Modernista masterpiece, long considered one of the city's most important hospitals. The complex, including 16 unique pavilions – together with the Palau de la Música Catalana, a joint World Heritage Site – is lavishly decorated.

 ## Don't Miss
Casa Batlló

One of the strangest residential buildings in Europe, this is Gaudí at his hallucinogenic best. The facade, sprinkled with bits of blue, mauve and green tiles and studded with wave-shaped window frames and balconies, rises to an uneven blue-tiled roof with a solitary tower.

Locals know Casa Batlló variously as the *casa dels ossos* (house of bones) or *casa del drac* (house of the dragon). It's easy enough to see why. The balconies look like the bony jaws of some strange beast and the roof represents Sant Jordi (St George) and the dragon. Even the roof was built to represent the shape of an animal's back, with shiny scales – the 'spine' changes colour as you walk around. Before going inside, take a look at the pavement. Each paving piece carries stylised images of an octopus and a starfish, Gaudí designs originally cooked up for Casa Batlló.

When Gaudí was commissioned to refashion this building, he went to town inside and out. The internal light wells shimmer with tiles of deep sea blue. Gaudí eschewed the straight line, and so the staircase wafts you up to the 1st (main) floor, where the salon looks on to Passeig de Gràcia. Everything swirls: the ceiling is twisted into a vortex around its sunlike lamp; the doors, window and skylights are dreamy waves of wood and coloured glass. The attic is characterised by Gaudí's trademark hyperboloid arches. Twisting tiled chimney pots add a surreal touch to the roof.

NEED TO KNOW

Map p144; ☎ 93 216 03 06; www.casabatllo.es; Passeig de Gràcia 43; adult/child under 7yr/student, child 7-18yr & senior €18.15/free/14.55; ⏱ 9am-8pm; Ⓜ Passeig de Gràcia

Domènech i Montaner wanted to create a unique environment that would also cheer up patients. Among artists who contributed statuary, ceramics and artwork was the prolific Eusebi Arnau. The hospital facilities have been transferred to a new complex on the premises, freeing up the century-old structures, which are being restored to their former glory in a plan to convert the complex into an international centre on the Mediterranean.

Guided tours are the only way the curious get inside this unique site – but the building might one day open up for more regular visits.

Museu de la Música
Museum

(Map p136; 🕿93 256 36 50; www.museumusica. bcn.cat; Carrer de Lepant 150; adult/senior & student €5/4, 3-8pm Sun free; ⊙10am-6pm Mon & Wed-Sat, to 8pm Sun; MMonumental) Some 500 instruments (less than a third of those held) are on show in this museum housed on the 2nd floor of the admin-

istration building in L'Auditori, the city's main classical-music concert hall.

Fundació Suñol
Gallery

(Map p144; 🕿93 496 10 32; www.fundaciosunol. org; Passeig de Gràcia 98; adult/concession €5/3; ⊙4-8pm Mon-Sat; MDiagonal) Rotating exhibitions of portions of this private collection of mostly 20th-century art (some 1200 works in total) offer anything from Man Ray's photography to sculptures by Alberto Giacometti.

Museu Egipci
Museum

(Map p144; 🕿93 488 01 88; www.museuegipci. com; Carrer de València 284; adult/senior & student €11/8; ⊙10am-8pm Mon-Sat, to 2pm Sun; MPasseig de Gràcia) Hotel magnate Jordi Clos has spent much of his life collecting ancient Egyptian artefacts, brought together in this private museum. It's divided into different thematic areas (the Pharaoh, religion, funerary practices, mummification, crafts etc) and boasts an interesting variety of exhibits.

Left: Museu del Modernisme Català (p138);
Below: Palau del Baró Quadras (p141)

FREE Palau del Baró Quadras — Architecture

(Casa Asia; Map p144; ☏93 368 08 36; www. casaasia.es; Avinguda Diagonal 373; ☉10am-8pm Tue-Sat, to 2pm Sun; MDiagonal) Puig i Cadafalch designed Palau del Baró Quadras (built 1902–06) in an exuberant Gothic-inspired style. The main facade is its most intriguing, with a soaring, glassed-in gallery. Take a closer look at the gargoyles and reliefs – the pair of toothy fish and the sword-wielding knight clearly have the same artistic signature as the architect behind Casa Amatller.

Església de la Puríssima Concepció I Assumpció de Nostra Senyora — Church

(Map p144; Carrer de Roger de Llúria 70; ☉8am-1pm & 5-9pm; MPasseig de Gràcia) One hardly expects to run into a medieval church on the grid-pattern streets of the late-19th-century city extension, yet that is just what this is. Transferred stone by stone from the old centre in 1871–88, this 14th-century church has a pretty 16th-century cloister with a peaceful garden.

Palau Montaner — Architecture

(Map p144; ☏93 317 76 52; www.rutadelmodern isme.com; Carrer de Mallorca 278; adult/child & senior €6/3; ☉guided visit in English 10.30am & in Spanish 12.30pm Sat, in Catalan 10.30am, in Spanish 11.30am & in Catalan 12.30pm Sun; MPasseig de Gràcia) Interesting on the outside and made all the more enticing by its gardens, this creation by Domènech i Montaner is spectacular on the inside. Completed in 1896, its central feature is a grand staircase beneath a broad, ornamental skylight. The interior is laden with sculptures (some by Eusebi Arnau), mosaics and fine woodwork.

FREE Fundació Joan Brossa — Gallery

(Map p144; ☏93 467 69 52; www.fundaciojoan brossa.cat; Carrer de Provença 318; ☉10am-

141

VINCENZO LOMBARDO / GETTY IMAGES ©

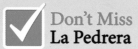

Don't Miss
La Pedrera

This undulating beast is another madcap Gaudí masterpiece, built in 1905–10 as a combined apartment and office block. Formally called Casa Milà after the businessman who commissioned it, it is better known as La Pedrera (the Quarry) because of its uneven grey stone facade, which ripples around the corner of Carrer de Provença. Pere Milà had married the older – and far richer – Roser Guardiola, the widow of Josep Guardiola, and clearly knew how to spend his new wife's money. Milà was one of the city's first car owners and Gaudí built parking space into this building, itself a first. When commissioned to design this apartment building, Gaudí wanted to top anything else done in L'Eixample.

The Fundació Caixa Catalunya has opened the top-floor apartment, attic and roof, together called the Espai Gaudí (Gaudí Space), to visitors. The roof is the most extraordinary element, with its giant chimney pots looking like multicoloured medieval knights. Gaudí wanted to put a tall statue of the Virgin up here too: when the Milà family said no, fearing it might make the building a target for anarchists, Gaudí resigned from the project in disgust.

One floor below the roof, where you can appreciate Gaudí's taste for parabolic arches, is a modest museum dedicated to his work. The next floor down is the apartment (El Pis de la Pedrera). It is fascinating to wander around this elegantly furnished home, done up in the style a well-to-do family might have enjoyed in the early 20th century. There are sensuous curves and unexpected touches in everything from light fittings to bedsteads, from door handles to balconies.

NEED TO KNOW

Casa Milà; Map p144; ☏ 902 400973; www.fundaciocaixacatalunya.es; Carrer de Provença 261-265; adult/student/child €15/13.50/7.50; ☉ 9am-8pm Mar-Oct, to 6.30pm Nov-Feb; Ⓜ Diagonal

2pm & 3-7pm Mon-Fri; **M**Diagonal) Pop into this basement gallery to get an insight into the mind of one of the city's cultural icons, Joan Brossa, a difficult-to-classify mix of poet, artist, theatre man, Catalan nationalist and all-round visionary.

FREE **Museu de Carrosses Fúnebres** Museum
(Map p136; 📞902 076902; Carrer de Sancho d'Àvila 2; 🕑10am-1pm & 4-6pm Mon-Fri, 10am-1pm Sat, Sun & holidays; **M**Marina) If late-18th-century to mid-20th-century hearses (complete with period-dressed dummies) are your thing, then this museum, probably the city's weirdest sight, is where to contemplate the pomp and circumstance of people's last earthly ride.

 Eating

Most of this huge area's many varied and enticing restaurants are concentrated in the Quadrat d'Or between Carrer de Pau Claris and Carrer de Muntaner, Avinguda Diagonal and Gran Via de les Corts Catalanes.

La Dreta de L'Eixample

Tapaç 24 Tapas €€
(Map p144; www.carlesabellan.com; Carrer de la Diputació 269; mains €10-20; 🕑9am-midnight Mon-Sat; **M**Passeig de Gràcia) Carles Abellán, master of Comerç 24 in La Ribera, runs this basement tapas haven known for its gourmet versions of old faves. Specials include the *bikini* (toasted ham and cheese sandwich – here the ham is cured and the truffle makes all the difference) and a thick black *arròs negre de sípia* (squid-ink black rice). The inventive McFoie-Burguer is fantastic and, for dessert, choose *xocolata amb pa, sal i oli* (delicious balls of chocolate in olive oil with a touch of salt and wafer). You can't book but it's worth the wait.

Can Kenji Japanese €
(Map p136; 📞93 476 18 23; www.cankenji.com; Carrer del Rosselló 325; mains €6-12; 🕑1-3.30pm

& 8.30-11.30pm Mon-Sat; **M**Verdaguer) The chef of this understated little *izakaya* (the Japanese version of a pub/eatery) gets his ingredients fresh from the city's markets, with traditional Japanese recipes getting a Mediterranean touch, so you'll get things like sardine tempura with an aubergine, miso and anchovy puree, or *tataki* (lightly grilled meat) of bonito (tuna) with *salmorejo* (a Córdoban cold tomato and bread soup).

Alkímia Catalan €€€
(📞93 207 61 15; www.alkimia.cat; Carrer de l'Indústria 79; set menu €38-84; 🕑lunch & dinner Mon-Fri Sep-Jul; **M**Verdaguer) Jordi Vila, a culinary alchemist, serves up refined Catalan dishes with a twist in this elegant, white-walled locale well off the tourist trail. Dishes such as his *arròs de nyore i safrà amb escamarlans de la costa* (saffron and sweet-chilli rice with crayfish) earned Vila his first Michelin star.

Noti Mediterranean €€
(Map p144; 📞93 342 66 73; http://noti-universal.com; Carrer de Roger de Llúria 35; mains €10-15; 🕑lunch & dinner Mon-Fri, dinner Sat; **M**Passeig de Gràcia) Once home to the *Noticiero Universal* newspaper, Noti has an ample dining room plastered with mirrors that seem to multiply the steely designer tables. Try the fresh fish from the Boqueria market with ratatouille of courgette and lemon butter or perhaps a meat dish – anything from steak tartare to chicken curry. Start the evening with the cocktail of the day at the bar.

Patagonia South American €
(Map p144; 📞93 304 37 35; Gran Via de les Corts Catalanes 660; meals €40-45; 🕑lunch & dinner daily; **M**Passeig de Gràcia) An elegant Argentinean beef-fest awaits in this stylish restaurant. Start with empanadas (tiny meat-crammed pies). You might want to skip the *achuras* (offal) and head for a hearty meat main, such as a juicy beef *medallón con salsa de colmenillas* (a medallion in a morel sauce) or such classics as *bife de chorizo* (sirloin) or Brazilian *picanha* (rump).

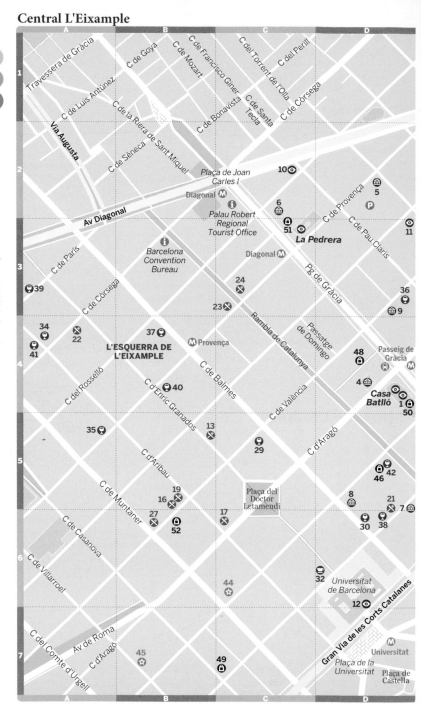

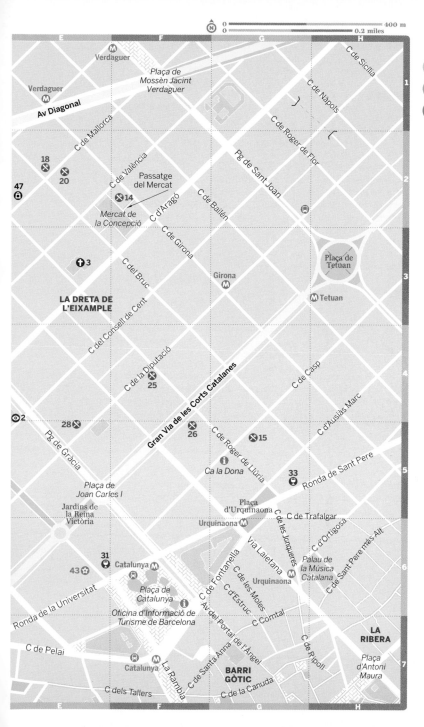

Verdaguer

Plaça de
Mossèn Jacint
Verdaguer

Verdaguer

Av Diagonal

C de Sicília

C de Nàpols

C de Roger de Flor

C de Mallorca

18

20

47

C de València

Passatge
del Mercat

14

Mercat de
la Concepció

C d'Aragó

C de Bailèn

Pg de Sant Joan

3

C del Bruc

C de Girona

Girona

Plaça de
Tetuan

LA DRETA DE
L'EIXAMPLE

C del Consell de Cent

Tetuan

C de Casp

C de la Diputació

25

Gran Via de les Corts Catalanes

C d'Ausiàs Marc

2

28

26

15

Pg de Gràcia

C de Roger de Llúria

Ca la Dona

33

Ronda de Sant Pere

Plaça de
Joan Carles I

Plaça
d'Urquinaona

C de Trafalgar

C d'Ortigosa

Jardins de
la Reina
Victòria

Urquinaona

C de les Jonqueres

Via Laietana

Palau de
la Música
Catalana

C de Sant Pere més Alt

31

43

Catalunya

Plaça de
Catalunya

Oficina d'Informació de
Turisme de Barcelona

C de Fontanella

C d'Estruc

C de les Moles

Urquinaona

LA
RIBERA

Plaça
d'Antoni
Maura

C de Pelai

Ronda de la Universitat

Catalunya

La Rambla

C de Santa Anna

Av del Portal de l'Àngel

C Comtal

BARRI
GÒTIC

C de Ripoll

C dels Tallers

C de la Canuda

145

Central L'Eixample

Casa Calvet
Catalan €€

(Map p144; ☎ 93 412 40 12; www.casacalvet. es; Carrer de Casp 48; mains €15-30; ⊙ lunch & dinner Mon-Sat; ⓂUrquinaona) An early Gaudí masterpiece loaded with his trademark curvy features now houses a swish restaurant (just to the right of the building's main entrance). Dress up and ask for an intimate *taula cabina* (wooden booth). You could opt for sole and lobster on mashed leeks, with balsamic vinegar and Pedro Ximénez reduction, and artichoke chips.

De Tapa Madre
Catalan €€

(Map p144; ☎ 93 459 31 34; www.detapama dre.cat; Carrer de Mallorca 301; mains €8-15; ⊙8am-1am Mon-Sat; ⓂVerdaguer) A chatty atmosphere greets you from the bar from the moment you swing open the door. A few tiny tables line the window, but head upstairs for more space in the gallery, which hovers above the array of tapas on the bar below, or go deeper inside past the bench with the ham legs. The *arròs caldós amb llagostins* (a hearty rice dish with king prawns) is delicious.

Embat
Mediterranean €€

(Map p144; ☎ 93 458 08 55; www.restaurantem bat.es; Carrer de Mallorca 304; mains €10-20; ⊙lunch Tue & Wed, lunch & dinner Thu-Sat; ⓂGirona) Enthusiastic young chefs turn out beautifully presented dishes in this basement eatery, the brown and cream decor of which might not enchant all comers. You can eat three fish or meat courses for around €20 to €25 at lunch.

Indulge perhaps in *raviolis de pollo amb bacon i calabassó* (chicken ravioli bathed in a sauce of finely chopped bacon, zucchini and other vegetables) followed by melt-in-the-mouth *lluç amb pa amb tomàquet, carxofes i maionesa de peres* (a thick cut of hake on a tomato-drenched clump of bread dressed with artichoke slices and a pear mayonnaise).

Casa Amalia
Catalan €

(Map p144; 🖉93 458 94 58; Passatge del Mercat 4-6; mains €8-16; ⏱lunch & dinner Tue-Sat, lunch Sun Sep-Jul; Ⓜ Girona) This formal restaurant is popular for its hearty Catalan cooking using fresh produce, mainly sourced from the busy market next door. On Thursdays during winter it offers the Catalan mountain classic, *escudella*. Otherwise, you might try light variations on local cuisine, such as the *bacallà al allioli de poma* (cod in an apple-based aioli sauce). The four-course *menú del día* is exceptional lunchtime value at €12.

L'Esquerra de L'Eixample

Cata 1.81
Tapas €€

(Map p144; 🖉93 323 68 18; www.cata181.com; Carrer de València 181; tapas €7-12; ⏱dinner Mon-Sat; Ⓜ Passeig de Gràcia) A beautifully designed venue (with lots of small lights, some trapped in birdcages), this is the place to come for fine wines and dainty gourmet dishes like *raviolis amb bacallà* (salt-cod dumplings) or *truita de patates i tòfona negre* (thick potato tortilla with a delicate trace of black truffle).

Taktika Berri
Basque, Tapas €€

(Map p144; Carrer de València 169; mains €15; ⏱lunch & dinner Mon-Fri, lunch Sat; Ⓜ Hospital Clínic) Get in early as the bar teems with punters from far and wide, anxious to wrap their mouths around some of the best Basque tapas in town. The hot morsels are all snapped up as soon as they arrive from the kitchen, so keep your eyes peeled. The seated dining area out the back is also good. In the evening, it's all over by about 10.30pm.

Speakeasy
International €€

(Map p144; 🖉93 217 50 80; www.drymartinibcn. com; Carrer d'Aribau 162-166; mains €10-15; ⏱lunch & dinner Mon-Fri, dinner Sat Sep-Jul; Ⓜ Diagonal) This clandestine restaurant lurks behind the Dry Martini (p150) bar. You will be shown a door through the open kitchen area to the 'storeroom', lined with hundreds of bottles of backlit, quality tipples. Dark decorative tones, a few works of art, low lighting, light jazz music and smooth service complete the setting. The menu has tempting options like the huge hunk of burrata cheese with white asparagus and strips of ravishing *jamón* (cured ham).

🖉 Fastvínic
Cafe €

(Map p144; 🖉93 487 32 41; www.fastvinic.com; Carrer de la Diputació 251; sandwiches €6-10; ⏱noon-midnight Mon-Sat; Ⓜ Passeig de Gracia) A project in sustainability all round, this is slow food done fast, with ingredients, wine and building materials all sourced from Catalonia. It's all sandwiches on the menu, with some wonderful choices of roast beef, mustard and honey, or more adventurous crunchy suckling pig, banana chutney and coriander; there is also a self-service wine machine with quality Spanish choices.

Cinc Sentits
International €€

(Map p144; 🖉93 323 94 90; www.cincsentits. com; Carrer d'Aribau 58; mains €10-20; ⏱lunch & dinner Tue-Sat ; Ⓜ Passeig de Gràcia) Enter this somewhat overlit realm of the 'Five Senses' to indulge in a tasting menu (from €49 to €69) consisting of a series of small, experimental dishes. A key is the use of fresh local produce, such as fish landed on the Costa Brava and top-quality suckling pig from Extremadura. Less ambitious, but cheaper, is the set lunch at €30.

Melton
Italian €€

(Map p136; 🖉93 363 27 76; Carrer de Muntaner 189; mains €12-20; ⏱Tue-Sat; Ⓜ Hospital Clínic) You know you're onto something when Italians recommend an Italian restaurant. This slick place offers well-prepared pasta and risotto dishes (the latter, for example, with foie gras) and a tempting array of meat and fish mains. For an unusual pasta option, try the *lasagnetta de tòfona negra i múrgules* (little lasagna with black truffle and morel mushrooms). There is a tasting menu at €55.

Alba Granados Spanish, Mediterranean €€

(Map p144; ☏ 93 454 61 16; Carrer d'Enric Granados 34; mains €12; ⓘlunch & dinner Mon-Sat, lunch Sun; Ⓡ FGC Provença) In summer ask for one of the romantic tables for two on the 1st-floor balcony. Overlooking the trees, it is a unique spot, with little traffic. The menu offers a little of everything but the best dishes revolve around meat, such as *solomillo a la mantequilla de trufa con tarrina de patata y beicon* (sirloin in truffle butter, potato and bacon terrine).

Terrabacus Tapas €€

(Map p136; ☏ 93 410 86 33; www.terrabacus. com; Carrer de Muntaner 185; mains €12-15, menú del día €18; ⓘlunch & dinner Tue-Fri, dinner Mon & Sat; ⓜHospital Clínic) Food exists to accompany wine, or so one could be led

to believe here. In this 'Land of Bacchus', one of the joys is sampling from the extensive wine list and choosing bites to go down with the nectar. You might try the various cheese platters or select a dish of high-grade Joselito cured ham. More substantial dishes range from risotto to steak tartare.

Cerveseria Brasseria Gallega Tapas €€

(Map p136; ☏ 93 439 41 28; Carrer de Casanova 238; mains €10-20; ⓘlunch & dinner Mon-Sat; ⓜHospital Clínic) You could walk right by this modest establishment without giving it a second glance. If you did, you'd notice it was chock-full of locals immersed in animated banter and surrounded by plates of abundant Galician classics. The fresh *pulpo a la gallega* (spicy octopus chunks with potatoes) as starter confirms this place is a cut above the competition.

La Bodegueta Provença Tapas €

(Map p144; ☏ 93 215 17 25; Carrer de Provença 233; mains €7-10; ⓘlunch & dinner daily; ⓜDiagonal) The 'Little Wine Cellar' offers classic tapas presented with a touch of class, from *calamares a la andaluza* (lightly battered calamari rings) to *cecina* (dried cured veal meat). The house speciality is *ous estrellats* (literally 'smashed eggs') – a mix of scrambled egg white, egg yolk, potato and then ingredients ranging from foie gras to *morcilla* (black pudding). Wash it all down with a good Ribera del Duero or *caña* (little glass) of beer.

Koyuki Japanese €€

(Map p144; Carrer de Còrsega 242; mains €14; ⓘlunch & dinner Tue-Sat, dinner Sun; ⓜDiagonal) This unassuming basement Japanese diner is one of those rough-edged diamonds that it pays to revisit. Sit

Tapas

at a long table and order from the cheesy menu complete with pictures courtesy of the Japanese owner – you won't be disappointed. The variety of *sashimi moriawase* is generous and constantly fresh. The *tempura udon* is a hearty noodle option.

El Rincón Maya · Mexican €
(Map p144; ☎93 451 39 46; Carrer de València 183; mains €5-10; ⏱lunch & dinner Tue-Sat, dinner Mon; Ⓜ Passeig de Gràcia) The setting is warm, modest and simple. The pocket-sized serves of nachos, guacamole and fajitas all burst with flavour. You'll also discover lesser-known items like *tacos de pibil* (pork tacos) and *tinga,* little pasta pockets of chicken. There are also more substantial dishes for €9.50. The owner-chef spent much of his life in the restaurant business in Mexico City.

Amaltea · Vegetarian €
(Map p136; www.amalteaygovinda.com; Carrer de la Diputació 164; mains €5; ⏱lunch & dinner Mon-Sat; ☍; Ⓜ Urgell) The ceiling fresco of blue sky sets the scene in this popular vegetarian eatery. The weekday set lunch (€10.50) offers a series of dishes that change frequently with the seasons. At night, the set two-course dinner (€15) offers good value. The place is something of an alternative lifestyle centre, with yoga, t'ai chi and belly-dancing classes.

Escribà · Desserts €
(Map p136; ☎93 454 75 35; www.escriba.es; Gran Via de les Corts Catalanes 546; pastries from €2; ⏱8am-3pm & 5-9pm Mon-Fri, 8am-9pm Sat, Sun & holidays; Ⓜ Urgell) Antoni Escribà carries forward a family tradition (since 1906) of melting *barcelonins'* hearts with remarkable pastries and criminal chocolate creations. Escribà has another branch in a Modernista setting at La Rambla de Sant Josep 83.

Mauri · Pastelería €
(Map p144; ☎93 215 10 20; Rambla de Catalunya 102; pastries from €1.50; ⏱8am-9pm Mon-Sat, to 3pm Sun; Ⓜ Diagonal) Since it opened in 1929, this grand old pastry shop has had its regular customers salivating over the endless range of sweets, chocolate croissants and gourmet delicatessen items.

Cremeria Toscana · Gelateria €
(Map p136; ☎93 539 38 25; Carrer de Muntaner 161; gelati from €1.50; ⏱1-9pm Tue-Sun Oct-Easter, 1pm-midnight Tue-Sun Easter-Sep; Ⓜ Hospital Clínic) Yes, you can stumble across quite reasonable ice cream in Barcelona, but close your eyes and imagine yourself across the Mediterranean with the real ice-cream wizards. Creamy *stracciatella* and wavy *nocciola*…and myriad other flavours await at the most authentic gelato outlet in town.

Drinking & Nightlife

Much of middle-class L'Eixample is dead at night, but several streets are exceptions. Noisy Carrer de Balmes is lined with a rowdy adolescent set. Much more interesting is the cluster of *locales* lining Carrer d'Aribau between Avinguda Diagonal and Carrer de Mallorca. They range from quiet cocktail bars to '60s retro joints. Lower down, on and around Carrer del Consell de Cent and Carrer de la Diputació, is the heart of Gaixample, with several gay bars and clubs.

L'Esquerra de L'Eixample

Monvínic · Wine Bar
(Map p144; ☎932 72 61 87; www.monvinic. com; Carrer de la Diputació 249 ; ⏱wine bar 1.30-11.30pm, restaurant 1.30-3.30pm & 8.30-10.30pm; Ⓜ Passeig de Gracia) Proclaimed as 'possibly the best wine bar in the world' by the Wall Street Journal, and apparently considered unmissable by El Bulli's sommelier, Mondvínic is an ode, a rhapsody even, to wine loving. The interactive wine list sits on the bar for you to browse on a digital tablet similar to an iPad and boasts more than 3000 varieties.

At the back is the restaurant that specialises in Mediterranean cuisine, with ingredients that are sourced locally from Catalan farmers.

La Fira · Bar
(Map p144; www.lafiraclub.com; Carrer de Provença 171; admission €8-12; ⏱10.30pm-3am

Wed-Sat; ®FGC Provença) A designer bar with a difference. Wander in past distorting mirrors and ancient fairground attractions from Germany. Put in coins and listen to hens squawk. Speaking of squawking, the music swings wildly from whiffs of house through '90s hits to Spanish pop classics.

Dry Martini — Bar
(Map p144; ☑93 217 50 72; www.drymartinibcn. com; Carrer d'Aribau 162-166; ⊗5pm-3am; ⓂDiagonal) Waiters with a discreetly knowing smile will attend to your cocktail cares here. The house drink, taken at the bar or in one of the plush green leather lounges, is a safe bet. The gin and tonic comes in an enormous mug-sized glass – a couple of these and you're well on the way! Out the back is a restaurant, Speakeasy (p147).

Cosmo — Cafe
(Map p144; www.galeriacosmo.com; Carrer d'Enric Granados 3; ⊗10am-10pm Mon-Thu, noon-2am Fri & Sat, noon-10pm Sun; 🛜; ⓂUniversitat) This groovy space – with psychedelic colouring in the tables and bar stools, high white walls out back for exhibitions and events, a nice selection of teas, pastries and snacks, all set on a pleasant pedestrian strip just behind the university – is perfect for a morning session on your laptop or a civilised evening tipple while admiring the art.

Café San Telmo — Bar
(Map p136; ☑934 39 17 09; www.cafesantelmo. com; Carrer de Buenos Aires 60; ⊗9am-2.30pm Mon-Fri, 9am-3.30pm Sat & Sun; ⓂDiagonal) This narrow bar has an appealingly busy feel, with big windows along Carrer de Casanova revealing the crowds and traffic of nearby Avinguda Diagonal. Perch at the bar for a couple of low-key afternoon drinks while you ponder the evening ahead (some of the area's key bars and clubs are just over the other side of Avinguda Diagonal).

Mediterráneo — Bar
(Map p144; ☑678 211253; Carrer de Balmes 129; ⊗11pm-3am; ⓂDiagonal) This smoky, studenty jam joint is a great hang-out that attracts a mostly casual student set. Sometimes the young performers are surprisingly good.

Museum — Gay Bar
(Map p136; Carrer de Sepúlveda 178; ⊗6.30pm-3am; ⓂUniversitat) 'Kitsch gone mad' is the artistic theme here, where chandeliers meet mock Renaissance sculpture and light pop. Twinks and muscle builders mix happily in this gay starter bar perfectly located for a hop over to Metro later on.

Premier — Bar
(Map p144; Carrer de Provença 236; ⊗6pm-2.30am Mon-Thu, to 3am Fri & Sat; ®FGC Provença) A little cross-pollination has happened in this funky little French-run wine bar. Hug the bar, sink into a lounge or hide up on the mezzanine. Later in the evening, a DJ adds to the ambience.

Quilombo — Bar
(Map p144; ☑93 439 54 06; Carrer d'Aribau 149; ⊗7pm-2.30am daily Jun-Sep, Wed-Sun Oct-May; ®FGC Provença) Some formulas just work, and this place has been working since the 1970s. Set up a few guitars in the back room, which you pack with tables and chairs, add some cheapish pre-prepared mojitos and plastic tubs of nuts, and let the punters do the rest.

Aire — Lesbian Club
(Map p144; ☑93 487 83 42; www.arenadisco. com; Carrer de València 236; ⊗11pm-3am Thu-Sat; ⓂPasseig de Gràcia) A popular locale for lesbians, the dance floor is spacious and there is usually a DJ in command of the tunes, which range from hits of the '80s and '90s to techno.

Arena Madre — Gay Club
(Map p144; ☑93 487 83 42; www.arenadisco. com; Carrer de Balmes 32; admission €6-12; ⊗12.30am-5.30am; ⓂPasseig de Gràcia) Popular with a hot young crowd, Arena Madre is one of the top clubs in town for boys seeking boys.

City Hall — Club
(Map p144; ☑93 238 07 22; www.grupo-ottozutz. com; Rambla de Catalunya 2-4; admission €12; ⊗midnight-5am Mon-Thu, to 6am Fri & Sat; ⓂCatalunya) A corridor leads to the dance floor of this place, located in a former theatre. House and other electric sounds

dominate, including a rather forward-sounding session of cutting-edge funk called Get Funkd! on Tuesdays.

Metro
Gay Club

(Map p136; ☎93 323 52 27; www.metrodiscobcn.com; Carrer de Sepúlveda 185; ⏰1am-5am Mon, midnight-5am Sun & Tue-Thu, midnight-6am Fri & Sat; Ⓜ Universitat) Metro attracts a casual gay crowd with its two dance floors, three bars and very dark room.

Opium Cinema
Club

(Map p144; ☎93 414 63 62; www.opiumcinema.com; Carrer de París 193-197; ⏰9pm-2.30am Tue-Thu, to 3am Fri & Sat; Ⓜ Diagonal) Reds, roses and yellows dominate the colour scheme in this wonderful former cinema. Barcelona's beautiful people, from a broad range of ages, gather to drink around the central rectangular bar, dance a little and eye one another up.

Roxy Blue
Club

(Map p144; ☎93 272 66 97; www.roxyblue.es; Carrer del Consell de Cent 294; ⏰midnight-5am Wed & Thu, to 6am Fri & Sat; Ⓜ Passeig de Gràcia) Blue is indeed the predominant colour in this split-level miniclub. Tastes in music

swing from New York beats to Brazil night on Sunday.

La Dreta de L'Eixample

Les Gens Que J'Aime
Bar

(Map p144; Carrer de València 286; ⏰6pm-2.30am Sun-Thu, to 3am Fri & Sat; Ⓜ Passeig de Gràcia) This intimate basement relic of the 1960s follows a deceptively simple formula: chilled jazz music in the background, minimal lighting from an assortment of flea-market lamps and a cosy, cramped scattering of red velvet-backed lounges around tiny dark tables.

Dboy
Gay Club

(Map p144; ☎93 453 05 10; Ronda de Sant Pere 19-21; ⏰midnight-6am Sat; Ⓜ Urquinaona) With pink laser lights and dense crowds of fit young lads, this is one of the big dance-club locations on a Saturday night.

Entertainment

Bel-Luna Jazz Club
Jazz

(Map p144; ☎93 302 22 21; www.bel-luna.com; Rambla de Catalunya 5; admission €5-15;

Dry Martini

⏰9pm-2am Sun-Thu, to 3am Fri & Sat; Ⓜ Catalunya) This basement restaurant-cum-bar-cum-club is not the prettiest location but attracts a full jazz program, seven nights a week, with local and visiting acts.

Dietrich Gay Teatro Café   Cabaret

(Map p144; ☎93 451 77 07; Carrer del Consell de Cent 255; ⏰10.30pm-3am; Ⓜ Universitat) It's show time at 1am, with at least one drag-queen gala each night in this cabaret-style locale dedicated to Marlene Dietrich. Soft house is the main musical motif and the place has an interior garden.

L'Auditori   Classical Music

(Map p136; ☎93 247 93 00; www.auditori.org; Carrer de Lepant 150; admission €10-60; ⏰box office 3-9pm Mon-Sat; Ⓜ Monumental) Barcelona's modern home for serious music lovers, L'Auditori (designed by Rafael Moneo) puts on plenty of orchestral, chamber, religious and other music.

Teatre Nacional De Catalunya   Performing Arts

(Map p136; ☎93 306 57 00; www.tnc.cat; Plaça de les Arts 1; admission €12-32; ⏰box office 3-7pm Wed-Fri, 3-8.30pm Sat, 3-5pm Sun & 1hr

before show; Ⓜ Glòries or Monumental) Ricard Bofill's ultra-neoclassical theatre, with the bright, airy foyer, hosts a wide range of performances, principally drama (anything from King Lear in Catalan to La Fura dels Baus) but occasionally dance and other performances.

Méliès Cinemes   Cinema

(Map p144; ☎93 451 00 51; www.cinesmelies.net; Carrer de Villarroel 102; admission €3-5; Ⓜ Urgell) A cosy cinema with two screens, the Méliès specialises in old classics from Hollywood and European cinema.

Renoir Floridablanca   Cinema

(Map p136; ☎93 426 33 37; www.cinesrenoir.com; Carrer de Floridablanca 135; Ⓜ Sant Antoni) With seven screens, this is one of a small chain of art-house cinemas in Spain showing quality flicks.

🔓 Shopping

Most of the city's classy shopping spreads across the heart of L'Eixample, in particular along Passeig de Gràcia, Rambla de Catalunya and adjacent streets.

Cacao Sampaka

IMAGEBROKER / ALAMY ©

All about are dotted a surprising array of specialty stores, selling anything from gloves to glues.

Vinçon
Homewares

(Map p144; [phone] 93 215 60 50; www.vincon.com; Passeig de Gràcia 96; [clock] 10am-8.30pm Mon-Sat; [M] Diagonal) An icon of the Barcelona design scene, Vinçon has the slickest furniture and household goods (particularly lighting), both local and imported. Not surprising, really, since the building, raised in 1899, belonged to the Modernista artist Ramon Casas. Head upstairs to the furniture area – from the windows and terrace you get close side views of La Pedrera.

Els Encants Vells
Market

(Fira de Bellcaire; Map p136; [phone] 93 246 30 30; www.encantsbcn.com; Plaça de les Glòries Catalanes; [clock] 7am-6pm Mon, Wed, Fri & Sat; [M] Glòries) Also known as the Fira de Bellcaire, the 'Old Charms' flea market is the biggest of its kind in Barcelona. It's all here, from antique furniture through to secondhand clothes.

El Bulevard dels Antiquaris
Antiques

(Map p144; [phone] 93 215 44 99; www.bulevarddels antiquaris.com; Passeig de Gràcia 55-57; [clock] 10.30am-8.30pm Mon-Sat; [M] Passeig de Gràcia) More than 70 stores (most are open from 11am to 2pm and from 5pm to 8.30pm) are gathered under one roof (on the floor above the more general Bulevard Rosa arcade) to offer the most varied selection of collector's pieces, ranging from old porcelain dolls through to fine crystal, from Asian antique furniture to old French goods, and from African and other ethnic art to jewellery.

Xampany
Drink

(Map p144; [phone] 610 845011; Carrer de València 200; [clock] 4.30-10pm Mon-Fri, 10am-2pm Sat;

[M] Passeig de Gràcia) Since 1981, this 'Cathedral of Cava' has been distributing bubbly to the local citizenry. It's a veritable Aladdin's cave of *cava* (Catalan version of champagne), with bottles of the stuff crammed high and into every possible chaotic corner of this dimly lit locale.

Cacao Sampaka
Food

(Map p144; [phone] 93 272 08 33; www.cacaosampaka. com; Carrer del Consell de Cent 292; [clock] 9am-9pm Mon-Sat; [M] Passeig de Gràcia) Chocoholics will be convinced they have died and passed on to a better place. Load up in the shop or head for the bar out the back where you can have a classic *xocolata calenta* (hot chocolate) and munch on exquisite chocolate cakes, tarts, ice cream, sweets and sandwiches.

Cubiña
Homewares

(Map p144; [phone] 93 476 57 21; www.cubinya.es; Carrer de Mallorca 291; [M] Verdaguer) Even if interior design doesn't ring your bell, a visit to this extensive temple to furniture, lamps and just about any home accessory your heart might desire is worth it just to see this Domènech i Montaner building.

Nosotraos
Gay & Lesbian

(Map p144; [phone] 93 451 51 34; http://nosotras.cat; Carrer de Casanova 56; [M] Urgell) Everything from gay girl calendars to bear T-shirts and books appear in this multifacted gay and lesbian store in the heart of the 'Gaixample'.

Regia
Perfume

(Map p144; [phone] 93 216 01 21; www.regia.es; Passeig de Gràcia 39; [clock] 9.30am-8.30pm Mon-Fri, 10.30am-8.30pm Sat; [M] Passeig de Gràcia) Reputed to be one of the best perfume stores in the city and in business since 1928, Regia stocks all the name brands and also has a private perfume museum (p138) out the back.

Montjuïc

Montjuïc is home to some of the city's finest art collections – Museu Nacional d'Art de Catalunya, CaixaForum and Fundació Joan Miró. It also hosts several lesser museums, curious sights like the Poble Espanyol, the sinister Castell de Montjuïc and the beautiful remake of Mies van der Rohe's 1920s German pavilion Pavelló Mies van der Rohe. The bulk of the Olympic installations of the 1992 games are also here. Come at night and witness the spectacle of Font Màgica, several busy theatres and a couple of nightclubs. Throw in various parks and gardens and you have the makings of an extremely full couple of days.

You can approach the hill from Plaça d'Espanya on foot and take advantage of a series of escalators up to Avinguda de l'Estadi. Alternatively, and spectacularly, you can get onto a cable car from Barceloneta and take in the beautiful aerial views of the verdant hill.

Museu Nacional d'Art de Catalunya (p160)

Montjuïc
Highlights

Museu Nacional d'Art de Catalunya (p160)

Rising from its stately perch in Montjuïc, the building itself, an imposing neobaroque palace known as the Palau Nacional, is the first and most impressive exhibit of this popular art museum. It was built for the 1929 International Exhibition and converted into a museum in 1995. Once inside, decipher the details of one of the best ensembles of Romanesque painting in Europe.

1

2

Fundació Joan Miró (p170)

Contrarian, surrealist, experimentalist and, above all, Catalan, Miró was a local boy who went global with cutting-edge art that provoked and inspired. Barcelona can't claim Picasso as a native but it can gloat about Miró, a talented artistic conjurer who, along with Dalí, dragged surrealism into the mainstream. Fundació Joan Miró is the world's largest single collection of his work. Fundació Joan Miró; architect: Josep Lluis Ser

Poble Espanyol (p163)

This microcosmic Spanish 'village' was the brainchild of Modernista architect Josep Puig i Cadafalch and is a bit like an all-Castilian Disneyland. Every region of Spain is architecturally represented, from Andalucía to the Basque Country. Village-like streets and plazas, full-scale replicas of famous buildings, craft workshops (pottery, glassmaking, textiles) and half a dozen restaurants (and a popular nightclub) mean you won't run out of things to do.

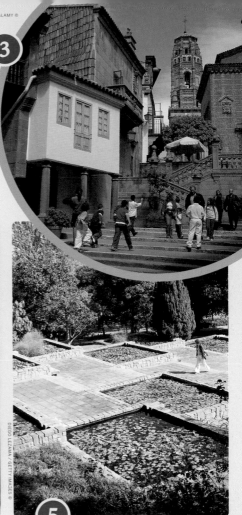

Font Màgica (p163)

If you take the dictionary definition of 'magic' as 'something that seems to cast a spell', Font Màgica is aptly named. A grandiose aquatic feature built for the 1929 International Exhibition, the fountain forms the centrepiece of a series of terraces and waterfalls cascading from the Palau Nacional. For full psychedelic effect, catch a nightly sound and light show.

Gardens of Montjuïc (p162)

Montjuïc is also home to large pockets of greenery. These lush environs harbour everything from fragrant botanical gardens planted with exotic species to manicured parks, dotted with sculptures, gurgling fountains and terraced lawns. The views are superb. To make the most of your time, bring a picnic (the Mercat de la Boqueria makes a fine stop before heading uphill).

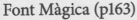

Jardins de Mossèn Cinto de Verdaguer

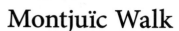

Montjuïc Walk

Montjuïc's pretty gardens and scenic views seem a world away from the bustle of downtown Barcelona. This leisurely stroll takes you from the Castell de Montjuïc on a winding (generally downhill) route toward the Font Màgica, passing by manicured flower-filled gardens. Bring along a picnic.

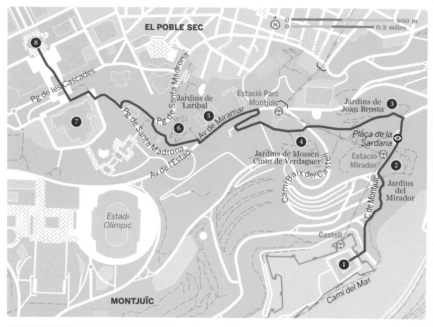

WALK FACTS

- **Start** Castell de Montjuïc
- **Finish** Font Màgica
- **Distance** 2.5km
- **Duration** 90 minutes

① Castell de Montjuïc

Long synonymous with oppression, the dark history of **Castell de Montjuïc** (p162) is today overshadowed by the fine views it commands over the city and sea. The Telefèric is the perfect way to get up and from there on it's all refreshingly downhill through amassing greenery.

② Jardins del Mirador

A short stroll down the road or the parallel Camí del Mar pedestrian trail leads to another fine viewpoint over the city and sea, the **Jardins del Mirador** (p163). Take the weight off your feet on one of the park benches, or pick up a snack and grab some reflection time.

③ Jardins de Joan Brossa

Further downhill is the multitiered **Jardins de Joan Brossa** (p163). The entrance is on the left just beyond Plaça de la Sardana, with the sculpture of people engaged in the classic Catalan folk dance. More fine city views can be had from among the many Mediterranean trees and plants.

4 Jardins de Mossèn Cinto de Verdaguer

Exiting the Jardins de Joan Brossa at the other (west) side, cross Camí Baix del Castell to the painstakingly laid-out **Jardins de Mossèn Cinto de Verdaguer** (p163). This is a beautiful setting for a slow meander among the tulip beds and water lilies, which act as both relaxant and inspiration.

5 Fundació Joan Miró

Joan Miró left a broad collection of his works to the city in his specially designed hillside **foundation** (p170). You can discover his earliest, tentative artistic attempts and continue right through to the characteristic broad canvases for which he is known. Get close-up views of sculptures in the adjacent garden.

6 Jardins de Laribal

Dropping away behind the Fundació Joan Miró, the **Jardins de Laribal** are a combination of terraced gardens linked by paths and stairways. The pretty sculpted watercourses along some of the stairways were inspired by Granada's Muslim-era palace of El Alhambra. Stop for a snack and contemplate a Moorish paradise.

7 Museu Nacional d'Art de Catalunya

Whichever direction you are coming from, it is worth making the effort to reach this huge ochre beast of a **museum** (p160) to see one of Europe's finest collections of Romanesque art, salvaged from countless churches and chapels sprinkled over northern Catalonia. Further collections range from Gothic to Modernista.

8 Font Màgica

Descending from the museum past the Plaça de les Cascades to the **Font Màgica** (p163) is as magic as the name suggests, particularly if you've stretched this walk long enough (easily done) to arrive here after dark – in time for the rather splendid sound and light show.

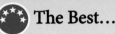 **The Best...**

PLACES TO EAT

Tickets The celebrated new restaurant by Ferran Adrià, one of the world's best chefs. (p167)

Quimet i Quimet An old-time favourite with superb tapas. (p168)

Xemei Mouth-watering Venetian fare. (p168)

Barramòn A buzzing space for sampling Canarian cooking. (p168)

Taverna Can Margarit Great old-fashioned ambience and classic Catalan fare. (p168)

PLACES TO DRINK

La Caseta del Migdia An open-air charmer hidden in the thickets of Montjuïc. (p171)

Tinta Roja A bohemian, cabaret-like atmosphere prevails at this Poble Sec bar. (p171)

Terrazza Lovely summertime dance spot in Poble Espanyol. (p171)

Barcelona Rouge For something different, this place has a decadent, bordello-esque vibe. (p171)

VIEWS

Castell de Montjuïc The castle offers commanding views. (p162)

Miramar The first-rate cuisine is only slightly upstaged by the view. (p169)

Jardins de Mossèn Cinto de Verdaguer (p163)
DIEGO LEZAMA / GETTY IMAGES ©

Don't Miss
Museu Nacional d'Art de Catalunya

From across the city, the bombastic neobaroque silhouette of the Palau Nacional can be seen rising up from the slopes of Montjuïc. Built for the 1929 World Exhibition and restored in 2005, it houses a vast collection of mostly Catalan art spanning the early Middle Ages to the early 20th century. The high point is the collection of extraordinary Romanesque frescoes, which is considered the most important concentration of early medieval art in the world.

MNAC

Map p164

📞 93 622 03 76

www.mnac.es

Mirador del Palau Nacional

adult/senior & child under 15yr/student €10/free/7, 1st Sun of month free

🕐 10am-7pm Tue-Sat, 10am-2.30pm Sun & holidays, library 10am-6pm Mon-Fri, to 2.30pm Sat

Ⓜ Espanya

Romanesque Masterpieces

Rescued from neglected country churches across northern Catalonia in the early 20th century, the Romanesque collection consists of 21 frescoes, woodcarvings and painted altar frontals (low-relief wooden panels that were the forerunners of the elaborate altarpieces that adorned later churches). The insides of several churches have been recreated and the frescoes – in some cases fragmentary, in others extraordinarily complete and alive with colour – have been placed as they were when in situ.

Gothic Collection

Opposite the Romanesque collection is the museum's Gothic art section with Catalan works and paintings from other Spanish and Mediterranean regions. Look out for the work of Bernat Martorell and Jaume Huguet. Images of the martyrdom of St Vincent and St Llúcia feature among Martorell's works. Huguet's *Consagració de Sant Agustí*, in which St Augustine is depicted as a bishop, is dazzling.

Cambò Bequest & Thyssen-Bornemisza Collection

As the Gothic collection draws to a close, you pass through two eclectic collections, which span the history of European painting between the 14th century and the beginning of the 19th century.

Modern Catalan Art

Up on the next floor, after a series of rooms devoted to mostly minor works by a variety of 17th-century Spanish Old Masters, the collection turns to modern Catalan art. The collection is an uneven affair, but it's worth looking out for Modernista painters Ramon Casas and Santiago Rusiñol, as well as the recently deceased Antoni Tàpies.

Also on show are items of Modernista furniture and decoration, including a mural by Ramon Casas of himself and Pere Romeu on a tandem bicycle. The furniture collection comes from the original Modernista houses and includes a great display of decorative objects.

Don't Miss List

BY NÚRIA ROCAMORA, CULTURAL MANAGER AND MNAC GUIDE.

1 PALAU NACIONAL

The building itself was conceived as the main pavilion for the 1929 Barcelona International Exposition and was designed in a mannerist style, inspired in part by the Spanish Renaissance.

2 CENTRAL APSE OF SANT CLIMENT DE TAÜLL

Seeing the magnificent Romanesque works is a highlight of any visit to MNAC. One of the masterpieces was taken from the central apse of the 12th century Catalan church Sant Climent in Taüll. Here you see a Christin Majesty, inscribed in a mandorla, seated on the arc of Heaven and joined by the four Evangelists, various key saints and the Virgin Mary.

3 SAINT FRANCIS OF ASSISI AFTER THE VISION OF POPE NICHOLAS V

One of the great masters of the 17th century was Spanish painter Francisco Zurbarán, whose exquisite, dramatically lit portraits sometimes earn him comparison with Caravaggio. In this evocative painting of Saint Francis, Zurbarán depicts the saint near the moment of rapture, capturing profound religious feeling while avoiding stylistic cliches.

4 RAMON CASAS AND PERE ROMEU ON A TANDEM

This simple, funny work that's utterly representative of the whole Catalan Modernista style. It's subject: just one of the most important artists of this period and his friend riding a bicycle. Two years later, Ramon Casas painted a second version of this work of art, but with the two driving in a car!

5 NUMISMATIC CABINET

The often overlooked Numismatic Cabinet is a staggering collection of rare coins, some of which date back to the 6th century BC. Highlights include the first silver coins minted in the Iberian Peninsula by the Greeks of Emporion, pieces made during the 17th-century Reapers' War and local notes issued during the Spanish Civil War.

Discover Montjuïc

See p160.

Getting There & Away

○ **Metro** Metro Línia 3 runs through El Poble Sec. The closest stops to Montjuïc are Espanya, Poble Sec and Paral.lel.

○ **Bus** Bus 50 runs to Montjuïc along Gran Via de les Corts Catalanes via Plaça de l'Universitat and Plaça d'Espanya. Bus 61 runs on weekdays along Avinguda del Paral.lel to Montjuïc via Plaça d'Espanya. Bus 55 runs across town via Plaça de Catalunya and Carrer de Lleida, terminating at the Estació Parc Montjuïc funicular station. The 193 (Parc de Montjuïc) line does a circle trip from Plaça d'Espanya to the Castell de Montjuïc.

○ **Funicular** Take the Metro (Línia 2 or 3) to the Paral.lel stop and pick up the funicular railway, part of the Metro fare system, to Estació Parc Montjuïc.

◉ Sights

Museu Nacional d'Art de Catalunya   Museum
See p160.

CaixaForum   Gallery
(www.fundacio.lacaixa.es; Avinguda de Francesc Ferrer i Guàrdia 6-8; adult/student & child €3/2, first Sunday of the month free; ◷10am-8pm Tue-Fri & Sun, to 10pm Sat; Ⓜ Espanya) The Caixa building society prides itself on its involvement in (and ownership of) art, in particular all that is contemporary. The setting is a completely renovated former factory, the Fàbrica Casaramona, an outstanding Modernista brick structure designed by Puig i Cadafalch.

Now it is home to major exhibition space. On occasion portions of La Caixa's own collection of 800 works of modern and contemporary art go on display, but more often than not major international exhibitions are the key draw.

FREE Castell de Montjuïc   Fortress, Gardens
(◷9am-9pm Tue-Sun Apr-Sep, to 7pm Tue-Sun Oct-Mar; ☐193, Telefèric de Montjuïc (Castell de Montjuïc)) The forbidding Castell (castle or fort) de Montjuïc domi-nates the southeastern heights of Montjuïc and enjoys command-ing views over the Mediterranean. It dates, in its present form, to the late 17th and 18th centuries. For most of its dark history, it has been used to watch over the city and as a political prison and killing ground.

Anarchists were executed here around the end of the 19th century, fascists during the civil war and Republicans after

Poble Espanyol

it – most notoriously Lluís Companys in 1940. The castle is surrounded by a network of ditches and walls (from which its strategic position over the city and port become clear).

In the coming years, it is planned to establish an international peace centre in the castle, as well as a display on its history. There will also be an interpretation centre dedicated to Montjuïc.

The views from the castle and the surrounding area looking over the sea, port and city below are the best part of making the trip up. Catalan and Spanish speakers can join free guided tours of the castle on Saturdays and Sundays (11.30am in Catalan, 1pm in Spanish). Group tours (€65 to €80) can also be booked (also in English and French).

Around the seaward foot of the castle is an airy walking track, the **Camí del Mar**, which offers breezy views of city and sea. Towards the foot of this part of Montjuïc, above the thundering traffic of the main road to Tarragona, the **Jardins de Mossèn Costa i Llobera** (admission free; 10am-sunset; Transbordador Aeri (Miramar)) have a good collection of tropical and desert plants – including a veritable forest of cacti. Near the Estació Parc Montjuïc funicular/Telefèric station are the ornamental **Jardins de Mossèn Cinto de Verdaguer** (admission free; 10am-sunset; Funicular Parc de Monjuïc). These sloping, verdant gardens are home to various kinds of bulbs and aquatic plants. Many of the former (some 80,000) have to be replanted each year. They include tulips, narcissus, crocus, varieties of dahlia and more. The aquatic plants include lotus and water lilies.

From the **Jardins del Mirador** (Telefèric de Montjuïc (Mirador)), opposite the Mirador Transbordador Aeri (Telefèric) station, you have fine views over the port of Barcelona. A little further downhill, the **Jardins de Joan Brossa** (admission free; 10am-sunset; Telefèric de Montjuïc (Mirador)) are charming, landscaped gardens on the site of a former amusement park near **Plaça de la Sardana**. These gardens contain many Mediterranean species, from cypresses to pines and a few palms.

There are swings and things, thematic walking trails and some good city views.

Estadi Olímpic   Stadium
(Avinguda de l'Estadi; 10am-8pm; 50, 61 or 193) The Estadi Olímpic was the main stadium of Barcelona's Olympic Games. The stadium was opened in 1929 and restored for 1992.

Museu Olímpic i de l'Esport   Museum
(www.museuolimpicbcn.com; Avinguda de l'Estadi 60; adult/student €4/2.50; 10am-8pm; 50, 61 or 193) The Museu Olímpic i de l'Esport is an information-packed interactive museum dedicated to the history of sport and the Olympic Games. After picking up tickets, you wander down a ramp that snakes below ground level and is lined with displays on the history of sport, starting with the ancients.

Font Màgica   Fountain
(Avinguda de la Reina Maria Cristina; every 30min 7-9pm Fri & Sat Oct-late Jun, 9-11.30pm Thu-Sun late Jun-Sep; Espanya) The main fountain of a series that sweeps up the hill from Avinguda de la Reina Maria Cristina to the grand facade of the Palau Nacional, Font Màgica is a unique performance in which the water can look like seething fireworks or a mystical cauldron of colour.

With a flourish, the 'Magic Fountain' erupts into a feast of musical, backlit aquatic life. On hot summer evenings especially, this 15-minute spectacle (repeated several times throughout the evening) mesmerises onlookers. On the last evening of the Festes de la Mercè in September, a particularly spectacular display includes fireworks.

Poble Espanyol   Cultural Centre
(www.poble-espanyol.com; Avinguda de Francesc Ferrer i Guàrdia; adult/child €9.50/5.60; 9am-8pm Mon, to 2am Tue-Thu, to 4am Fri, to 5am Sat, to midnight Sun; ; 50, 61 or 193, Espanya) Welcome to Spain! All of it! This 'Spanish Village' is both a cheesy souvenir hunters' haunt and an intriguing scrapbook of Spanish architecture built for the Spanish crafts section of the 1929 World Exhibition.

Montjuïc

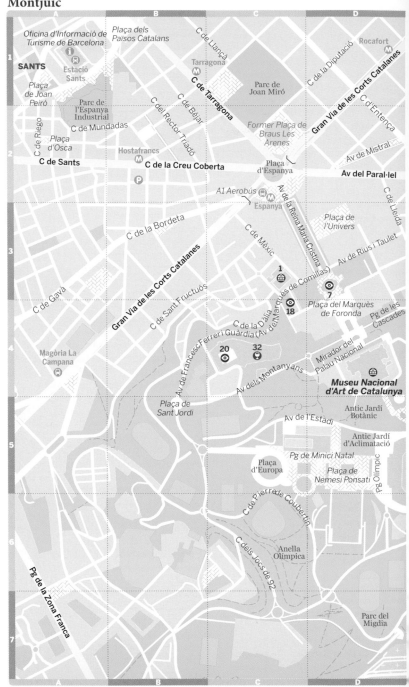

Oficina d'Informació de Turisme de Barcelona

Plaça dels Països Catalans

C de Llançà

Rocafort

Tarragona

C de la Diputació

Gran Via de les Corts Catalanes

SANTS

Estació Sants

C de Tarragona

Parc de Joan Miró

Plaça de Joan Peiró

Parc de l'Espanya Industrial

C del Rector Triadó

C de Béjar

C d'Entença

C de Mundadas

Former Plaça de Braus Les Arenes

Av de Mistral

C de Riego

Plaça d'Osca

C de Sants

Hostafrancs

C de la Creu Coberta

Plaça d'Espanya

Av del Paral·lel

A1 Aeròbus

Espanya

Av de la Reina Maria Cristina

C de Lleida

C de la Bordeta

Plaça de l'Univers

C de Mèxic

Av de Rius i Taulet

Gran Via de les Corts Catalanes

Av del Marquès de Comillas

1

7

C de Sant Fructuós

18

Plaça del Marquès de Foronda

Pg de les Cascades

C de Gavà

C de la Dàlia

Av de Francesc Ferrer i Guàrdia (Av del

20

32

Mirador del Palau Nacional

Magòria La Campana

Av dels Montanyans

Museu Nacional d'Art de Catalunya

Plaça de Sant Jordi

Av de l'Estadi

Antic Jardí Botànic

Antic Jardí d'Aclimatació

Pg de Minici Natal

Plaça d'Europa

Plaça de Nemesi Ponsatí

Pg Olímpic

C de Pierre de Coubertin

C dels Jocs de 92

Anella Olímpica

Pg de la Zona Franca

Parc del Migdia

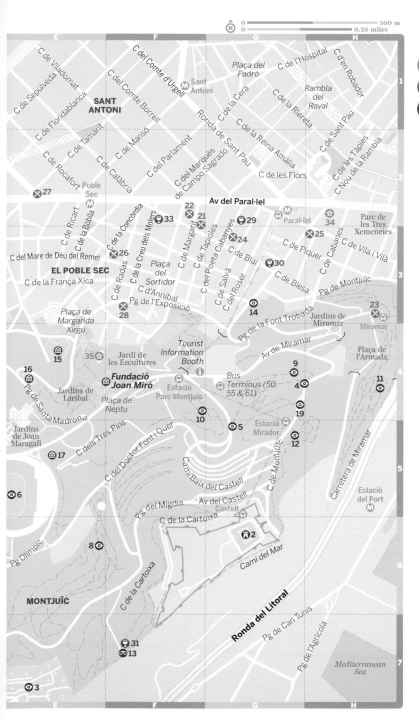

Montjuïc

You can meander from Andalucía to the Balearic Islands in the space of a couple of hours, visiting surprisingly good copies of Spain's characteristic buildings.

You enter from beneath a towered medieval gate from Ávila. Inside, to the right, is an information office with free maps. Straight ahead from the gate is the Plaza Mayor (Town Square), surrounded with mainly Castilian and Aragonese buildings. It is sometimes the scene of summer concerts. Elsewhere you'll find an Andalucian *barri*, a Basque street, Galician and Catalan quarters and even a Dominican monastery (at the eastern end). The buildings house dozens of restaurants, cafes, bars, craft shops and workshops (such as glassmakers), and some souvenir stores.

At night the restaurants, bars and especially the discos become a lively corner of Barcelona's nightlife.

Pavelló Mies van der Rohe
Architecture
(☎93 423 40 16; www.miesbcn.com; Avinguda de Francesc Ferrer i Guàrdia; adult/child under 18yr/student €4.75/free/2.60; ⊙10am-8pm; Ⓜ Espanya) The Pavelló Mies van der Rohe is not only a work of breathtaking beauty and simplicity, it is a highly influential building emblematic of the modern movement. The structure has been the subject of many studies and interpretations, and it has inspired several generations of architects. Designed in 1929 by Ludwig Mies van der Rohe (1886–1969) as the Pavelló Alemany (German Pavilion) for the World Exhibition, it was removed after the show and reconstructed only in 1980, after the building had been consistently referred to as one of the key works of modern architecture.

Museu d'Arqueologia de Catalunya (MAC)
Museum
(Archaeology Museum; www.mac.cat; Passeig de Santa Madrona 39-41; adult/student €3/2.10; ⊙9.30am-7pm Tue-Sat, 10am-2.30pm Sun; ☐55 or 193) This archaeology museum, housed in what was the Graphic Arts palace during the 1929 World Exposition, covers Catalonia and other Spanish cultures. Items range from copies of pre-Neanderthal

skulls to lovely Carthaginian necklaces and jewel-studded Visigothic crosses.

Museu Etnològic Museum

(www.museuetnologic.bcn.cat; Passeig de Santa Madrona 16-22; adult/senior & student €3.50/1.75; ⏲noon-8pm Tue-Sat, 11am-3pm Sun; 🚌55) Barcelona's ethnology museum presents a curious permanent collection that explores how various societies have worked down the centuries, as seen through collections of all sorts of objects. The entire museum was closed at the time of writing for major refurbishments. Check the website for reopening date.

Jardí Botànic Gardens

(www.jardibotanic.bcn.es; Carrer del Doctor Font i Quer 2; adult/student €3.50/1.70; ⏲10am-8pm; 🚌50, 61 or 193) This botanical garden is dedicated to Mediterranean flora and has a collection of some 40,000 plants and 1500 species that thrive in areas with a climate similar to that of the Mediterranean, such as the Eastern Mediterranean, Spain (including the Balearic and Canary Islands), North Africa, Australia, California, Chile and South Africa.

Cementiri del Sud-Oest Cemetery

(⏲8am-6pm; 🚌193) On the hill to the south of the Anella Olímpica stretches this huge cemetery, the Cementiri del Sud-Oest or Cementiri Nou, which extends down the southern side of the hill. Among the big names are Joan Miró, Carmen Amaya (the flamenco dance star from La Barceloneta), Jacint Verdaguer (the 19th-century priest and poet to whom the rebirth of Catalan literature is attributed), Francesc Macià and Lluís Companys (nationalist presidents of Catalonia; Companys was executed by Franco's henchmen in the Castell de Montjuïc in 1940), Ildefons Cerdà (who designed L'Eixample) and Joan Gamper (the founder of the FC Barcelona football team, aka Hans Gamper). Many victims of Franco's postwar revenge were buried in unmarked graves here – the last of them in 1974. From the 193 bus stop, it's about an 800m walk southwest. Otherwise, bus 38 from Plaça de Catalunya stops close to the cemetery entrance.

MUHBA Refugi 307 Historic Site

(☎93 256 21 22; www.museuhistoria.bcn.cat; Carrer Nou de la Rambla 169; admission incl tour €3; ⏲tours 11am-2pm Sat & Sun; Ⓜ Paral·lel) Part of the Museu d'Història de Barcelona (MUHBA), this is a shelter that dates back to the days of the Spanish Civil War. Barcelona was the city most heavily bombed from the air during the Spanish Civil War and had more than 1300 air-raid shelters. Local citizens started digging this one under a fold of Montjuïc in March 1937.

In the course of the next two years, the web of tunnels was slowly extended to 200m, with a theoretical capacity for 2000 people. The half-hour tours (in Catalan or Spanish; book ahead for English or French) explain all this and more.

Eating

Montjuïc is largely bereft of notable eating options, for the obvious reason that it is mostly parks and gardens. In gruff old El Poble Sec, however, you'll turn up all sorts of priceless nuggets, from historic taverns offering Catalan classics to a handful of smart, new-wave eateries.

El Poble Sec

Tickets Spanish **€€**

(www.ticketsbar.es; Avinguda del Paral·lel 164; tapas from €4-12; ⏲lunch & dinner; Ⓜ Paral·lel) This is, literally, one of the sizzling tickets in the restaurant world. It's the new tapas bar opened by Ferran Adrià, of the legendary El Bulli, and his brother Albert. And unlike El Bulli, it's an affordable venture – if you can book a table, that is (you can only book online, and two months in advance).

It's a fairly flamboyant and modern affair in terms of decor, playing with circus images and theatre lights, while the food has kept some of the El Bulli greats such as the 'air baguette' – a crust larded with Iberico ham, or the slightly bonkers 'cotton candy tree', with fruit-studded candyfloss clouds served up on a small bush. The seafood bar serves a slightly more serious option of oysters, tuna belly, and delicate fish skin in a paper cone. At

the back is the bar, 41° – go through the curtain for cocktail classics with an Adrià twist: the ice has had the oxygen sucked out so it sparkles like a diamond.

Quimet i Quimet
Tapas €€

(Carrer del Poeta Cabanyes 25; tapas €3-11; ⏱lunch & dinner Mon-Fri, noon-6pm Sat; Ⓜ Paral·lel) Quimet i Quimet is a family-run business that has been passed down from generation to generation. There's barely space to swing a calamari in this bottle-lined, standing-room-only place, but it is a treat for the palate. Look at all those gourmet tapas waiting for you! Let the folk behind the bar advise you, and order a drop of fine wine to accompany the food.

Xemei
Italian €€

(☎93 553 51 40; Passeig de l'Exposició 85; mains €10-20; ⏱Wed-Mon; Ⓜ Paral·lel) Xemei ('twins' in Venetian, because it is run by a pair of twins from Italy's lagoon city) is a wonderful slice of Venice in Barcelona. To the accompaniment of gentle jazz, you might try an entrée of mixed *cicheti*

(Venetian seafood tapas), followed with *bigoi in salsa veneziana* (thick spaghetti in an anchovy and onion sauce).

Barramòn
Canarian €

(☎934 42 30 80; www.barramon.es; Carrer de Blai 28; mains €6-14; Ⓜ Paral.lel) On the lively Carrer de Blai, Barramòn is a great little bar that serves Canarian food and is a bit rock and roll at the same time. Try the Ropa Vieja (an infinitely more flavour-some version of its eponymous Cuban cousin), a wonderful stew of chickpeas and shredded pork; *papas arrugadas* (baked new potatoes with a spicy sauce); and *almogrote* (cured cheese topped with olive oil, garlic and red pepper).

Taverna Can Margarit
Catalan €€

(Carrer de la Concòrdia 21; mains €8-10; ⏱dinner Mon-Sat; Ⓜ Poble Sec) For decades this former wine store has been dishing out dinner to often raucous groups. Traditional Catalan cooking is the name of the game. Surrounded by aged wine barrels, take your place at old tables and benches

Left: Torre Telefonica, designed by Santiago Calatrava, at Estadi Olímpic (p163); **Below:** Quimet i Quimet

(LEFT) LONELY PLANET / GETTY IMAGES ©; (BELOW) DIEGO LEZAMA / GETTY IMAGES ©

and perhaps order the *conejo a la jumillana* (fried rabbit served with garlic, onion, bay leaves, rosemary, mint, thyme and oregano).

La Bella Napoli   Pizza €

(☎93 442 50 56; www.bellanapoli.net; Carrer de Margarit 14; pizzas €7-21; ⏱lunch & dinner daily; Ⓜ Paral.lel) There are pizza joints all over Barcelona. And then there's the real thing: the way they make it in Naples. This place even *feels* like Naples. The waiters are mostly from across the Med and have that cheeky southern Italian approach to food, customers and everything else.

Restaurant Elche   Spanish €€

(☎93 441 30 89; Carrer de Vila i Vilà 71; mains €10-12; ⏱lunch & dinner; Ⓜ Paral.lel) With tables spreading over two floors, and old-world style in service and settings, this spot has been doing some of Barcelona's best paella (of various types) and *fideuá* (vaguely similar to paella, but made with vermicelli noodles) since the 1960s.

Monjuïc

Miramar   Mediterranean, Asian €€

(☎93 443 66 27; www.club-miramar.es; Carretera de Miramar 40; mains €10-15, lunchtime 3-course fixed menu €19.50; ⏱lunch & dinner Tue-Sat, lunch Sun; ☒50 & 193) With several terraces and a cool designer main dining area, this restaurant's key draw is the views it offers over Barcelona's waterfront. Hovering just above the Transbordador Aeri cable-car station, you can linger over a coffee or tuck into an elegant meal with a creative Catalan and Mediterranean slant, or opt for an extensive Asian menu.

☻ Drinking & Nightlife

A couple of curious bars in El Poble Sec (literally 'Dry Town'!) make a good prelude to the clubs that hold sway up in the

GRAFICART.NET / ALAMY © ARCHITECT: JOSEP LLUIS SERT

Don't Miss
Fundació Joan Miró

Joan Miró, the city's best-known 20th-century artistic progeny, bequeathed this art foundation to his home town in 1971. The foundation rests amid the greenery of the mountains and holds the greatest single collection of the artist's work, comprising around 220 of his paintings, 180 sculptures, some textiles and more than 8000 drawings spanning his entire life. Only a small portion is ever on display.

The exhibits give a broad impression of Miró's artistic development. The first couple of rooms (11 and 12) hold various works, including a giant tapestry in his trademark primary colours. Room 13, a basement space called Espai 13, leads you downstairs to a small room for temporary exhibitions.

Next comes room 16, the Sala Joan Prats, with works spanning the years until 1931, entitled The Early Years and Paris and Surrealism. Here, you see how Miró moved away, under surrealist influence, from relative realism (for instance his 1917 painting *Ermita de Sant Joan d'Horta*) towards his unique style that uses primary colours and morphed shapes symbolising the moon, the female form and birds.

This theme is continued upstairs in room 17, the Sala Pilar Juncosa (named after his wife), which covers the years 1932–55, his surrealist years. Rooms 18–19 contain masterworks of the years 1956–83, and room 20 a series of paintings done on paper. Room 21 hosts a selection of the private Katsuka collection of Miró works from 1914 to the 1970s. Room 22 rounds off the permanent exhibition with some major paintings and bronzes from the 1960s and 1970s. On the way here, you will see Mercury Fountain by Alexander Calder, a rebuilt work that was originally built for the 1937 Paris Fair and represented Spain at the Spanish Republic's Pavilion.

NEED TO KNOW

www.bcn.fjmiro.es; Plaça de Neptu; adult/senior & child €10/7; ⊙10am-8pm Tue, Wed, Fri & Sat, to 9.30pm Thu, to 2.30pm Sun & holidays; 🚌50, 55, 193, Paral·lel wonderfully weird fantasy world of the Poble Espanyol.

La Caseta Del Migdia
Bar

(☎617 956572, 93 301 91 77; www.lacaseta.org; Mirador del Migdia; ⏱6pm-2.30am Thu-Sat, noon-1am Sun Jun-Sep, noon-7pm Sat & Sun Oct-May; Ⓜ Paral.lel,) The effort of getting to what is, to all intents and purposes, a simple *chiringuito* (makeshift cafe-bar) is well worth it. Stare out to sea over a beer or coffee by day. As sunset approaches the atmosphere changes, as lounge music (from samba to funk) wafts out over the hammocks. Walk below the walls of the Montjuïc castle along the dirt track or follow Passeig del Migdia (watch out for signs for the **Mirador del Migdia**).

Tinta Roja
Bar

(Carrer de la Creu dels Molers 17; ⏱8.30pm-2am Thu, to 3am Fri & Sat; Ⓜ Poble Sec) A succession of nooks and crannies, dotted with what could be a flea market's collection of furnishings and dimly lit in violets, reds and yellows, makes the 'Red Ink' an intimate spot for a drink and the occasional show in the back – with anything from actors to acrobats.

Barcelona Rouge
Bar

(☎93 442 49 85; Carrer del Poeta Cabanyes 21; ⏱11pm-2am Tue-Thu, to 3am Fri & Sat; 📶; Ⓜ Poble Sec) Decadence is the word that springs to mind in this bordello-red lounge-cocktail bar, with acid jazz, drum and bass and other soothing sounds drifting along in the background.

Gran Bodega Saltó
Bar

(http://bodegasalto.net; Carrer de Blesa 36; ⏱7pm-3am Wed-Sat, noon-2am Sun; Ⓜ Paral. lel) You can tell by the ranks of barrels that this was once an old-fashioned wine store. Now, after a little homemade psychedelic redecoration, with odd lamps, figurines and old Chinese beer ads, this is a magnet for an eclectic barfly crowd.

Terrazza
Club

(www.laterrrazza.com; Avinguda de Francesc Ferrer i Guàrdia; admission €10-20; ⏱midnight-5am Thu, to 6am Fri & Sat; Ⓜ Espanya) One of the city's top summertime dance locations, Terrrazza attracts squadrons of the beautiful people, locals and foreigners alike, for a full-on night of music and cocktails partly under the stars inside the Poble Espanyol complex.

⭐ Entertainment

Sala Apolo
Live Music

(☎93 441 40 01; www.sala-apolo.com; Carrer Nou de la Rambla 113; admission €6-12; ⏱12.30-6am Fri & Sat, midnight-5am Sun-Thu; Ⓜ Paral-lel) This is a fine old theatre, where red velvet dominates and you feel as though you're in a movie-set dancehall scene featuring Eliot Ness. Earlier in the evening, concerts generally take place. Tastes are as eclectic as possible, from local bands to international acts.

Park Güell, Camp Nou & La Zona Alta

The undulating terrain north of L'Eixample is dominated by the fairy-tale setting of Park Güell, one of Gaudí's most extraordinary creations. From its hillside perch, it has stellar views over Barcelona.

South of here is Gràcia, a separate village until 1897. It still has a distinct vibe and is home to artists, hipsters, expats and young families. Its pretty plazas are ringed with bars and cafes, and there's a plethora of restaurants, vintage shops and drinking dens in its narrow lanes.

West of Gràcia lies the vast Zona Alta, the affluent 'High Zone'. Scattered here are a handful of worthwhile sites, including the serene Pedralbes monastery and the charming neighbourhood of Sarria. Further north is Tibidabo, the city's high point, with acres of green space, fine views and an amusement park. Further south, near the Sants neighbourhood is Camp Nou, the hallowed home stadium of FC Barcelona.

Park Güell (p178)

Park Güell, Camp Nou & La Zona Alta Highlights

Park Güell (p178)

Imagine a Disney fairy tale, scripted by Tolkien and filmed by Fellini, and you've conjured a picture of Park Güell. The park's construction was initiated in 1900 when Count Eusebi Güell bought a scrubby hillside and hired Antoni Gaudí to create a miniature city of posh houses in landscaped grounds. The project was a commercial flop, but the abandoned site was saved i the 1920s and soon garnered a dedicated following.

Camp Nou (p183)

Spanish soccer is a sometimes bitter tal of two teams, Real Madrid and FC Barce lona, with the latter currently enjoying a spell as one of the best in the world, courtesy of such living legends as Lionel Messi and Xavi Hernández. The team's home stadium is the largest in Europe and its on-site museum is a manifestation of fervour, football and intense Catalan pride.

Cosmocaixa (p180)

3

This sprawling science museum, one of the largest in Europe, is packed with fascinating exhibits exploring the wonders of the natural world. You can wander through a mocked-up Amazonian rainforest, peer back in time at geologic formations and journey to the outer limits of the solar system. Interactive hands-on exhibits make Cosmocaixa a perennial kid-pleaser. It's easy to spend a half-day or more here.

4

Museu-Monestir de Pedralbes (p181)

The city's periphery hides occasional oases of peace, including this impressive and beautifully preserved 14th-century Catalan-Gothic monastery. Highlights include the three-story cloister, a mural-filled chapel and a fascinating series of rooms that help conjure up life among the Poor Clares. The former sleeping quarters have been transformed into a gallery of religious art dating back to the 1500s.

5

Parc de Collserola (p187)

When Barcelona feels like it's closing in on you, find breathing space amid the rolling hills and dirt trails of rugged Parc de Collserola. Comprising 8000 hectares (22 times the size of New York's Central Park), Collserola is the largest municipal park in the world. Its view-laced ridges provide enough terrain to run multiple marathons, cycle a mini Tour de España and spot everything from wild boars to eagles.

Park Güell, Camp Nou & La Zona Alta Walk

This walk offers a window into centuries past when the Zona Alta was home to lavish summer estates, manicured gardens and sleepy age-old villages.

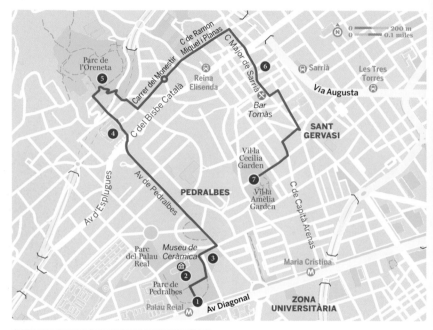

WALK FACTS
- **Start** Jardins del Palau de Pedralbes
- **Finish** Vil·la Amèlia & Vil·la Cecilia Gardens
- **Distance** 5km
- **Duration** Two hours

1 Jardins del Palau de Pedralbes

Although it's located on busy Avinguda Diagonal, this elegant little **park** feels like a peaceful escape from the bustling city beyond its gates. Pathways lead past manicured shrubbery, cedar and cypress trees, and a vine-covered pergola designed by Antoni Gaudí. A few sculptures dot the pathways, including a 17th-century urn and a nude by Enric Casanovas – one of the pivotal sculptors of the Noucentisme movement of the early 20th century.

2 Palau Reial de Pedralbes

At the north end of the park stands the **Palau Reial de Pedralbes** (p181), an Italian neoclassical design built between 1926 and 1929. The estate belonged to the family of Eusebi Güell (Gaudí's patron) until it was handed over to the city to serve as a royal residence. King Alfonso XIII stayed here when visiting the city and in 1936 the *palau* became the official residence of Manuel Azaña, the last president of the Spanish Republic. Today it houses the Museu de Ceràmica.

③ Pavellons Güell

Over by Avinguda de Pedralbes are the stables and porter's lodge designed by Gaudí for the Finca Güell, as the Güell estate here was called. Known also as the **Pavellons Güell**, they were built in the mid-1880s, when Gaudí was strongly impressed by Islamic architecture. A magnificent wrought-iron dragon guards the gate.

④ Museu-Monestir de Pedralbes

A stroll uphill along tree-lined Avinguda de Pedralbes leads to an oasis of another time, the peaceful **Museu-Monestir de Pedralbes** (p181). This Gothic convent with its enchanting cloister provides a tantalising glimpse into the life of nuns down the centuries.

⑤ Parc de l'Oreneta

Just behind the Museu-Monestir de Pedralbes rise the green slopes of this somewhat scrubby **woodland**. You can walk amid eucalypts, pines and oaks in a park that attracts few visitors on weekdays. Weekend activities bring out families with pony rides and train rides on a miniature locomotive. Various lookouts provide views over Barcelona.

⑥ Sarrià

Go east along the peaceful Carrer del Monestir for a look at some of the elegant mansions dotting the neighbourhood. Turn right at Carrer Major de Sarrià, which leads you into the heart of what was once the medieval village of **Sarrià**. Wander the pleasant streets and squares in the immediate area and try the city's best *patates braves* (potato chunks in a slightly spicy tomato sauce) at **Bar Tomàs** (p188).

⑦ Vil·la Amèlia & Vil·la Cecilia Gardens

Further southwest, these two **gardens** were once part of a magnificent summer estate. Shaded pathways meander beneath cypress, date palms and magnolias, with statuary and pools lending an elegance to the greenery. The 19th-century Vil·la Amèlia today houses the Sarrià civic centre.

 The Best...

PLACES TO EAT

La Balsa First-rate Catalan cooking amid lovely garden-covered terraces with views. (p188)

Botafumeiro Decadent seafood feasts are served at this long-running Galician classic. (p183)

El Aasador de Aranda Excellent roast meats in a Modernista dining room. (p188)

PLACES TO DRINK

Mirablau Fun crowd and panoramic views from its Tibidabo perch. (p190)

Raïm A slice of old Havana with expert mojitos. (p189)

La Nena One of Gràcia's best-loved neighbourhood cafes. (p183)

VIEWPOINTS

Parc de Collserola An 8000-hectare park in the hills. (p187)

Temple del Sagrat Cor Giant Christ statue with lift to the top. (p187)

Torre de Collserola A 288m tower with a glass elevator to an observation deck. (p187)

Park Güell Architectural intrigue and breezy views over city and sea. (p178)

Observatori Fabra Telescopic views of outer space. (p181)

Torre de Collserola (p187)
ZEBRA0209 / SHUTTERSTOCK ©

Don't Miss
Park Güell

One of Antoni Gaudí's best-loved creations, Park Güell – a fantasy public park that was designed as a gated playground for Barcelona's rich – climbs a hillside north of the centre. This is where the master architect turned his hand to landscape gardening and the result is an expansive and playful stand of greenery interspersed with otherworldly structures that glitter with ceramic tiles. The lasting impression is of a place where the artificial almost seems more natural than the natural.

Map p184

☎ 93 413 24 00

Carrer d'Olot 7

admission free

🕙 10am-9pm Jun-Sep, 10am-8pm Apr, May & Oct, 10am-7pm Mar & Nov, 10am-6pm Dec-Feb

🚌 24, Ⓜ Lesseps or Vallcarca

Background

Park Güell originated in 1900, when Count Eusebi Güell bought a tree-covered hillside (then outside Barcelona) and hired Gaudí to create a miniature city of houses for the wealthy in landscaped grounds. The project was a commercial flop and was abandoned in 1914 – but not before Gaudí had created 3km of roads and walks, steps, a plaza and two gatehouses in his inimitable manner. In 1922 the city bought the estate for use as a public park.

Much of the park is still wooded, but it's laced with pathways. The best views are from the cross-topped Turó del Calvari in the southwest corner.

Sala Hipóstila

The steps up from the entrance, guarded by a mosaic dragon/lizard, lead to the Sala Hipóstila (the Doric Temple). This forest of 88 stone columns – some of which lean like mighty trees bent by the weight of time – was originally intended as a market. To the left curves a gallery whose twisted stonework columns and roof give the effect of a cloister beneath tree roots – a motif repeated in several places in the park.

Banc de Trencadís

On top of the Sala Hipóstila is a broad open space whose centrepiece is the Banc de Trencadís, a tiled bench curving sinuously around its perimeter and designed by one of Gaudí's closest colleagues, architect Josep Maria Jujol (1879–1949). With Gaudí, however, there is always more than meets the eye. This giant platform was designed as a kind of catchment area for rainwater washing down the hillside. The water is filtered through a layer of stone and sand, and it drains down through the columns to an underground cistern.

Casa-Museu Gaudí

The spired house to the right is the Casa-Museu Gaudí, where Gaudí lived for most of his last 20 years (1906–26). It contains furniture he designed (including items that were once at home in La Pedrera, Casa Batlló and Casa Calvet) and other memorabilia.

Local Knowledge

Don't Miss List

BY GONZALO SALAYA VENTURA, TOURIST GUIDE AT ICONO SERVEIS CULTURALS

1 ENTRANCE PAVILIONS
The entrance to Park Güell is flanked by two pavilions, best viewed from the public square up above. Here you'll see classic Gaudí features – hyperbolic shapes, the use of brick and ceramic and cross-topped towers, plus the incredible decoration.

2 SALAMANDER
The most famous creation in the park is this striking, mosaic-covered creature – perhaps a depiction of the legendary salamander associated with medieval alchemy. Like so much of Gaudí's works, this sculpture serves both aesthetic and practical purposes by linking water from an underground reservoir to the (mostly unbuilt) homes.

3 SALA HIPÓSTILA
Located underneath the (planned) main public square, the One Hundred Columns' Room, aka Sala Hipóstila, has an incredible ceiling composed of broken bits of ceramic and glass, including bottles. Here Gaudí created organic forms – suns, waves and other nature-inspired shapes – while employing the innovative technique of *trencadis* (p217).

4 CARYATID COLUMN
Descending from the right stairs leading off the public square to the salamander, you can access a 'diagonal' porch. Here you see dramatically slanting columns, one of Gaudí's trademarks. Nearly concealed amid the columns is a caryatid (a sculpted female figure which serves as a support). It harks back to Ancient Greece, but Gaudí has given the figure the more contemporary appearance of a washerwoman.

5 TURÓ DEL CALVARI
Christian symbols figure heavily in Gaudí's work and Park Güell is no exception. Most obvious are the three crosses atop the Turó del Calvari, evoking the crucifixion of Christ and two thieves atop Mt Calvary. When you find the right perspective, you can appreciate the clever design as the three crosses became one.

179

Discover Park Güell, Camp Nou & La Zona Alta

🔀 Getting There & Away

○ Metro Take Metro Línia 3 toward Canyelles for Gràcia (Fontana stop) and Park Güell (Vallcarca stop). Take Línia 3 toward Zona Universitária to reach Palau Reial de Pedralbes or Camp Nou (Palau Rail stop).

○ Train FGC trains are handy for getting near Tibidabo (Tibadabo stop), Sarrià (Sarrià stop) and Museu-Monestir de Pedralbes (Reina Elisenda stop).

○ Tram Outside Avinguda de Tibidabo station, the tramvia blau runs to Plaça del Doctor Andreu, where you can catch an onward funicular up to Tibidabo.

◉ Sights

Gràcia

Park Güell   Park

See p178.

FREE **Mercat de la Llibertat** Market
(Map p182; 📞 93 217 09 95; Plaça de la Llibertat; ⏰ 8am-8.30pm Mon-Fri, 8am-3pm Sat; ℝ FGC Gràcia) Built in the 1870s, the 'Liberty Market' was covered over in 1893 in typically fizzy Modernista style, employing generous whirls of wrought iron.

La Zona Alta

Cosmocaixa   Museum
(Museu de la Ciència; Map p184; 📞 93 212 60 50; www.fundacio.lacaixa.es; Carrer de Isaac Newton 26; adult/child €3/2; ⏰ 10am-8pm Tue-Sun; 🚌 60, ℝ FGC Avinguda Tibidabo) Kids (and kids at heart) are fascinated by displays here and the museum has become one of the city's most popular attractions. The single greatest highlight is the re-creation over 1 sq km of a chunk of flooded Amazon rainforest (Bosc Inundat). More than 100 species of Amazon flora and fauna (including anacondas, colourful poisonous frogs and caymans) prosper in this unique, living diorama in which you can even experience a tropical downpour. In another original section, the Mur Geològic, seven great chunks of rock (90 tonnes in all) have been assembled to create a Geological Wall.

These and other displays on the lower 5th floor (the bulk of the museum is underground) cover many fascinating

Palau Reial de Pedralbes
POSZTOS (COLORLAB.HU) / SHUTTERSTOCK ©

areas of science, from fossils to physics, and from the alphabet to outer space.

Palau Reial de Pedralbes   Palace
(Map p184; ☎ 93 256 34 65; Avinguda Diagonal 686; all collections adult/student & senior €5/3, 1st Sunday of the month & 3-6pm Sun free; ⏰ museum 10am-6pm Tue-Sun, 10am-3pm holidays, park 10am-6pm daily; Ⓜ Palau Reial) Fronted by pretty, manicured gardens, the Palau Reial is an elegant estate dating from the 1920s that houses the **Museu de Ceràmica** (Map p184; www.museuceramica. bcn.es). You'll find a superb collection of Spanish ceramics from the 10th to 19th centuries, including work by Picasso and Miró.

Observatori Fabra   Observatory
(Map p184; ☎ 93 431 21 39; www.fabra.cat; Carretera del Observatori; admission €10; 🚉 Avinguda Tibidabo, 🚋 tramvia blau) Inaugurated in 1904, this Modernista observatory is still a functioning scientific foundation. It can be visited on certain evenings to allow people to observe the stars through its grand old telescope. Visits, generally in Catalan or Spanish (Castilian)

have to be booked. From mid-June to mid-September, an option is to join in for the nightly Sopars amb Estrelles (Dinner under the Stars). The easiest way here is by taxi.

Museu-Monestir de Pedralbes

Museu-Monestir de Pedralbes   Monastery
(Map p184; ☎ 93 256 34 34; www.museuhistoria. bcn.cat; Baixada del Monestir 9; adult/child €7/5; ⏰ 10am-5pm Tue-Sat, to 8pm Sun; 🚉 FGC Reina Elisenda, 🚌 22, 63, 64 or 75) This peaceful old convent was first opened to the public in 1983 and is now a museum of monastic life (the few remaining nuns have moved into more modern neighbouring buildings).

The architectural highlight is the large, elegant, three-storey cloister, a jewel of Catalan Gothic, built in the early 14th century. Following its course to the right, stop at the first chapel, the Capella de Sant Miquel, whose murals were done in 1346 by Ferrer Bassá, one of Catalonia's earliest documented painters.

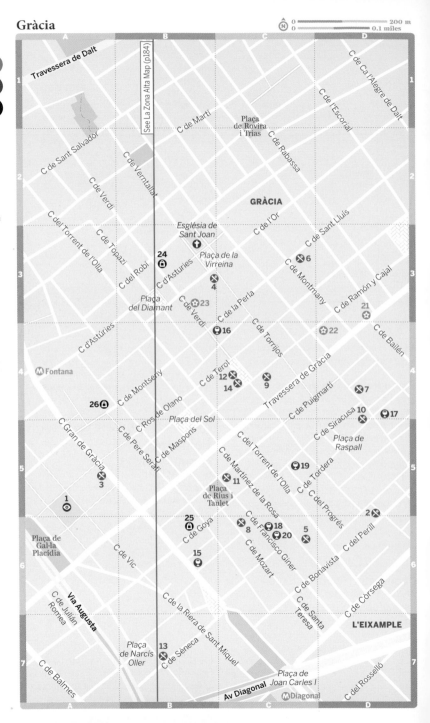

0 200 m
0 0.1 miles

Travessera de Dalt

See La Zona Alta Map (p184)

C de Ca l'Alegre de Dalt

C de l'Escorial

C de Martí

Plaça de Rovira i Trias

C de Rabassa

C de Sant Salvador

C de Verdi

C de Verntallat

GRÀCIA

C de Topazi

C del Torrent de l'Olla

C de l'Or

C de Sant Lluís

Església de Sant Joan

24

C del Robí

C d'Astúries

Plaça de la Virreina

6

C de Montmany

C de Ramón y Cajal

4

21

Plaça del Diamant

23

C de Verdi

C de la Perla

16

C de Torrijos

22

C de Bailèn

C d'Astúries

Fontana

C de Montseny

C de Terol

12

14

9

Travessera de Gràcia

7

C de Puigmartí

10

17

C de Siracusa

26

C de Ròs de Olano

C de Pere Serafí

C de Maspons

Plaça del Sol

C del Torrent de l'Olla

Plaça de Raspall

C Gran de Gràcia

C de Martínez de la Rosa

19

C de Tordera

C del Progrés

11

3

Plaça de Rius i Taulet

1

25

C de Goya

8

18

20

5

15

C de Francisco Giner

C del Perill

Plaça de Gal·la Placídia

C de Vic

C de Mozart

C de Bonavista

C de Còrsega

C de Santa Teresa

Via Augusta

C de Julián Romea

C de la Riera de Sant Miquel

L'EIXAMPLE

Plaça de Narcís Oller

13

C de Sèneca

C de Balmes

Plaça de Joan Carles I

Av Diagonal

Diagonal

C del Rosselló

Gràcia

⊙ Sights

Camp Nou   Stadium

(Map p184; ☎ **93 496 36 00; www.fcbarcelona. com; Carrer d'Aristides Maillol; adult/child €23/17;** ☺ **10am-8pm Mon-Sat, to 2.30pm Sun;** Ⓜ **Palau Reial)** Among Barcelona's most-visited sites is the massive stadium of Camp Nou (which means New Field in Catalan), home to the legendary Futbol Club Barcelona. Football fans who aren't able to attend a game can get a taste of all the excitement at the museum, with its multimedia exhibits, and a stadium tour.

 Eating

Gràcia

Spread across this busy *barri* are all sorts of enticing options, from simple tapas bars to top-class seafood. Gràcia is loaded with Middle Eastern and, to a lesser extent, Greek restaurants, which are chirpy and good value. Several classic Catalan taverns tick along nicely with a strong local following. There's little of interest, however, around Park Güell.

Botafumeiro   Seafood €€

(Map p182; ☎ **93 218 42 30; www.botafumeiro. es; Carrer Gran de Gràcia 81; meals €15-25;** ☺ **1pm-1am;** Ⓜ **Fontana)** It is hard not to mention this classic temple of Galician shellfish and other briny delights, long a magnet for VIPs visiting Barcelona. Try the *percebes*, the strangely twisted goose barnacles harvested along Galicia's north Atlantic coast, which many Spaniards consider the ultimate seafood delicacy.

Sureny   Catalan €

(Map p182; ☎ **93 213 75 56; Plaça de la Revolució de Setembre de 1868; meals €8-10;** ☺ **Tue-Sun;** Ⓜ **Fontana)** Appearances can be deceiving: the cooks in this unremarkable-looking corner restaurant dedicate themselves to producing gourmet tapas and *raciones*, ranging from exquisite *vieiras* (scallops) to a serving of *secreto ibérico*, a particular tasty cut of pork meat (near the porcine equivalent of the armpit, perhaps that's the 'secret').

O'Gràcia!   Mediterranean €€

(Map p182; Plaça de la Revolució de Setembre de 1868 15; meals €10-12; ☺ **Tue-Sat;** Ⓜ **Fontana)** This is an especially popular lunch option, with the *menú del día* outstanding value at €10.50. The *arròs negre de sepia* (black rice with cuttlefish) makes a good first course, followed by a limited set of meat and fish options with vegetable sides.

La Nena   Cafe, Chocolate €

(Map p182; ☎ **93 285 14 76; Carrer de Ramon i Cajal 36; snacks €2-4;** ☺ **9am-2pm & 4-10pm Mon-Sat, 10am-10pm Sun & holidays;** ⊞; Ⓜ **Fontana)**

183

La Zona Alta

0   500 m
0   0.25 miles

VALLVIDRERA

To Tibidabo

Parc de la
Collserola

Carretera del Vallvidrera
al Tibidabo

Funicular de Vallvidrera

Túnel de Vallvidrera

Túnel de Vallvidrera

Peu del
Funicular

3

Funicular
del Tibidabo

Plaça del
Doctor
Andreu

Ronda de Dalt

1

11

5

Cosmocaixa

C de la
Infanta Isabel

7

Av del Tibidabo

8

Av Tibidabo

C de Balmes

C d'Esteve Terradas

Parc de la
Creueta del
Coll

Pg de la Mare
de Déu del Coll

VALLCARCA

Vallcarca

Penitents

Av de l'Hospital Militar

Jardins
del Turó
del Puget

SANT
GERVASI DE
CASSOLES

Park Güell

EL
CARMEL

Plaça
de Lesseps

Lesseps

Av del Príncep d'Astúries

GRÀCIA

Fontana

Travessera de Dalt

C de Lincoln   Gràcia

12

C de Vallirana

C de Saragossa

Molina

Pàdua

C de Balmes

Sant Gervasi

Via Augusta

Ronda del General Mitre

C de Muntaner

C de Mandri

El Putxet

C de Sant Joan de la Salle

C del Bellesguard

SARRIÀ –
SANT GERVASI

C d'Iradier

C d'Angli

SARRIÀ

C Major de Sarrià

Reina
Elisenda

Plaça de
Sarrià

Sarrià

6

Pg de la Bonanova

C de Ganduxer

C de les Escoles Pies

C d'Iradier

Plaça de
Adrià

C de Copèrnic

C de Freixa

Parc de
l'Oreneta

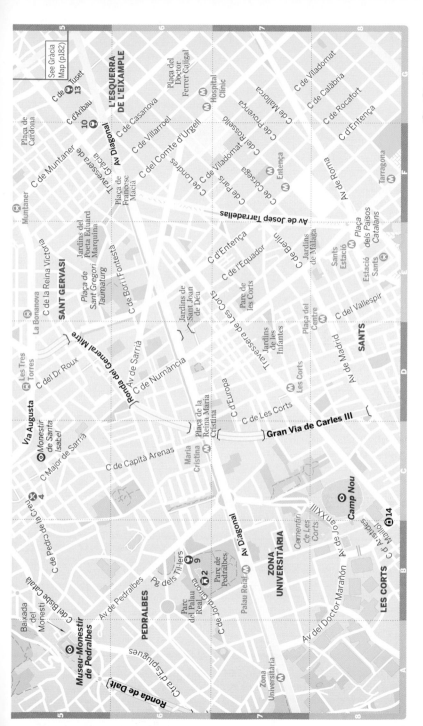

See Gràcia Map (p182)

C de Tuset **13**

L'ESQUERRA DE L'EIXAMPLE

C d'Aribau **10**

Plaça de Cardona

C de Muntaner

Travessera de Gràcia

Av Diagonal

C de Casanova

C de Villarroel

C del Comte d'Urgell

Plaça de Francesc Macià

Plaça del Doctor Ferrer Cajigal

Hospital Clínic

C de Rosselló

C de Provença

C de Mallorca

C de Viladomat

C de Calàbria

C de Rocafort

C d'Entença

Muntaner

Les Tres Torres

SANT GERVASI

La Bonanova

C de la Reina Victòria

Jardins del Poeta Eduard Marquina

Plaça de Sant Gregori Taumaturg

C de Bori i Fontestà

C de Londres

C de Còrsega

C de París

C de Viladomat

Entença

Av de Roma

Tarragona

Av de Josep Tarradellas

C d'Entença

C de l'Equador

C de Berlín

Jardins de Màlaga

Sants Estació

Plaça dels Països Catalans

Estació Sants

SANT GERVASI

C del Dr Roux

Ronda del General Mitre

Av de Sarrià

C de Numància

Jardins de Sant Joan de Déu

Parc de les Corts

Plaça del Centre

C del Vallespir

SANTS

Via Augusta

Monestir de Santa Isabel

C Major de Sarrià

Plaça de la Reina Maria Cristina

Travessera de Les Corts

Jardins de les Infantes

C de Les Corts

Les Corts

Av de Madrid

Maria Cristina

C d'Europa

Gran Via de Carles III

C de Capità Arenas

C de Pedro de la Creu

Baixada del Monestir

C del Bisbe Català

Museu-Monestir de Pedralbes

Ctra d'Esplugues

Ronda de Dalt

PEDRALBES

Av de Pedralbes

Pg dels Tillers **9**

2

Parc del Palau Reial

C de Jordi Girona

Parc de Pedralbes

Av Diagonal

Palau Reial

ZONA UNIVERSITÀRIA

Cementiri de Les Corts

Av de Joan XXIII

Camp Nou

14

C d'A. i Isidre

C de Mallol

LES CORTS

Av del Doctor Marañón

Zona Universitària

Museu-Monestir de Pedralbes

185

La Zona Alta

A French team has created this delightfully chaotic space for indulging in cups of rich hot chocolate (known as *suïssos*) served with a plate of heavy homemade whipped cream and *melindros* (spongy sweet biscuits), fine desserts and even a few savoury dishes (including crêpes).

Restaurant Roig Robí   Catalan €€
(Map p182; ✆93 218 92 22; www.roigrobi.com; Carrer de Sèneca 20; meals €15-20; ⏰lunch & dinner Mon-Fri, dinner Sat; Ⓜ Diagonal) This is an altar to refined traditional cooking. Try the *textures de carxofes amb vieires a la plantxa* (artichokes with grilled scallops) for the delicate scent of artichoke wafting over the prized shellfish. The restaurant also does several seafood-and-rice dishes and offers half portions for those with less of an appetite.

Con Gracia   Fusion €€€
(Map p182; ✆93 238 02 01; www.congracia.es; Carrer de Martínez de la Rosa 8; set menus €59; ⏰lunch & dinner Tue-Fri, dinner Sat; Ⓜ Diagonal)

This teeny hideaway (seating about 20 in total) is a hive of originality, producing delicately balanced Mediterranean cuisine with Asian touches. At lunch, only groups are accepted. Book ahead.

Ipar-Txoko   Basque €€€
(Map p182; ✆93 218 19 54; Carrer de Mozart 22; meals €40-50; ⏰Tue-Sat Sep-Jul; Ⓜ Diagonal) Inside this Basque eatery, the atmosphere is warm and traditional. Getxo-born Mikel turns out traditional cooking from northern Spain, including a sumptuous *chuletón* (T-bone steak for two – look at the size of that thing!) or a less gargantuan *tortilla de bacalao* (a thick salted-cod omelette).

Bilbao   Spanish €€
(Map p182; ✆93 458 96 24; Carrer del Perill 33; meals €10-15; ⏰Mon-Sat; Ⓜ Diagonal) It doesn't look much from the outside, but Bilbao is a timeless classic, where reservations for dinner are imperative. The back dining room, with bottle-lined walls, stout timber tables and a yellow light evocative of a country tavern, will appeal to carnivores especially, although some fish dishes are also on offer.

Lac Majùr   Italian €€€
(Map p182; ✆93 285 15 03; Carrer de Tordera 33; meals €25; ⏰Mon-Sat; Ⓜ Verdaguer) Inside this cosy slice of northwest Italy, all sorts of home-cooking delights await, including the house pasta specials, gnocchi and trofie.

El Glop   Catalan €€€
(Map p182; ✆93 213 70 58; www.tavernael glop.com; Carrer de Sant Lluís 24; meals €25; Ⓜ Joanic) This raucous eatery is decked out in country Catalan fashion, with gingham tablecloths and no-nonsense, slap-up meals. The secret is hearty serves of simple dishes, such as *bistec a la brasa* (grilled steak), perhaps preceded by *albergínies farcides* (stuffed aubergines) or *calçots* (spring onions) in winter.

Himali   Nepalese €€
(Map p182; ✆93 285 15 68; Carrer de Milà i Fontanals 60; meals €15-20; ⏰Tue-Sun; ✆;

M Joanic) Spacious and simple, with gruff service and paper placemats, this is a great spot for Nepalese chow and vegetarian dishes.

Nou Candanchú   Tapas €
(Map p182; ☏ 93 237 73 62; Plaça de la Vila de Gràcia 9; meals €5-7; ☺ Wed-Mon; M Fontana) The liveliest locale on the square, Nou Candanchú is a long-time favourite for various reasons. Many flock to its sunny terrace just for a few drinks. Accompany the liquid refreshment with one of the giant *entrepans* (filled rolls) for which this place is famous.

Cantina Machito   Mexican €
(Map p182; ☏ 932 17 34 14; www.cantinamachito. com; Carrer Torrijos 47; meals €8-11; ☺ 1-4pm, 7pm-1.30am daily; M Fontana or Joanic) On the leafy Torrijos street, the colourful Machito – which seems devoted to the image of Frida Kahlo – gets busy with locals, and the outside tables are a great place to eat and drink until late. You'll find all the standard Mexican delights like quesadillas, tacos, enchiladas and so on, and some wonderfully refreshing iced water flavoured with honey and lime, mint and fruit.

La Zona Alta

Some of the grandest kitchens in the city are scattered across La Zona Alta, from Tibidabo across Sant Gervasi (as far down as Avinguda Diagonal, west of Gràcia) to Pedralbes.

Tibidabo

Framing the north end of the city, the forest-covered mountain of Tibidabo, which tops out at 512m, is the highest peak in Serra de Collserola. Aside from the superb views from the top, the highlights of Tibidabo include an 8000-hectare park, an old-fashioned amusement park, a telecommunications tower with viewing platform and a looming church that's visible from many parts of the city.

Barcelonins (people of Barcelona) needing an escape from the city without heading too far into the countryside seek out the vast **Parc de Collserola** (☏ 93 280 35 52; www.parcnaturalcollserola.cat; Carretera de l'Església 92; ☺ Centre d'Informació 9.30am-3pm, Can Coll 9.30am-3pm Sun & holidays, closed Jul & Aug; ☒ FGC Peu del Funicular, Baixador de Vallvidrera) in the hills. It is a great place to hike and bike and bristles with eateries and snack bars. Pick up a map from the Centre d'Informació.

The **Temple del Sagrat Cor** (Church of the Sacred Heart; ☏ 93 417 56 86; Plaça de Tibidabo; admission free, lift €2; ☺ 8am-7pm, lift 10am-7pm), looming above the top funicular station, was built from 1902 to 1961 in a mix of styles with some Modernista influence, and is as visible as its Parisian namesake, Sacre Cœur.

The reason most *barcelonins* come up to Tibidabo is for some thrills in the amusement park, **Parc d'Atraccions** (☏ 93 211 79 42; www.tibidabo.cat; Plaça de Tibidabo 3-4; adult/child €25.20/9; ☺ closed Jan-Feb), close to the top funicular station.

Sir Norman Foster designed the 288m-high **Torre de Collserola** (Map p184; ☏ 93 406 93 54; www.torredecollserola.com; Carretera de Vallvidrera al Tibidabo; adult/child €5/3; ☺ noon-2pm & 3.15-8pm Wed-Sun Jul & Aug, noon-2pm & 3.15-6pm Sat, Sun & holidays Sep-Jun, closed Jan & Feb; ☒ 111, Funicular de Vallvidrera) telecommunications tower, which was completed in 1992. The visitors' observation area, 115m up, offers magnificent views – up to 70km on a clear day.

La Balsa
Mediterranean €€€

(Map p184; ☎93 211 50 48; www.labalsares
taurant.com; Carrer de la Infanta Isabel 4; mains
€18-24; ⏱lunch Tue-Sun, dinner Mon-Sat, in
Aug dinner only 9pm-midnight; ☒FGC Avinguda
Tibidabo) With its grand ceiling and the
scented gardens that surround the main
terrace dining area, La Balsa is one of
the city's top dining experiences. The
menu changes frequently and is a mix of
traditional Catalan and off-centre inven-
tiveness. Lounge over a cocktail at the bar
before being ushered to your table.

El Asador de Aranda
Spanish €€€

(Map p184; ☎93 417 01 15; www.asadordearanda.
com; Av del Tibidabo 31; mains €20-22; ⏱closed
Sun dinner; ☒Av Tibidabo) A great place for
a meal after visiting Tibidabo, El Asador
de Aranda is set in a striking art nouveau
building, complete with stained-glass
windows, Moorish-style brick arches and
elaborate ceilings. You'll find a fine assortment of tapas plates for sharing, though
the speciality is the meat (roast lamb,

spare ribs, beef), beautifully prepared in a
wood oven.

La Molina
Catalan €€

(Map p184; ☎93 417 11 24; Passeig de Sant
Gervasi 65; mains €9-16; ⏱1pm-12.30am
Mon-Fri, 11am-5pm Sat & Sun; ☒FGC Avinguda
Tibidabo) La Molina looks like a typical
tapas bar at first glance – sidewalk tables,
nondescript bar in front – but head to the
back room, and you'll discover one of the
great unsung Catalan restaurants in the
neighbourhood.

Bar Tomàs
Tapas €

(Map p184; ☎93 203 10 77; Carrer Major de
Sarrià 49; tapas €3-5; ⏱noon-10pm Thu-Tue;
☒FGC Sarrià) Many *barcelonins* have long
claimed that Bar Tomàs is by far the best
place in the city for *patates braves* (potato
chunks in a slightly spicy tomato sauce),
prepared here with a special variation
on the traditional sauce. The place is a
rough-edged bar, but that doesn't stop
the well-off citizens of Sarrià piling in,
particularly for lunch on weekends.

Foix De Sarrià
Pastelería €

(Map p184; ☑93 203 04 73; www.foixde
sarria.com; Plaça de Sarrià 12-13; Desserts €2-5;
⏰8am-8pm; 🚇FGC Reina Elisenda) Since
1886 this exclusive pastry shop has been
selling the most exquisite cakes and
sweets.

🍷 Drinking & Nightlife

Gràcia is a quirky place. In many ways
it's its own world, with rowdy young beer
swillers, trendy music bars and a couple
of the city's big clubs.

Gràcia

Raïm
Bar

(Map p182; www.raimbcn.com; Carrer del Progrés
48; ⏰8pm-2.30am; 🚇Diagonal) The walls
in Raïm are alive with black-and-white
photos of Cubans and Cuba. Tired old
wooden chairs of another epoch huddle
around marble tables, while grand old
timber-lined mirrors hang from the walls.
They just don't make old Spanish taverns
like this anymore.

Alfa
Bar

(Map p182; ☑93 415 18 24; Carrer Gran de
Gràcia 36; ⏰11pm-3.30am Thu-Sat; 🚇Diagonal)
Aficionados of good old-fashioned rock
love this unchanging bar-cum-minidisco,
a Gràcia classic.

La Baignoire
Bar

(Map p182; Carrer de Verdi 6; ⏰7pm-2.30am
Sun-Thu, 7pm-3am Fri & Sat; 🚇Fontana) This
inviting, tiny wine bar is always packed.
Grab a stool and high table and order fine
wines by the glass (beer and cocktails
available too). It's perfect before and after
a movie at the nearby Verdi cinema.

La Cigale
Bar

(Map p182; ☑93 457 58 23; http://poesia
lacigale.blogspot.co.uk; Carrer de Tordera 50;

☼6pm-2.30am Sun-Thu, 6pm-3am Fri & Sat; Ⓜ Joanic) A very civilised place for a cocktail (or two for €8 before 10pm) and hearing some poetry readings. Prop up the zinc bar, sink into a secondhand lounge chair around a teeny table or head upstairs. Music is chilled, conversation lively and you're likely to see Charlie Chaplin in action on the silent flat-screen TV.

Le Journal   Bar
(Map p182; ☎93 218 04 13; Carrer de Francisco Giner 36; ☼6pm-2.30am Sun-Thu, 6pm-3am Fri & Sat; Ⓜ Fontana) Students love the conspiratorial basement air of this narrow bar, whose walls and ceiling are plastered with newspapers (hence the name). Read the headlines of yesteryear while reclining in an old lounge.

Sabor A Cuba   Bar
(Map p182; Carrer de Francisco Giner 32; ☼10pm-2.30am Mon-Thu, 10pm-3am Fri & Sat; Ⓜ Diagonal) Ruled since 1992 by the charismatic Havana-born Angelito is this home of *ron y son* (rum and sound). A mixed crowd of Cubans and fans of the Caribbean island come to drink mojitos and shake their stuff in this diminutive, good-humoured hang-out.

La Zona Alta

North of Avinguda Diagonal, the *pijos* (cashed-up mamma's boys and papa's girls) are in charge. Whether you sample the bars around Carrer de Marià Cubí (and surrounding streets) or try the clubs around Carrer d'Aribau or Tibidabo, expect to be confronted by perma-tanned Audi- and 4WD-driving folks in designer threads.

Mirablau   Bar
(Map p184; Plaça del Doctor Andreu; ☼11am-4.30am Sun-Thu, to 5am Fri & Sat; ℞Avinguda Tibidabo, ☒tramvia blau) Gaze out over the entire city from this privileged balcony restaurant on the way up to Tibidabo. Wander downstairs to join the folk in the tiny dance space. In summer you can step out onto the even smaller terrace for a breather.

Elephant   Club
(Map p184; ☎93 334 02 58; www.elephantbcn. com; Passeig dels Til·lers 1; ☼11.30pm-4am Thu, to 5am Fri & Sat ; Ⓜ Palau Reial) Getting in here is like being invited to a private fantasy party in Beverly Hills. Models and wannabes mix with immaculately groomed lads who most certainly didn't come by taxi. A big tentlike dance space is the main game here, but smooth customers slink their way around a series of garden bars in summer too.

Otto Zutz   Club
(Map p184; www.ottozutz.com; Carrer de Lincoln 15; admission €15; ☼midnight-6am Tue-Sat; ℞FGC Gràcia) Beautiful people only need apply for entry to this three-floor dance den. Shake it all up to house on the ground floor, or head upstairs for funk and soul.

Sutton The Club   Club
(Map p184; www.thesuttonclub.com; Carrer de Tuset 13; admission €15; ☼midnight-5am Wed-Thu, midnight-6am Fri & Sat, 10.30pm-4am Sun; Ⓜ Diagonal) A classic disco with mainstream sounds on the dance floor, some hopping house in a side bar and a fair spread of eye candy, this place inevitably attracts just about everyone pouring in and out of the nearby bars at some stage of the evening.

Luz de Gas   Club
(Map p184; ☎93 209 77 11; www.luzdegas.com; Carrer de Muntaner 246; admission up to €20; ☼11.30pm-6am; ☒6, 7, 15, 27, 32, 33, 34, 58 or 64, Ⓜ Diagonal) Several nights a week this club, set in a grand former theatre, stages concerts ranging through soul, country, salsa, rock, jazz and pop. From about 2am, the place turns into a club that attracts a well-dressed crowd with varying musical tastes, depending on the night.

☆ Entertainment

Heliogàbal   Live Music
(Map p182; www.heliogabal.com; Carrer de Ramón i Cajal 80; ☼9pm-2am Sun-Thu, 9pm-3am Fri & Sat; Ⓜ Joanic) This compact bar is a veri-

table hive of cultural activity where you never quite know what to expect. Aside from art exhibitions and poetry readings, you will often be pleasingly surprised by the eclectic live-music program.

Elèctric Bar
Live Music

(Map p182; www.electricbarcelona.com; Travessera de Gràcia 233; ⊗7pm-2am Sun-Thu, 7pm-3am Fri & Sat; MJoanic) Concerts get under way between 10pm and 11pm in this long and somewhat dingy bar. Generally, we're looking at home-grown bands revelling in the chance to bring jazz, blues, funk, bossa nova and much more to a small stage and appreciative crowd.

Verdi
Cinema

(Map p182; ✐93 238 79 90; www.cines-verdi. com; Carrer de Verdi 32; MFontana) A popular original-language movie house in the heart of Gràcia, handy to lots of local eateries and bars for pre- and post-film enjoyment.

 Shopping

Gràcia

A wander along the narrow lanes of Gràcia turns up all sorts of surprises, mostly tiny enterprises producing a variety of pretty garments and trinkets. Carrer de Verdi has plenty of interesting clothes shops.

A Casa Portuguesa
Food

(Map p182; ✐933 68 35 28; www.acasaportuguesa.com; Carrer de Verdi 58; ⊗5-10pm Tue-Fri, 11am-3pm & 5-10pm Sat & Sun, closed Mon; MFontana) Come here to try Barcelona's best Portuguese custard tarts, *pastéis de Belém*. The gourmet shop also sells other Portuguese goodies – cheeses, pastries and wines – and a new restaurant is in the works.

Hibernian
Books

(Map p182; ✐93 217 47 96; Carrer de Montseny 17; ⊗4-8.30pm Mon, 10.30am-8.30pm Tue-Sat; MFontana) The biggest secondhand English bookshop in Barcelona stocks thousands of titles covering all sorts of subjects, from cookery to children's classics.

Érase una Vez
Fashion

(Map p182; ✐93 217 29 77; Carrer de Goya 7; MFontana) 'Once Upon a Time' is the name of this fanciful boutique, which brings out the princess in you (if you have one in there, that is). Local designers such as Llamazares y de Delgado and Zazo & Brull are behind these sometimes-sumptuous creations.

La Zona Alta

FC Botiga
Souvenirs

(Map p184; ✐93 492 31 11; http://shop.fcbarcelona.com; Carrer de Arístides Maillol; ⊗10am-9pm Mon-Sat; MCollblanc) Here you will find footballs, shirts, scarves, socks, wallets, bags, sneakers, iPhone covers – pretty much anything you can think of, all featuring Barça's famous red-and-blue insignia. It has branches all over town, including at **Maremàgnum** and **Carrer de Jaume I 18** (Map p58; ✐93 269 15 32; Carrer de Jaume I 18; ⊗10am-9pm; MJaume I).

Day Trips

Girona (p194)

A splendid cathedral, a maze of narrow cobbled streets and Catalonia's finest medieval Jewish quarter are part of this riverside town's charms.

Montserrat (p196)

Catalonia's most important shrine in a mountain monastery, complete with Europe's oldest choir and superb scenic walks.

Sitges (p197)

A string of beaches, great nightlife and a hedonistic carnival await visitors at Costa Daurada's premier seaside town.

Montserrat basilica (p197)

Girona

Girona's big draw is its Old Town, a tight huddle of ancient arcaded houses, grand churches and climbing cobbled streets, so head first for the star attraction – the Catedral – either by strolling along the lazy Río Onyar or by taking the high road along the medieval walls, followed by a visit to the Call (medieval Jewish quarter) and the excellent Museu d'Història dels Jueus de Girona before taking your pick of the restaurants in the nearby streets.

After lunch, continue your exploration of other Old Town sights, such as the wonderfully intact Banys Àrabs or the attractive cloisters and verdant grounds of the Monestir de Sant Pere de Galligant, before finding a bar around the Plaça Independencia to while away the evening.

Getting There & Away

Car Take the AP-7 freeway via Granollers.

Train At least 20 trains run daily from Barcelona Sants station (from €9.70, up to 1½ hours).

Girona

Need to Know

○ **Area Code** 972

○ **Location** 85km northeast of Barcelona

○ **Tourist Office** (972 22 65 75; www.girona. cat/turisme; Rambla de la Llibertat 1; 9am-8pm Mon-Fri, 9am-2pm & 4-8pm Sat, 9am-2pm Sun)

◉ Sights

Catedral   Cathedral
(www.catedraldegirona.org; Plaça de la Catedral; museum adult/child €5/1.20, Sun free; 10am-8pm) The billowing baroque facade of the cathedral seems all the grander, standing at the head of the 86 steps rising from Plaça de la Catedral. Though the Romanesque **cloister** dates back to the 12th century, most of the building has been repeatedly altered down the centuries, giving it the second-widest Gothic nave (23m) in Christendom. The cathedral's **museum** contains numerous ecclesiastic treasures, including the masterly Romanesque *Tapís de la Creació* (Tapestry of the Creation) and a Mozarabic illuminated *Beatus* manuscript, dating from 975.

MAURIZIO BORGESE / GETTY IMAGES ©

Museu d'Història dels Jueus de Girona
Museum

(Carrer de la Força 8; adult/child €2/free; ☾10am-8pm Mon-Sat, 10am-2pm Sun Jul & Aug, shorter hr rest of yr) The restored Centre Bonstruc ća Porta, named after Jewish Girona's most illustrious figure – a 13th-century cabbalist philosopher and mystic – houses the excellent Museu d'Història dels Jueus de Girona, which shows genuine pride in Girona's Jewish heritage without shying away from the less salubrious aspects, such as persecution by the Inquisition and forced conversions.

Banys Àrabs
Bathhouse

(www.banysarabs.org; Carrer de Ferran Catòlic; adult/child €2/1; ☾10am-7pm Mon-Sat Apr-Sep, shorter hr rest of yr, 10am-2pm Sun & holidays) This is the only public bathhouse discovered from 12th-century Christian Spain. Possibly in reaction to Muslim enthusiasm for water and cleanliness (and a widely held view that water carried disease), washing almost came to be regarded as ungodly.

Monestir de Sant Pere de Galligants
Monastery

(www.mac.cat/cat/Seus/Girona; Carrer de Santa Llúcia; adult/senior & child €2.30/free; ☾10.30am-1.30pm & 4-7pm Tue-Sat Jun-Sep, 10am-2pm Sun & holidays) This 11th- and 12th-century Romanesque Benedictine monastery has a lovely cloister, featuring otherworldly animals and mythical creatures on its pillars, and is home to the **Museu Arqueològic** (adult/senior & child €2.30/free), with exhibits that range from prehistoric to medieval times.

Museu d'Història de la Ciutat
Museum

(www.girona.cat; Carrer de la Força 27; adult/student/child €4/2/free; ☾10am-2pm & 5-7pm Tue-Sat, 10am-2pm Sun & holidays) The engaging and well-presented museum does Girona's long and impressive history justice, its displays covering everything from the city's Roman origins, through the siege of the city by Napoleonic troops to the *sardana* (Catalonia's national folk dance) tradition and edgy temporary art.

Sleeping in Girona

○ **Casa Cúndaro** (☎972 22 35 83; www.casacundaro.com; Pujada de la Catedral 9; d €60-80; 🛜) Medieval Jewish house featuring five sumptuous rooms and four self-catering apartments – all combining original exposed stone walls with modern luxuries such as satellite TV. The location is practically on top of the cathedral.

○ **Bed & Breakfast Bells Oficis** (☎972 22 81 70; www.bellsoficis.com; Carrer dels Germans Busquets 2; r incl breakfast €40-85; ❄🛜) Six very desirable rooms in a 19th-century building. Some have unusual pebble art in the bathrooms, while others share bathrooms and some have views over the street.

FREE Església de Sant Feliu
Church

(Plaça de Sant Feliu; ☾9.30am-2pm & 4-7pm Mon-Sat, 10am-noon Sun) The 17th-century main facade of Girona's second great church, with its landmark single tower, is on Plaça de Sant Feliu.

✕ Eating

L'Alqueria
Catalan €€

(☎972 22 18 82; www.restaurantalqueria.com; Carrer de la Ginesta 8; mains €18-22; ☾lunch & dinner Wed-Sat, lunch only Tue & Sun) This smart minimalist *arrocería* (a restaurant specialising in rice dishes) serves the finest *arròs negre* (rice cooked in cuttlefish ink) and *arrós a la Catalan* (Catalan paella, cooked in an earthenware pot, without saffron) in the city, as well as around 20 other superbly executed rice dishes. Book ahead for dinner.

+Cub
Tapas €

(Plaça de Catalunya; 3 tapas €10.40; ☾lunch daily, dinner Mon-Sat; 🖋) Ubercentral cafe-bar distinguished by the friendly service, innovative tapas – from black pudding with pistachio to salad with black fig sorbet – fresh fruit juice combos, shakes and Girona's own La Moska microbrew.

Montserrat

Though the monastery complex itself is compact, allow a whole day for the visit if you want to take advantage of the many splendid mountain walks. Take the earliest *cremallera* (rack-and-pinion train) or cable car up the mountain to beat the crowds and begin with the exploration of the monastery complex, paying a visit to the Virgin and then the worthwhile Museu de Montserrat before grabbing an early lunch at the cafeteria. Don't stray too far, as you wouldn't want to miss the 1pm performance by Europe's oldest boys' choir (www.escolania.cat) inside the basilica.

Afterwards, ride the funiculars, or else take a walk down to the Santa Cova – the spot where the Virgin was originally found – or up to the Sant Jeroni peak for a splendid view of the valley below.

Getting There & Away

Train, rack railway & cable car The R5 line trains operated by FGC (www.fgc.net) run hourly from Plaça d'Espanya station, starting at 8.36am (52 to 56 minutes). They connect with the cable car (www.aeridemontserrat.com) at the Montserrat Aeri stop (€5/7.90 oneway/return, 17 minutes, 9.40am to 7pm March to October, 10.10am to 5.45pm Monday to

Sleeping in Montserrat

○ **Hotel Abat Cisneros** (☏93 877 77 01; s/d €60/104; P ❄) The only hotel in the monastery complex has modern, comfortable rooms, some of which look over Plaça de Santa Maria. It has a good restaurant serving imaginative Catalan dishes (meals €36).

Saturday, 10.10am to 6.45pm Sunday & holidays November to February) and the cremallera (www.cremallerademontserrat.com) at the following stop, Monistrol de Montserrat (€6/9 one way/return, five minutes).

Need to Know

○ **Area Code** ☏938

○ **Location** 50km northwest of Barcelona

○ **Tourist Office** (☏938 77 77 01; www.montserratvisita.com; ◷9am-5.45pm Mon-Fri, to 6.45pm Sat & Sun)

Sights

Monestir de Montserrat Monastery (www.abadiamontserrat.net; ◷9am-6pm) The monastery – the second most important pilgrimage centre in Spain after Santiago de Compostela – was founded in 1025 to commemorate a vision of the Virgin on the mountain, seen by – you've guessed it – shepherds, after which the Black Virgin icon, allegedly carved by St Luke and hidden in the mountains by St Peter to protect it from the Moors, was discovered. Wrecked by Napoleon's troops in 1811, the monastery was rebuilt from 1858. Today a community of about 80 monks lives here. Pilgrims come from far and wide to venerate the Virgen de Montserrat, affectionately known as **La Moreneta** ('the little brown one' or 'the Black Madonna'), a 12th-century Romanesque wooden sculpture of a regal-looking Mary, holding the infant Jesus, the wood stained dark by centuries of smoke. She has been Catalonia's patron since 1881 and her blessing is particularly sought by newly married couples; Barcelona FC dedicate their victories to her and during the civil war she was courted by Franco.

Museu de Montserrat Museum (Plaça de Santa Maria; adult/student €6.50/5.50; ◷10am-6pm) The two-part Museu de Montserrat has an excellent collection, ranging from an Egyptian mummy and Gothic altarpieces to art by El Greco, Monet, Degas and Picasso, as well as modern art and some fantastic 14th-century Russian icons.

EDDIE LINSSEN / ALAMY ©

Basilica
Church

(admission €5; ⏰7.30am-8pm) From Plaça de Santa Maria, you enter the courtyard of the 16th-century Renaissance basilica. Stairs lead to the narrow **Cambril de la Mare de Déu** (⏰7-10.30am & noon-6.30pm), which houses La Moreneta.

Sant Jeroni
Mountain

You can explore the mountain above the monastery on a web of paths leading to some of the peaks and to 13 empty and picturesquely dilapidated hermitages. The **Sant Joan funicular** (one way/return €5.05/8; ⏰every 20min 10am-6.50pm, closed Jan & Feb) will carry you up the first 250m from the monastery. If you prefer to walk, the road past the funicular's bottom station leads to its top station in about one hour (3km).

From the top station, it's a 20-minute stroll (signposted) to the **Sant Joan chapel**, with fine westward views. More exciting is the one-hour walk northwest to Montserrat's highest peak, Sant Jeroni, from where there's an awesome sheer drop on the north face.

Santa Cova
Chapel

To see the chapel on the spot where the holy image of the Virgin was discovered (currently housing a replica La Moreneta), take the **Santa Cova funicular** (one way/return €2/3.20; ⏰every 20min 10am-5.30pm) or else just stroll down, then follow the precipitous mountain path with fabulous views of the valley below.

Eating

Cafeteria
Fast Food €

(meals €15-20; ⏰lunch noon-4pm) At this central self-service spot you can grab a sandwich or more substantial mains: *calamares a la romana* (deep-fried calamari rings), meatballs, burgers – the usual suspects.

Sitges

Sitges is perfect for seafront promenading and sun worshipping, so in warmer weather you'll find the most central beaches quite crowded. Luckily, there are quite a few to choose from, so pick your spot for a morning of sunbathing (or skinny dipping off the nudist beach) before choosing a seafood restaurant nearby.

197

If you have an interest in contemporary art and in the modernism (Catalan Art Nouveau) movement, the Museu Cau Ferrat (p198) is well worth an hour of your time in the afternoon, followed by a central tapas bar for an afternoon drink. If you're particularly hardcore, you will then stay on and party until daybreak at one of the many clubs on the outskirts of town.

Getting There & Away

Car The best road from Barcelona is the C-32 tollway. More scenic is the C-31, which hooks up with the C-32 after Castelldefels, but it is often busy and slow.

Train Four R2 *rodalies* trains an hour, from about 6am to 10pm, run from Barcelona's Passeig de Gràcia and Estació Sants to Sitges (€3.60, 27 to 46 minutes depending on stops).

Need to Know

○ **Area Code** ☏938

○ **Location** 32km southwest of Barcelona

○ **Tourist Office** (☏938 11 06 11; Passeig de la Ribera; ☉10am-2pm & 4-8pm)

Sights

Beaches
Beaches

There are 12 beaches altogether in Sitges: the main beach, flanked by the attractive seafront **Passeig Maritim**, dotted with *chiringuitos* (beachside bars) and divided into nine sections with different names by a series of breakwaters, as well as Sant Sebastiá, Balmins and D'aiguadolç beaches running east of the headland that's crowded with museums and graced by the striking **Església de Sant Bartomeu i Santa Tecla**. Though Bassa Rodona used to be the unofficial 'gay beach', gay sunbathers are now spread out pretty evenly, while Balmins is the sheltered bay favoured by nudists.

Museu Cau Ferrat
Museum

(Carrer de Fonollar) Built in the 1890s as a house-cum-studio by artist Santiago Rusiñol (a pioneer of the modernism movement whose statue graces the main beach), this whitewashed mansion is full of his own art and that of his contemporaries, including his friend Picasso, as well as a couple of El Grecos. Under renovation at the time of writing, the museum should have reopened by the time you read this.

Eating & Drinking

eF & Gi International €€ (www.efgirestaurant.com; Carrer Major 33; meals €35-50; ☉dinner Tue-Sat mid-Jan–mid-Dec) Fabio and Greg (eF & Gi) are not afraid to experiment and the results are startlingly good: the mostly Mediterranean menu with touches of Asian inspiration throws out such delights as char-

Sitges

grilled beef infused with lemongrass and kaffir lime, and tuna loin encrusted with peanuts and calamata olives with mango chutney.

El Pou
Tapas €€

(www.elpoudesitges.com; Carrer de Sant Pau 5; meals €30; ☺lunch & dinner Wed-Mon) The tiny Wagyu beef burgers at this friendly gourmet tapas place are an absolute delight, and the rest doesn't lag far behind; the traditional *patatas bravas* sit alongside the likes of *mojama* (salted dried tuna) with almonds and fried aubergine with cane molasses.

Sweet Pachá Club
Club

(www.sweetpacha.com; Avinguda Port d'Aiguadolç 9) The white leather seats are perfect for a pause inbetween cocktail-fuelled sessions on the dance floor and there's a decent seafood restaurant for those wanting a quieter night. It's located just back from the Aiguadolç marina, 1.2km east along the coast from the Museu Maricel del Mar.

Sleeping in Sitges

○ **Hotel Romàntic** (☏93 894 83 75; www.hotelromantic.com; Carrer de Sant Isidre 33; s/d from €70/100; ✻) These three adjoining 19th-century villas are presented in sensuous Modernista style, with a leafy dining courtyard and friendly service, though the rooms are smallish and could do with sprucing up. Just around the corner is its charming sister hotel, **Hotel La Renaixença** (☏93 894 06 43; www.hotelromantic.com; Carrer d'Illa de Cuba 45; s/d from €70/100), which is actually better value.

L'Atlàntida Club
Club

(www.clubatlantida.com; Platja de Les Coves; ☺Fri & Sat plus 2 more nights per week Jun-Sep) An Ibiza-esque big mama of a beachside nightclub with a large open-air dance floor, about 3.5km west of the centre.

Barcelona
In Focus

Rambla de Mar (p110)
PHOTOGRAPHER: KRZYSZTOF DYDYNSKI / GETTY IMAGES ©

Barcelona Today

> *regardless of financial forecasts, most barcelonins couldn't imagine living anywhere else*

belief systems
(% of population)

90 Roman Catholic

10 Other

if Barcelona were 100 people

62 would be Catalan
24 would be other Spanish
14 would be non-Spanish

population per sq km

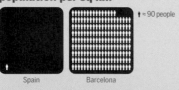

♦ ≈ 90 people

Spain

Barcelona

Economic Woes

In 2012, the Spanish economy slipped into recession for its second time in three years. Unemployment levels in the city have risen above 20% (slightly lower than Spain's nearly 24%). Meanwhile austerity measures pre-scribed by bureaucrats – slashing budgets, raising taxes and freezing public sector pay – have done nothing to alleviate the hardship.

Anger at the labour reforms and dramatic spending cuts has led to nationwide strikes, with tens of thousands marching in the streets of Barcelona in 2012 (joining millions of protesting Spaniards nationwide).

Reinventing Neighbourhoods

The financial crisis has stalled some projects like Norman Foster's dramatic (some would say psychedelic) €250 million redesign of the Camp Nou football stadium. Yet the city has pushed ahead on other major developments. Ongoing expansion work continues on the Metro, with new stations planned (including

ANNA SERRANO / SIME / 4CORNERS ©

the Parc del Fòrum is the largest of any European city. Catalonia also announced plans to quintuple wind capacity by 2020.

Barcelona's shared bike program, Bicing, which was launched in 2007, has helped reduce traffic on the road.

No Smoke, No Bull

Other ways the air is getting a little cleaner: Spain's strict antismoking ban went into effect in 2011. Bars, restaurants and nightclubs are now smoke-free, as is Camp Nou. Speaking of bans, in 2012 Catalonia officially outlawed bullfighting, becoming the first region in mainland Spain to prohibit the practice.

A Catalan Nation

Sensitivity over regional identity is never far from Spanish political debates, particularly as public perception has been that Catalonia makes substantial financial contributions to the state but often gets a proportionally tiny piece of the pie. Perhaps angered by this, Barcelona staged a symbolic referendum on Catalan independence in 2011. Little more than 20% of eligible voters turned out, although 90% of them voted in favour of independence.

one out to the airport) and overall accessibility greatly improving travel options for those with limited mobility.

New buildings like the Filmoteca de Catalunya with exhibition space and cinemas have added to the city's creative credibility; the film centre is the latest in a series of major art spaces (including the Richard Meier–designed MACBA and the cutting-edge CCCB) that have contributed to El Raval's ongoing revitalisation.

Sustainable Initiatives

The first Smart City Expo and World Congress was held in Barcelona in 2011 to discuss urban planning, the environment and other increasingly important urban issues. Barcelona was chosen as the host city because of intelligent strategies in the urban landscape. Since 2000, the city has required all new buildings to install solar panels to provide most of their hot water. Its massive solar panel near

Food Frontiers

In the realm of cuisine, Barcelona continues to lead the way. Ferran Adrià, the mastermind behind molecular gastronomy, has opened a new restaurant in the city. He and other innovative chefs continue to bring bold new ideas to the Catalan table. Food, culture, design – it's boom days in Barcelona – though of course the economy says otherwise. But regardless of financial forecasts, most *barcelonins* couldn't imagine living anywhere else.

203

History

Parlament de Catalunya (p95)

CARSTEN LEUZINGER / IMAGEBROKE

The storied settlement of Barcelona has seen waves of immigrants and conquerors over its 2000-plus years of existence, including Romans, Visigoths, Franks and later Catalans. Barcelona has seen its fortunes rise and fall over the years – from the golden era of princely power in the 14th century to dark days of civil war and the Franco era. Throughout, a fierce independent streak has always run through Barcelona.

Wilfred the Hairy & Mediterranean Expansion

It was the Romans who first etched Barcino onto Europe's map in the 3rd century BC, though the nascent settlement long played second fiddle to their provincial capital in Tarragona. The Visigoths came next, followed by the Moors, whose relatively brief occupation was usurped when the Franks put the city under the control of local counts in 801

circa AD 15

Settlement of Barcino first mentioned in Roman chronicles under control of Tarraco (Tarragona).

as a buffer zone against the still Muslim-dominated caliphate to the south.

Eccentrically named Wilfred the Hairy (Count Guifré el Pelós) moulded the entity we now know as Catalonia in the 9th century by wresting control over several neighbouring territories and establishing Barcelona as its key city. The hirsute one founded a dynasty that lasted nearly five centuries and developed almost independently from the Reconquista wars that were playing out in the rest of Iberia.

The counts of Barcelona gradually expanded their territory south and, in 1137, Ramon Berenguer IV, the Count of Barcelona, married Petronilla, heir to the throne of neighbouring Aragón. Thus, the combined Crown of Aragón was created.

In the following centuries the regime became a flourishing merchant empire, seizing Valencia and the Balearic Islands from the Muslims, and later taking territories as far flung as Sardinia, Sicily and parts of Greece.

Santa Eulàlia

Barcelona's first patron saint, Santa Eulàlia (290–304) was martyred for her faith during the persecutory reign of Diocletian. Her death involved 13 tortures (one for each year of her life), including being rolled in a glass-filled barrel, having her breasts cut off and crucifixion. Some artwork (such as a sculpture inside the Museu Frederic Marès) depicts Eulàlia holding a tray containing her excised breasts. The cathedral (p54), which is dedicated to her, holds her remains, as well as a cloister with 13 lily-white geese – also symbolic of Eulàlia's tender age at martyrdom.

Castilian Dominance

Overstretched, racked by civil disobedience and decimated by the Black Death, Catalonia began to wobble by the 14th century. When the last count of Wilfred the Hairy's dynasty expired without leaving an heir, the Crown of Aragón was passed to a noble of Castile. Soon these two Spanish kingdoms merged, with Catalonia left as a very junior partner. As business shifted from the Mediterranean to the Atlantic after the discovery of the Americas in 1492, Catalans were increasingly marginalised from trade.

Decline & Fall

The region, which had retained some autonomy in the running of its own affairs, was dealt a crushing blow when it supported the wrong side in the War of the Spanish

717
Barcelona captured by the Moors, who rule until the arrival of the Franks in 801.

1137
Barcelona's power increases as it allies with the Kingdom of Aragon through royal marriage.

1380s
Catalonia's Mediterranean empire extends as far as Sardinia, Sicily and Greece.

Succession (1702–14). Barcelona, under the auspices of British-backed archduke Charles of Austria, fell after a stubborn siege on 11 September 1714 (now celebrated as National Catalan Day) to the forces of Bourbon king Philip V, who established a unitary Castilian state. Barcelona now faced a long backlash as the new king banned the writing and teaching of Catalan, swept away the remnants of local legal systems and tore down a whole district of medieval Barcelona in order to construct an immense fort (on the site of the present-day Parc de la Ciutadella), whose sole purpose was to watch over Barcelona's troublemakers.

The Renaixença & the Road Back

Buoyed by the lifting of the ban on its trade with the Americas in 1778, Barcelona embarked on the road to industrial revolution, based initially on textiles but spreading to wine, cork and iron in the mid-19th century.

It soon became Spain's leading city. As the economy prospered, Barcelona outgrew its medieval walls, which were demolished in 1854–56. Work on the gridplan L'Eixample (the Extension) district began soon after. The so-called Renaixença (Renaissance) brought a revival of Catalan culture, as well as political activism. It sowed the seeds of growing political tension in the early 20th century, as demands for autonomy from the central state became more insistent.

The Masses Against the Classes

Adding to the fiery mix was growing discontent among the working class. The grand Catalan merchant-bourgeois families grew richer, displaying their wealth in a slew of whimsical private mansions built with verve and flair by Modernista architects such as Antoni Gaudí. At the same time, the industrial working class, housed in cramped quarters such as Barceloneta and El Raval, and oppressed by poverty and disease, became organised and, on occasion, violent. Spain's neutrality during WWI had boosted Barcelona's economy, and from 1900 to 1930 the population doubled to one million, but the postwar global slump hit the city hard. Waves of strikes, organised principally by the anarchists' Confederación Nacional del Trabajo, brought tough responses. Left- and right-wing gangs took their ideological conflict to the streets. Tit-for-tat assassinations became common currency and the death toll mounted.

When the Second Spanish Republic was created under a left-wing government in 1931, Catalonia declared independence. Later, under pressure, its leaders settled for devolution, which it then lost in 1934, when a right-wing government won power in Madrid. The election of a left-wing popular front in 1936 again sparked Catalan autonomy claims but also led General Franco to launch the Spanish Civil War (1936–39), from which he emerged the victor.

1714
Under siege, Barcelona falls to King Philip V in the War of the Spanish Succession. King Philip V

1860s
Barcelona outgrows its medieval city walls and work begins on L'Eixample (the Extension).

Revolutionary Fervour

The acting capital of Spain for much of the civil war, Barcelona was run by anarchists and the Partido Obrero de Unificación Marxista (Marxist Unification Workers' Party) Trotskyist militia until mid-1937. Unions took over factories and public services, hotels and mansions became hospitals and schools, everyone wore workers' clothes, bars and cafes were collectivised, trams and taxis were painted red and black (the colours of the anarchists), and one-way streets were ignored as they were seen to be part of the old system.

The more radical anarchists were behind the burning of most of the city's churches and the shooting of more than 1200 priests, monks and nuns. The anarchists in turn were shunted aside by the communists (directed by Stalin from Moscow) after a bloody internecine battle in Barcelona that left 1500 dead in May 1937. Later that year the Spanish Republican government fled Valencia and made Barcelona the official capital (the government had left besieged Madrid early in the war).

The Republican defeat at the hands of the Nationalists in the Battle of the Ebro in southern Catalonia in the summer of 1938 left Barcelona undefended. It fell to the Nationalists on 25 January 1939, triggering a mass exodus of refugees to France, where most were long interned in makeshift camps. Purges and executions under Franco continued until well into the 1950s. Former Catalan president Lluís Companys was arrested in France by the Gestapo in August 1940, handed over to Franco, and shot on 15 October on Montjuïc. He is reputed to have died with the words 'Visca Catalunya!' ('Long live Catalonia!') on his lips.

The Best... Places to Discover Barcelona's Past

1 Museu d'Història de Barcelona (p67)

2 Museu d'Història de Catalunya (p112)

3 Església de Santa Maria del Mar (p102)

4 Via Sepulcral Romana (p61)

5 Temple Romà d'August (p61)

6 Sinagoga Major (p61)

IN FOCUS HISTORY

The City Reborn

The Francoist Josep Maria de Porcioles was mayor from 1957 until his death in 1973, a grey time for Barcelona, marked by regular demonstrations against the regime, always brutally put down. When Franco himself died two years later, the city rejoiced. In 1977 Catalonia was granted regional autonomy.

1888

The first International Exposition in Barcelona paves the way for two decades of Modernisme architecture.

1936-39

Thousands die from bloody fighting in the Civil War before the city falls to Franco's fascist forces.

1977

After one million demonstrate peacefully on Barcelona's streets, Catalonia is granted regional autonomy.

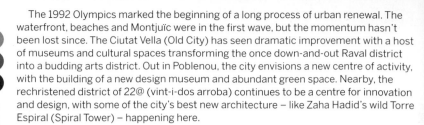

The 1992 Olympics marked the beginning of a long process of urban renewal. The waterfront, beaches and Montjuïc were in the first wave, but the momentum hasn't been lost since. The Ciutat Vella (Old City) has seen dramatic improvement with a host of museums and cultural spaces transforming the once down-and-out Raval district into a budding arts district. Out in Poblenou, the city envisions a new centre of activity, with the building of a new design museum and abundant green space. Nearby, the rechristened district of 22@ (vint-i-dos arroba) continues to be a centre for innovation and design, with some of the city's best new architecture – like Zaha Hadid's wild Torre Espiral (Spiral Tower) – happening here.

1992
Barcelona hosts a highly lauded Summer Olympics, ushering in another prolonged period of urban renewal.

2000s
Fresh immigration and slick modern buildings along the waterfront bring Barcelona into the 21st century.

2010
Pope Benedict XVI consecrates the basilica of Sagrada Família before an audience of 6500.

Playground in El Fòrum (p114)

OSO MEDIA / ALAMY ©

Barcelona offers abundant rewards to stimulate young minds. The city has running-around space in the parks and gardens of Montjuïc and Tibidabo, and the ample beaches near Barceloneta. It has quirks: fairy-tale Modernista architecture and the ever-revolving street theatre that is La Rambla. There are also activities aimed specifically at children, including a dreamlike aquarium, a hands-on science museum and an amusement park with panoramic views.

Catalan-Style

Going out to eat or sipping a beer on a late summer evening at a *terraza* (terrace) needn't mean leaving children with minders. Locals take their kids out all the time and don't worry about keeping them up late.

To make the most of your visit, try to adjust your child's sleeping habits to 'Spanish time' early on, or else you'll miss out on much of Barcelona. Also, be prepared to look for things 'outside the box': there's the childlike creativity of Picasso and Miró (give your children paper and crayons and take them around the museums), the Harry-Potter-meets-Tolkien fantasy of Park Güell and La Pedrera, and the wild costumes, human castle-building and street food at festivals.

Babysitters

Most of the midrange and top-end hotels in Barcelona can organise babysitting services. A company that many hotels use and that you can also contact directly is **5 Serveis** (☏93 412 56 76; www.5serveis.com; Carrer de Pelai 50). It has multilingual *canguros* (babysitters). Rates vary, but in the evening expect to pay around €12 an hour plus the cost of a taxi home for the babysitter. **Tender Loving Canguros** (☏647 605989; www.tlcanguros.com) offers English-speaking babysitters for a minimum of three hours (from €8 an hour).

Kids & Bikes

Barcelona has excellent bike hire facilities, with some companies offering special kids' bicycles. Barnabike (p235) rents out an assortment of bikes (including kick bikes) and karts, Trikkes (odd three-wheel contraptions), electric bikes and bikes for kids. Barcelonabiking.com (p235) rents bikes as well as baby seats.

Getting Around

The metro provides speedy access around town, and most stations have elevators. Sometimes getting from point A to point B can be the best part of the experience. If heading up to Tibidabo's amusement park (p187), the kids will love the old tram (tramvia blau) that rattles through the mansion-lined streets, followed by a ride on a funicular up the steep wooded hillside. Likewise, the aerial gondola ride from Barceloneta up to Montjuïc is another crowd-pleaser, with fantastic views of city and sea.

Eating with Kids

Barcelona – and Spain in general – is super friendly when it comes to eating with children. Spanish kids tend to eat the Mediterranean offerings enjoyed by their parents,

Need to Know

○ **Changing facilities** Not as ubiquitous as in North America, but generally good and clean.

○ **Cots** Usually available in hotels; reserve ahead.

○ **Health** High health-care standards. Make sure you have your child's **EHIC card** (www.applyehic.org) before you travel within the EU.

○ **Highchairs** Many restaurants have at least one; bring your own crayons.

○ **Nappies (diapers)** Nappies, dummies, creams and formula can be had at any of the city's many pharmacies. Nappies are cheaper in supermarkets.

○ **Strollers** Bring your own (preferably a fold-away).

○ **Transport** Barcelona's metro is accessible and great for families with strollers – just be mindful of your bags around the pickpockets who often target distracted parents.

but some restaurants have children's menus that serve up burgers, pizzas, tomato-sauce pasta and the like. Good local – and child-proof – food commonly found on tapas menus is *tortilla de patatas* (potato omelet) or *croquetas de jamon* (ham croquettes).

Top Kid-Friendly Eateries

Fastvínic (p147) is a good choice for an off-peak lunch or quick dinner while the kids entertain themselves drawing on the glass wall. At Le Cucine Mandarosso (p101), the incredible food means even the fussiest eaters will surrender – it's best for older kids since it can feel a bit cramped, but the little ones will be made to feel welcome too.

If you're after something sweet, La Nena (p183) is fantastic for chocolate and all manner of sweet things. There's also a play area and toys and books in a corner. And don't miss Granja Viader (p77). No kid will be left unimpressed – and without a buzz! – by the thick hot chocolate here.

The Best...
Kid-Friendly
Sights

IN FOCUS FAMILY TRAVEL

Food & Drink

Fideuà

PATTY ORLY / SHUTTERSTOCK

Barcelona has a celebrated food scene fueled by a combination of world-class chefs, imaginative recipes and magnificent ingredients fresh from farm and sea. Catalan culinary masterminds like Ferran Adrià and Carles Abellán have become international icons, reinventing the world of haute cuisine, while classic old-world Catalan recipes continue to earn accolades in dining rooms and tapas bars across the city.

New Catalan Cuisine

Since the closing of the El Bulli on the northern Catalonian coast – widely hailed as one of the world's best restaurants – in 2011, Ferran Adrià, along with his brother Albert, has turned his focus to Barcelona, with the opening of the tapas bar Tickets (p167) and creative cocktail bar 41°. Like El Bulli, there's plenty of imagination among 'deconstructed' dishes like liquid olives, 'air baguettes' (made with Iberian ham) and Parmesan ice cream.

Other great chefs who've followed on the heels of Adrià continue to redefine contemporary cuisine. Michelin-starred chef Carles Abellán at Comerc24 reinterprets traditional tapas with dishes like the bite-sized mini-pizza sashimi with tuna; *melón con jamón*, a millefeuille of layered caramelised Iberian ham and thinly sliced melon; oxtail with cauliflower puree; and a changing parade of other mouth-watering bites.

Other stars of the Catalan cooking scene include Jordi Vilà, who continues to wow diners with reinvented classics at Alkímia (p143), Fermi Puig, head chef at the five-star Hotel Majestic, and Xavier Pellicer at ABaC Barcelona.

Classic Catalan

Traditional Catalan recipes showcase the great produce of the Mediterranean: fish, prawns, cuttlefish, clams, pork, rabbit, game, first-rate olive oil, peppers and loads of garlic. Classic dishes also feature unusual pairings (seafood with meat, fruit with fowl): cuttlefish with chickpeas, cured pork with caviar, rabbit and prawns, goose with pears.

Sauces

The essence of Catalan food lies in its sauces for meat and fish. There are five main types: *sofregit* (fried onion, tomato and garlic), *samfaina* or *chanfaina* (*sofregit* plus red pepper and aubergine or courgette), *picada* (based on ground almonds, usually with garlic, parsley, pine nuts or hazelnuts, and sometimes breadcrumbs), *allioli* (a mayonnaise-style sauce of pounded garlic with olive oil) and *romesco* (an almond, red pepper, tomato, olive oil, garlic and vinegar sauce, used especially with *calçots*).

Paella & Fideuà

Arròs a la cassola or *arròs a la catalana* is the moniker given to Catalan paella. It's cooked in an earthenware pot without saffron, whereas *arròs negre* is rice cooked in squid ink – much tastier than it sounds. *Fideuà* is similar to paella, but uses vermicelli noodles rather than rice. It usually comes with a little side dish of *allioli* to mix in.

Seafood

Apart from more standard approaches such as serving up steamed, baked or fried fish, the Catalans like to mix it up a little, by way of fish soups and stews. *Suquet*, which combines several types of fish with potatoes, is the best known, while *sarsuela*

Need to Know

○ **Price Ranges** In our listings, the following price codes represent the cost of a main course:

€	less than 10
€€	10 to 20
€€€	over 20

○ **Opening Hours** Most restaurants open 1pm to 4pm, and 8.30pm to midnight.
○ **Reservations** At high-end restaurants, reserve ahead, especially for Thursday to Saturday nights.
○ **Tipping** A service charge is often included in the bill. If you are particularly happy, add 5% to 10% on top.
○ **Menú del Día** The *menú del día*, a multicourse set meal with water and wine, is a great way to cap prices at lunchtime. They range from €8 to €25.

The Best...
Tapas

includes a richer variety of fish ingredients. Other themed stews often go by the name of *caldereta*, where one item (usually lobster) is the star ingredient.

Calçots

Catalans are passionate about *calçots* (large, sweet spring onions), which are barbecued over hot coals, dipped in tangy *romesco* sauce and eaten voraciously when in season (between January and March). *Calçots* are usually the first course followed by copious meat and sausage dishes.

Tapas

Although tapas, Spain's quintessential bar snacks, were invented in Andalucía and weren't originally part of the Catalan eating tradition, they have been enthusiastically imported. Particularly popular are the Basque Country tapas known as *pintxos,* most of which come in the form of canapés. On slices of baguette are perched anything from *bacalao* (cod) to *morcilla* (black pudding). These are most refreshingly washed down with a slightly tart Basque white wine, *txacoli,* which is served like cider to give it a few (temporary) bubbles. Each *pintxo* comes with a toothpick, and payment is by the honour system – keep your toothpicks and present them for the final count when you ask for the bill.

In some gourmet spots, tapas have become something of an art form, while in many straightforward, beery bars you might just get a saucer of olives to accompany your tipple.

Cava

Welcome to *cava* country. That's sparkling wine to the uninitiated, or wine with significant levels of carbon dioxide either added after fermentation or produced during a second process of fermentation. Catalonia produces 95% of Spain's *cava* and the grapes are grown almost exclusively in the grape-rich Penedès region, most notably in the village of Sant Sadurni d'Anoia. Cava goes brilliantly with tapas. A couple of lively eat-drink *cava* spots where you can experience the magic include Xampanyeria Can Paixano (p121) and El Xampanyet (p104).

Architecture

Casa Batlló (p139)

Barcelona's architectural gift to the world was Modernisme, a flamboyant Catalan creation that erupted in the late 19th century. Barcelona's other great architectural epoch was during the Middle Ages, when mercantile wealth fuelled the creation of magnificent Gothic buildings. More recently, the city has continued to host cutting-edge designs and dramatic urban renewal projects that all began in the makeover before and after the 1992 Olympics.

Catalan Gothic

Barcelona's first great moment of creative electricity came when the city, grown rich on its Mediterranean trade and empire-building, transformed what is now the old city centre into the pageant of Gothic building that has survived in great part to this day.

Historically, Gothic sits between the Romanesque and Renaissance periods of medieval construction. It was an architectural style that emerged in France in the 1100s, but gradually spread throughout Europe, spawning numerous regional variations. The overlying themes, best exemplified in the ecclesial buildings of the day, were humungous scale (Gothic churches were the skyscrapers of their era), well-lit interiors, large windows, pointed arches, lofty pinnacles and spires, and majestic decoration.

The Best... Gothic Masterpieces

1 La Catedral (p54)

2 Església de Santa Maria del Mar (p102)

3 Museu Marítim (p115)

4 Església de Santa Maria del Pi (p57)

5 Museu d'Història de Barcelona (p67)

Most of these themes were employed in medieval Barcelona in a raft of buildings that spanned the whole era and later inspired a small neo-Gothic revival in the mid-19th century. The Església de Santa María del Mar is a fairly unembellished example of Levantino (14th-century) Gothic style at its height and is usually considered the city's greatest Gothic achievement. The more decorative Catedral is the synthesis of a Levantino Gothic base overlaid with a neo-Gothic facade.

The Modernistas

The second wave of Catalan creativity, also carried on the wind of boom times, came around the turn of the 20th century. The urban expansion program known as L'Eixample (the Extension), designed to free the choking population from the city's bursting medieval confines, coincided with a blossoming of unfettered thinking in architecture that arrived in the back-draft of the 1888 International Exposition of Barcelona.

The vitality and rebelliousness of the Modernistas is best summed up in the epithets modern, new, liberty, youth and secession. A key uniting element was the sensuous curve, implying movement, lightness and vitality. But the movement never stood still. Gaudí, in particular, repeatedly forged his own path. As he became more adventurous he appeared a lone wolf. With age he became almost exclusively motivated by stark religious conviction and devoted much of the latter part of his life to what remains Barcelona's call sign – the unfinished La Sagrada Família.

Paradoxically, Modernista architects often looked to the past for inspiration. Gothic, Islamic and Renaissance design all had something to offer. At its most playful, Modernisme was able to intelligently flout the rule books of these styles and create exciting new cocktails.

Antoni Gaudí

Leading the way was Antoni Gaudí. Born in Reus to a long line of coppersmiths, Gaudí was initially trained in metalwork. In childhood he suffered from poor health, including rheumatism, and became an early adopter of a vegetarian diet. He was not a promising student. In 1878, when he obtained his architecture degree the school's headmaster is reputed to have said: 'Who knows if we have given a diploma to a nutcase or a genius. Time will tell.'

As a young man, what most delighted Gaudí was being outdoors, and he became fascinated by the plants, animals and geology beyond his door. This deep admiration for the natural world would heavily influence his designs. 'This tree is my teacher,' he once said. 'Everything comes from the book of nature.' Throughout his work, he sought to emulate the harmony he observed in the natural world, eschewing the straight line and favouring curvaceous forms and more organic shapes.

The spiral of a nautilus shell can be seen in staircases and ceiling details, tight buds of flowers in chimney pots and roof ornamentation. Meanwhile undulating arches evoke a cavern, overlapping roof tiles mimic the scales of an armadillo and flowing walls resemble waves on the sea. Tree branches, spider webs, stalactites, honeycombs, starfish, mushrooms, shimmering beetle wings and many other elements from nature – all were part of the Gaudían vernacular.

Gaudí was a devout Catholic and a Catalan nationalist. In addition to nature, he drew inspiration from Catalonia's great medieval churches and took pride in utilising the building materials of the countryside: clay, stone and timber. In contrast to his architecture, Gaudí lived a simple life, and was not averse to knocking on doors, literally begging for money to help fund construction on the cathedral.

His masterpiece was La Sagrada Família (begun in 1882), and in it you can see the culminating vision of many ideas developed over the years. Its massive scale evokes the grandeur of Catalonia's Gothic cathedrals, while organic elements foreground its harmony with nature. As Gaudí became more adventurous he appeared as a lone wolf. With age he became almost exclusively motivated by stark religious conviction and devoted much of the latter part of his life to what remains Barcelona's call sign – the unfinished La Sagrada Família. He died in 1926, struck down by a streetcar while taking his daily walk to the Sant Felip Neri church. Wearing ragged clothes with empty pockets – save for an orange peel – Gaudí was initially taken for a beggar and taken to a nearby hospital where he was left in a pauper's ward. He died two days later. Thousands attended his funeral, in a half-mile procession to Sagrada Família where he was buried in the crypt.

Domènech i Montaner

Although overshadowed by Gaudí, Domènech i Montaner (1849–1923) was one of the great masters of Modernisme. He was a widely travelled man of prodigious intellect, with knowledge in everything from mineralogy to medieval heraldry, and he was an architectural professor, a prolific writer and a nationalist politician. The question of Catalan identity and how to create a national architecture consumed Domènech i Montaner, who designed over a dozen large-scale works in his lifetime.

The exuberant, steel-framed Palau de la Música Catalana is one of his masterpieces. Adorning the facade are elaborate Gothic-style windows, floral designs (Domènech i Montaner also studied botany) and sculptures depicting characters from Catalan folklore and the music world as well as everyday citizens of Barcelona. Inside, the hall leaves visitors dazzled with delicate floral-covered colonnades, radiant stained-glass walls and ceiling and a rolling, sculpture-packed proscenium referencing the epics of musical lore.

Puig i Cadafalch

Like Domènech, Puig i Cadafalch (1867–1956) was a polymath; he was an archaeologist, an expert in Romanesque art and one of Catalonia's most prolific architects. As a politician – and later president of the Mancomunitat de Catalunya (Commonwealth of Catalonia) – he was instrumental in shaping the Catalan nationalist movement.

One of his many Modernista gems is the Casa Amatller, a rather dramatic contrast to Gaudí's Casa Batlló next door. Here the straight line is very much in evidence, as is the foreign influence (the gables are borrowed from the Dutch). Puig i Cadafalch has designed a house

Trencadís

The Arabs invented the ancient technique of *trencadís*, but Gaudí was the first architect to revive it. The procedure involves taking ceramic tiles or fragments of broken pottery or glass and creating a mosaic-like sheath on roofs, ceilings, chimneys, benches, sculptures or any other surface. Noted art critic Robert Hughes even suggested that Gaudí's *trencadís* was undoubtedly influential on the development of Picasso's fragmented forms in his Cubist period.

The Best... Modernista Creations

of startling beauty and invention blended with playful Gothic-style sculpture.

Other important works by Puig i Cadafalch include the Casa Martí (better known as Els Quatre Gats), which was one of Barcelona's first Modernista-style buildings (from 1896), with Gothic window details and whimsical wrought-iron sculpture.

Barcelona Since the Olympic Games

Barcelona's latest architectural revolution began in the 1980s, when in the run up to the 1992 Olympics the city set about its biggest phase of renewal since the heady days of L'Eixample.

The Olympic makeover included the transformation of the Port Vell waterfront, the long road to resurrecting the 1929 International Exhibition sites in Montjuïc (including the refurbishment of the Olympic stadium) and the creation of landmarks such as Santiago Calatrava's (b 1951) Torre Calatrava.

Post-1992, landmark buildings still went up in strategic spots, usually with the ulterior motive of trying to pull the surrounding area up by its bootstraps.

One of the most emblematic of these projects was the gleaming white Museu d'Art Contemporani de Barcelona (MACBA), opened in 1995. The museum was designed by Richard Meier and incorporates the characteristic elements for which the American architect is so well known – the geometric minimalism, the pervasive use of all-white with glass and steel – and remains much debated in architectural circles.

Another big recent project (mostly completed in 2004) is Diagonal Mar, a whole district built in the northeast coastal corner of the city where before there was a void. Striking additions include high-rise apartments, waterfront office towers and a gigantic photovoltaic panel that provides some of the area's electricity.

The most visible addition to the skyline came in 2005. The shimmering, cucumber-shaped Torre Agbar is emblematic of the city's desire to make the developing hi-tech zone of 22@ (*vint-i-dos arroba*; www.22barcelona.com) a reality. Nearby, work continues (as of 2012) on the redevelopment of the Plaça de les Glòries Catalanes, which will add a high-tech design museum (new home of the Disseny Hub) and abundant green space surrounding it. Further east, work on Zaha Hadid's dynamic Spiral Tower adds yet more futurism to the city, with hopes that cutting-edge architecture will help boost ongoing development in the 22@ zone.

Modern Art

Fundació Antoni Tàpies (p135)

Barcelona is to modern art what Greece is to ruined temples. Three of the figures at the vanguard of 20th-century avant-gardism – Picasso, Miró and Dalí – were either born or spent their formative years here. Their powerful legacy is stamped all over Barcelona in museums and public installations. In the contemporary art world, Catalonia continues to be an incubator for innovative works, with instrumental figures like Antoni Tàpies leading the way.

The Crucial Three

Spain has been a giant in world art ever since Velázquez etched his haunting *Las Meninas* and ushered in the glittery Siglo de Oro (c 1492–1680), though Catalonia was a little late to the ball.

Picasso

It wasn't until the late 19th century that truly great artists began to emerge in Barcelona and its hinterland, led by dandy portraitist Ramón Casas (1866–1932). Casas, an early Modernista, founded a Barcelona bar known as Els Quatre Gats, which became the nucleus for the city's growing art movement, holding numerous shows and expositions. An early host was a young then unknown Malagueño named Pablo Picasso (1881–1973).

Picasso lived sporadically in Barcelona between the innocence-losing ages of 16 and 24, and the city heavily influenced his early painting. This was the period in which he amassed the raw materials for his Blue Period. In 1904 the then-mature Picasso moved to Paris where he found fame, fortune and Cubism, and went on to become one of the greatest artists of the 20th century.

Miró

Continuing the burst of brilliance was the Barcelona-born experimentalist Joan Miró (1893–1983), best remembered for his use of symbolic figures in primary colours. Declaring he was going to 'assassinate art', Miró wanted nothing to do with the constricting labels of the era, although he has often been called a pioneering surrealist, Dadaist and automatist.

Dalí

Rising on Miró's coattails was the extravagant Catalan surrealist and showman, Salvador Dalí (1904–89), from nearby Figueres, who mixed imaginative painting with posing, attention-seeking and shameless self-promotion. Dalí is hard to avoid anywhere in the world, especially Barcelona.

Public Art

The streets, squares and parks of Barcelona are littered with the signatures of artists past and present, famous and unknown. They range from Modernista sculptors, such as Josep Llimona, to international star sculptors, such as Roy Lichtenstein and Fernando Botero. Picasso and Joan Miró both left lasting reminders in the city.

Since the return of democracy in the late 1970s, the town hall has not been shy about encouraging the placement of sometimes grandiose and often incomprehensible contemporary works in the city's public spaces. Reactions range from admiration to perplexity.

Justly proud of its rich street-art heritage, the council has created an extensive archive of it all on the internet at www.bcn.cat (click on Art Públic, under Blog Barcelona). The site is rich in description of hundreds of items scattered across the city, and includes commentary on the history of the city through its street art. You can search particular items by district, period and key word.

The best thing about art in the streets is that it is open to all comers.

Art goes Informal

Picasso, Miró and Dalí were hard acts to follow. Few envied the task of Catalan Antoni Tàpies in reviving the red hot Modernista flame. An early admirer of Miró, Tàpies soon began pursuing his own esoteric path embracing 'art informal' (a Jackson Pollack–like use of spontaneity) and inventing painting that utilised clay, string and even bits of rubbish. In April 2010 King Juan Carlos I elevated Tàpies to the Spanish nobility for his contribution to postwar art with the hereditary title the 1st Marquess of Tàpies. He was arguably Spain's greatest living painter before his death in 2012.

Contemporary Art

In the wake of the big three, Barcelona has been a minor cauldron of activity, dominated by the figure of Antoni Tàpies (1923–2012). Early in his career (from the mid-1940s onwards) he seemed keen on self-portraits, but also experimented with collage using all sorts of materials, from wood to rice.

A poet, artist and man of theatre, Joan Brossa (1921–98) was a cultural beacon in Barcelona. His 'visual poems', lithographs and other artworks in which letters generally figure, along with all sorts of objects, make his world accessible to those who can't read his Catalan poetry.

Joan Hernández Pijuan (1931–2005), one of Barcelona's most important 20th-century abstract painters, produced work concentrating on natural shapes and figures, often using neutral colours on different surfaces.

Jaume Plensa (b 1955) is possibly Spain's best contemporary sculptor. His work ranges from sketches, through sculpture, to video and other installations that have been shown around the world.

Susana Solano (b 1946), one of Barcelona's best painters and sculptors, also works with video installations, collages and jewellery.

The Best... Places to See Modern Art

1 Museu Picasso (p92)

2 Fundació Joan Miró (p170)

3 Fundació Antoni Tàpies (p135)

4 MACBA (p81)

IN FOCUS MODERN ART

221

Football

FC Barcelona fans at Camp Nou (p183)

OSO MEDIA / ALA.

To understand a country – any country – you must first decipher its sporting rituals. In Barcelona that means football. Challenging the cathedral as the city's primary place of worship is Camp Nou, home of FC Barcelona – football club, international brand and fervent bastion of Catalan identity. Its blue-and-red stripes can be seen on everyone from football-mad Thai schoolkids to goat herders in the African bush.

A Cultural Force

The story starts on 29 November 1899, when Swiss Hans Gamper founded FC Barcelona, four years after English residents had first played the game here. His choice of club colours – the blue and maroon of his home town Winterthur – has stuck. By 1910 FC Barcelona was the premier club in a rapidly growing league and had picked up its first Spanish Cup. When Spain's La Liga was founded in 1929, Barcelona ran away with the first title, though its playing record became patchier as the decades wore on and the Franco regime suppressed all manifestations of Catalan-ness.

FC Barça's reemergence as a footballing and cultural force coincided with the death of Franco and an influx of foreign players, starting with Dutch midfield ace Johann Cruyff in 1973. More legends followed, with Diego Maradona arriving in 1982, the Brazilian

Ronaldo in 1996 and Ronaldinho in 2003. Fortunes went from good to better. FC Barça won La Liga four years in a row in the early '90s, took the Champions League in 2006, and in 2009 won an unprecedented 'treble' of La Liga, Spanish Cup and Champions League. They are led by the formidable talents of vertically challenged Argentine midfielder Lionel Messi, who is the club's all-time highest goal scorer and is widely considered one of the best active players on the planet.

The Best... Places to See a Game

1 Camp Nou (p183)

2 Polaroid (p65)

3 Dusk (p66)

4 Cafe San Telmo (p150)

Getting to See a Game

A match at Camp Nou (p183), the largest stadium in Europe, can be breathtaking. Don't pass up a chance to see the magic in person if you're in town when Barça is playing.

You can purchase tickets at the stadium box office, from FNAC and Carrerfour stores and from Servicaixa ATMs.Tickets can cost anything from €35 to upwards of €200, depending on seat and match. The ticket windows are open on Saturday morning and in the afternoon until the game starts. If the match is on Sunday, the ticket windows open Saturday morning only and then on Sunday until the match starts. Usually tickets are *not* available for matches with Real Madrid.

You will almost definitely find scalpers lurking near the ticket windows. They are often club members and can sometimes get you in at a significant reduction. Don't pay until you are safely seated.

If you can't catch a game, it's still worth a trip out to Camp Nou. You can relive the club's great moments over the years at the hi-tech museum, followed by a self-guided tour through the locker rooms and out onto the pitch.

The Other Team

The pub-quiz question pretty much guaranteed to stump all but the most in-the-know football geeks is: what is Barcelona's other team? The answer: RDC Espanyol, the city's perennial underachievers based at the **Estadi RCD Espanyol** (☏ 93 292 77 00; www.rcdespanyol.com; Avinguda del Baix Llobrega; ⓂCornellà Centre), which was built in 2009. The Barça–Espanyol rivalry is one of the most one-sided and divisive in football. While FC Barcelona is traditionally associated with Catalan nationalism, Espanyol is usually identified with Spanish immigrants from other parts of the country. Then there's the trophy haul: currently standing at Barcelona 79, Espanyol 4.

El Ingenio (p69)

GETTY IMAC

Mixing old junk with top name brands, and bohemian ethnicity with a penchant for Euro-chic, Barcelona does quirky shops like novelist Carlos Luís Zafón does Gothic thrillers. Whether you're an extravagant prince or a thrifty pauper matters not a jot. Hit the Passeig de Gràcia to tear metaphoric chunks out of your credit card. For bargain-hunting, ephemera and indie boutiques, gravitate towards shabby-chic El Raval or the ubertrendy La Ribera district.

The Cutting Edge

Prêt-à-porter giant Mango is one of Barcelona's main success stories. Emerging as one of the hippest local names on the world fashion catwalks is the youthful Custo Dalmau (aka Custo Barcelona), with a rapidly growing chain of stores in Spain and abroad. Other local names or Barcelona-based designers include Antonio Miró, Joaquim Verdú, David Valls, Josep Font, Armand Basi, Purificación García, Konrad Muhr, Sita Murt and TCN. All the big names of Spanish couture, from Adolfo Domínguez to Zara, are also present and there's barely an international brand that doesn't have outlets in Barcelona.

Twice a year the exclusive urban fashion salon Bread & Butter attracts hundreds of fashion producers and buyers from around the world to Barcelona. Founded in Berlin, the salon transferred to Barcelona in 2006 and is going from strength to strength.

Neighbourhood by Neighbourhood

In Barcelona, different enclaves offer different shopping experiences.

For high fashion, design, jewellery and many department stores, the main shopping axis starts on Plaça de Catalunya, proceeds up Passeig de Gràcia and turns left (west) into Avinguda Diagonal, along which it proceeds as far as Plaça de la Reina Maria Cristina. The densely packed section between Plaça de Francesc Macià and Plaça de la Reina Maria Cristina is good hunting ground.

The heart of L'Eixample – known as the Quadrat d'Or (Golden Square) – is jammed with all sorts of glittering shops. La Rambla de Catalunya is lined with chic stores, and it's not just about fashion. Carrer del Consell de Cent bursts with art galleries and the nearby streets are also busy with shopping options, from specialist wine purveyors to bookstores.

Shopkeepers in the Barri Gòtic think of their area as 'Barnacentre' (from Barna, slang for Barcelona). Some of the most curious old stores, whether milliners or candle-makers, lurk in the narrow lanes around Plaça de Sant Jaume. The once-seedy Carrer d'Avinyó has become a minor fashion boulevard, with creations by up-and-coming designers for a young (and young at heart) clientele. Antique stores abound on and around Carrer de la Palla and Carrer dels Banys Nous.

Over in La Ribera there are two categories of shops to look out for: some fine old traditional stores dealing in speciality foodstuffs, and a new crop of fashion and design stores (particularly along the stretch of Carrer del Rec between Passeig del Born and Avinguda del Marquès de l'Argentera), catering to the young professionals who have moved into the *barri*. Old-time stores abound in El Raval, where you'll also discover a cluster of preloved-clothes shops on Carrer de la Riera Baixa.

To Market, to Market

One of the greatest sound, smell and colour sensations in Europe is Barcelona's most central produce market, the Mercat de la Boqueria (p82). It spills over with all the rich and varied colour of plentiful fruit and vegetable stands, seemingly limitless varieties of sea critters, sausages, cheeses, meat and sweets. It is also sprinkled with half a dozen or so unassuming places to eat well, at lunchtime stalls. According to some chronicles, there has been a market on this spot since 1217. These days it's no easy task getting past the gawping tourists to get to the slippery slab of sole you're after.

The Urge to Rummage

Lovers of old books, coins, stamps and general bric-a-brac can indulge their habits uninhibited at several markets. They generally get going from 9am and wind down by late afternoon. Els Encants Vells (p153) is the biggest and best flea market in the city with all manner of bric-a-brac.

The Barri Gòtic is enlivened by an **art and crafts market** (Plaça de Sant Josep Oriol; Ⓜ Liceu) on Saturday and Sunday, the antiques-filled **Mercat Gòtic** (Plaça Nova; Ⓜ Liceu or Jaume I) on Thursday, and a **coin and stamp collectors' market** (Plaça Reial; Ⓜ Liceu) on Sunday morning.

On the waterfront on weekends you'll find a few small markets worth checking out. The Port Antic (p123) near the base of La Rambla has old photographs, frames, oil paintings, records, vintage toys and other antiques.

The Best... Shopping Secrets

Nearby, you can stroll along the pedestrian-only Rambla de Mar to reach the Mercado de Pintores (p123), with a broad selection of paintings both collectable and rather forgettable. Also in the area is the Feria de Artesanía del Palau de Mar (p123) vendors, who sell a range of crafty items, including jewellery, graphic t-shirts, handwoven hats, fragrant candles and soaps, scarves and decorative items. The market runs daily in July and August.

Just beyond the western edge of El Raval, the punters at the Modernista **Mercat de Sant Antoni (Carrer de Mallorca 157;** ☉**7am-8.30pm;** Ⓜ**Hospital Clínic)** dedicate Sunday morning to old maps, stamps, books and cards.

Once a fortnight, gourmands can poke about the homemade honeys, sweets, cheeses and other edible delights at the **Fira Alimentació (** Ⓜ**Liceu)** from Friday to Sunday.

Refunds

Non-EU residents are entitled to a refund of the 18% IVA (the Spanish equivalent of VAT or GST) on purchases of more than €90.16 from any shop if they take the goods out of the EU within three months. Ask the shop for a Cashback (or similar) refund form, which you present (with goods, prior to check-in) at the customs booth for IVA refunds when you leave Spain. At Barcelona airport, look for the customs booth opposite the bar on the ground floor of Terminal A. Note that IVA is expected to rise to 20% in 2013.

Survival
Guide

Mercat de la Boqueria (p82)
PHOTOGRAPHER: HANS BLOSSEY / IMAGEBROKER ©

Sleeping

Barcelona has an excellent range of accommodation, with high-end luxury hotels, small-scale boutique lodgings and a varied spread of midrange and budget selections. There is a great choice in settings, from exploring historic districts to facing the seaside or being in the thick of charming neighbourhoods packed with restaurants and nightlife. The continuing economic crisis has slowed price increases, making the city reasonable value overall.

Accommodation Types

Hotels

Hotels cover a broad range. At the bottom end there is often little to distinguish them from better *pensiones* and *hostales*, and from there, they run up the scale to five-star luxury. Some of the better features to look out for include rooftop pools and lounges, views (either of the sea or a cityscape such as La Sagrada Família, Montjuïc or the Barri Gòtic) and of course proximity to the important sights.

B&Bs

Barcelona has a growing number of B&B-style accom-modation. These tend to be in historic or heritage buildings in the Ciutat Vella (Old City) and L'Eixample, with boutique-style charm. Most have between three and ten rooms. Attractive common areas and an extensive cooked breakfast are common features. Not all will have private bathrooms.

Pensiones & Hostales

The city has plenty of hostels. If dorm living is not your thing but you are still looking for a budget deal, check out the many *pensiones* and *hostales*. These are family-run, small-scale hotels, often housed in sprawling apartments. Some are fleapits, others immacu-lately maintained gems.

If your budget is especially tight, look at the economical options on www.Barcelona30. com.

Apartment & Room Rentals

A cosier (and sometimes more cost-effective) alternative to hotels can be short-term apartment rental. A plethora of firms organise short lets across town, including **Air Bnb** (www.airbnb.com). Typical prices are around €80 to €100 for two people per night. For four people you might be looking at an average of €160 a night. In addition to full apartments, the site also lists rooms available, which can be a good way to meet locals and/or other travellers if you don't mind sharing common areas. Prices for a room range from €30 to €60 on average.

Costs

Depending on the season and the hostel, you will pay from €15 to €25 for a dorm bed in a youth hostel. In small *pen-*

PRICE GUIDE

These € signs indicate the price of a double room per night during high season. Prices include a private bathroom unless otherwise stated.

- ○ €   under €75
- ○ €€   €75 to €200
- ○ €€€   over €200

ROOM TAX

Virtually all accommodation is subject to IVA, the Spanish version of value-added tax, at 8%. As of November 2012, the city also levies an additional tax of €0.75 per night.

RESERVATIONS

Booking ahead is recommended, especially during peak periods such as Easter, Christmas/ New Year, trade fairs and throughout much of summer.

CHECK-IN & CHECK-OUT TIMES

Check-in time is around 2pm or 3pm. Check-out time is generally noon.

siones or hostales you are looking at a minimum of around €35/55 for basic individual/doble (single/double) rooms, mostly without a private bathroom. It is occasionally possible to find cheaper rooms, but they can be unappetising. For around €100 to €140, there are extensive options for good doubles across a broad range of hotels and areas. The top-end category starts at €250 for a double, but can easily rise to €500 (and beyond for suites).

Some hotels, particularly at the lower and mid levels, maintain the same prices year round. Others vary the rates for temporada alta (high season), temporada media (midseason) and temporada baja (low season). Low season is roughly November to Easter, except during the Christmas/New Year period.

Whenever there is a major trade fair (they are frequent), high-season prices generally apply. Conversely, business-oriented hotels often consider weekends, holiday periods and other slow business times to be low season. Booking on the web is often cheaper than turning up at the door.

Rooms for Travellers with Disabilities

Many hotels claim to be equipped for guests with disabilities but reality frequently disappoints. Check out www.barcelona-access.com for help with finding genuinely accessible accommodation.

Useful Websites

Lonely Planet (hotels.lonelyplanet.com) A large selection of accommodations at all price levels.

Oh-Barcelona (www.oh-barcelona.com) Well-curated selection of hotels, hostels and apartment rentals, plus helpful profiles and articles on Barcelona.

Air BnB (www.airbnb.com) One of the best options for apartment rentals or shares, with hundreds of listings.

Barcelona 30 (www.barcelona30.com) Top choice for budget-minded travellers.

Where to Stay

NEIGHBOURHOOD	FOR	AGAINST
BARRI GÒTIC & LA RAMBLA	Close to major sights – perfect area for exploring on foot. Good nightlife and dining options.	Very touristy and noisy. Some rooms are small, lack windows.
EL RAVAL	Central option, with good local nightlife and access to sights. Bohemian vibe with few tourists.	Can be noisy, seedy and run-down in parts. Feels unsafe to walk late at night.
LA RIBERA	Great restaurant scene and neighbourhood exploring. Central with top sights.	Can be noisy, overly crowded and touristy.
BARCELONETA & THE WATERFRONT	Excellent seafood restaurants, easy-going vibe and handy access to the waterfront.	Few sleeping options. Outside of Barceloneta, it's far from the action and aimed at business travellers.
LA SAGRADA FAMÍLIA & L'EIXAMPLE	Close to Modernista sights with good restaurants and nightlife. Prime gay scene.	Can be very noisy with lots of traffic. Not great for walking. A little far from the Ciutat Vella.
MONTJUÏC	Near the museums, gardens and views of Montjuïc. Great local exploring in Poble Sec.	Somewhat out of the way. Can be a bit gritty up by El Sants train station.
PARK GÜELL, CAMP NOU & LA ZONA ALTA	Youthful, local scene with lively restaurants and bars.	Far from the Ciutat Vella with few hotels. La Zona Alta is geared more towards business travellers.

Best Places to Stay

NAME		REVIEW
HOTEL 1898 €€€	Barri Gòtic & La Rambla	Luxury hotel with spa, pool and roof deck. Rooms have hardwood floors and tasteful furniture.
HOTEL NERI €€€	Barri Gòtic & La Rambla	Beautifully designed rooms in a centuries-old building next to tranquil Plaça de Sant Felip Neri.
HOTEL COLÓN €€	Barri Gòtic & La Rambla	Rooms range from modest singles to elegant doubles; the best have magical views of La Catedral.
EL JARDÍ €€	Barri Gòtic & La Rambla	Average doubles unless you nab one with a balcony overlooking one of Barcelona's prettiest squares.
HOSTAL CAMPI €	Barri Gòtic & La Rambla	Friendly, central hostal with bright rooms and clean faciliites in an 18th-century building.
CASA CAMPER €€€	El Raval	Eccentric designer hotel with Camper slippers, Vinçon furniture and hanging gardens.
WHOTELLS €€	El Raval	Fully functional apartments decked out with Muji furniture and near Mercat de la Boqueria.
BARCELÓ RAVAL €€	El Raval	Designer hotel with rooftop terrace and a stylish bar-restaurant; has slick gadget-filled rooms.
HOTEL SAN AGUSTÍN €€	El Raval	Opened in 1840, this is the city's oldest hotel with light-filled rooms overlooking a curious square.
HOSTAL CHIC & BASIC €€	El Raval	Rooms have touches that include plasma-screen TVs and iPod docks.
HOSTAL GAT RAVAL €	El Raval	A hip *hostal* on a bar-lined lane. The individual rooms are pleasant; some have private bathrooms.
GRAND HOTEL CENTRAL €€	La Ribera	Spacious designer rooms with high ceilings, dark timber floors and subtle lighting. Rooftop pool.
CHIC & BASIC €€	La Ribera	Cool hotel, with 31 spotlessly white rooms and original features, including a marble staircase.
HOTEL BANYS ORIENTALS €€	La Ribera	Magnetically popular boutique hotel with cool blue tones and dark-hued floors.
W BARCELONA €€€	Barceloneta & the Waterfront	A spinnaker-shaped tower with chic rooms. Amenities include a spa, massive pool and top-floor bar.
EUROSTARS GRAND MARINA HOTEL €€	Barceloneta & the Waterfront	A maritime flavour that continues into the rooms, with lots of polished timber. Rooftop pool.
HOTEL MARINA FOLCH €	Barceloneta & the Waterfront	Good-value family-run hotel with 10 rooms. The best have small balconies facing out towards the marina.
EQUITY POINT SEA HOSTEL €	Barceloneta & the Waterfront	A cramped party hostel (bring earplugs) with fantastic beachfront location.
HOTEL ARTS BARCELONA €€€	Barceloneta & the Waterfront	One of Barcelona's most fashionable hotels, with a Michelin-starred restaurant and unbeatable views.

PRACTICALITIES	BEST FOR
☎ 93 552 95 52; www.hotel1898.com; La Rambla 109; d €230-350; ❄ @ 🛜 ⛱; Ⓜ Liceu	Luxurious setting on La Rambla
☎ 93 304 06 55; www.hotelneri.com; Carrer de Sant Sever 5; d from €270; ❄ @ 🛜; Ⓜ Liceu	Superb Barri Gòtic location
☎ 93 301 14 04; www.hotelcolon.es; Avinguda de la Catedral 7; s/d from €110/170; ❄ @; Ⓜ Jaume I	Unrivaled cathedral views
☎ 93 301 59 00; www.eljardi-barcelona.com; Plaça de Sant Josep Oriol 1; d €65-120; ❄ 🛜; Ⓜ Liceu	Peaceful location
☎ 93 301 35 45; www.hostalcampi.com; Carrer de la Canuda 4; d €70, s/d without bathroom €35/60; @ 🛜; Ⓜ Catalunya	Location and price
☎ 93 342 62 80; www.casacamper.com; Carrer d'Elisabets 11; s/d €240/270; ❄ @; Ⓜ Liceu	Quirky style
☎ 93 443 08 34; www.whotells.com; Carrer de Joaquín Costa 28; apt from €180; ❄ @ 🛜; Ⓜ Universitat	Self-catering in El Raval
☎ 93 320 14 90; www.barceloraval.com; Rambla del Raval 17-21; d €160-230; ❄ @; Ⓜ Liceu	Designer digs
☎ 93 318 16 58; www.hotelsa.com; Plaça de Sant Agustí 3; r from €80-180; ❄ @ 🛜; Ⓜ Liceu	Good, central location
☎ 93 302 51 83; www.chicandbasic.com; Carrer de Tallers 82; s €80, d €103-124; ❄ @; Ⓜ Universitat	Good-value rooms
☎ 93 481 66 70; www.gataccommodation.com; Carrer de Joaquín Costa 44; s/d without bathroom €63/82; ❄ @ 🛜; Ⓜ Universitat	Exploring nightlife
☎ 93 295 79 00; www.grandhotelcentral.com; Via Laietana 30; d €235; ❄ @ ⛱; Ⓜ Jaume I	Designer style
☎ 93 295 46 52; www.chicandbasic.com; Carrer de la Princesa 50; s €96, d €132-192; ❄ @; Ⓜ Jaume I	Artful design
☎ 93 268 84 60; www.hotelbanysorientals.com; Carrer de l'Argenteria 37; s/d €88/105, ste €130; ❄ @; Ⓜ Jaume I	Superb location
☎ 93 295 28 00; www.w-barcelona.com; Plaça de la Rosa del Vents 1; r from €310; Ⓟ ❄ @ 🛜 ⛱; 🚍 17, 39, 57 or 64, Ⓜ Barceloneta	Style and beachside location
☎ 902 932424; www.grandmarinahotel.com; Moll de Barcelona; r €240-350; ❄ @ 🛜 ⛱; Ⓜ Drassanes	Sea breezes
☎ 93 310 37 09; www.hotelmarinafolchbcn.com; Carrer del Mar 16; s/d/tr €45/65/85; ❄ 🛜; Ⓜ Barceloneta	Price and marine location
☎ 93 231 20 45; www.equity-point.com; Plaça del Mar 1-4; dm €19-28; ❄ @ 🛜; 🚍 17, 39, 57 or 64, Ⓜ Barceloneta	Beachfront on a budget
☎ 93 221 10 00; www.hotelartsbarcelona.com; Carrer de la Marina 19-21; r from €480; Ⓟ ❄ @ 🛜 ⛱; Ⓜ Ciutadella Vila Olímpica	Style and beachside location

NAME		REVIEW
HOTEL ME €€	Barceloneta & the Waterfront	Plush rooms with sea or city views. There's a popular 6th-floor terrace bar-club and swimming pool.
POBLENOU BED & BREAKFAST €€	Barceloneta & the Waterfront	Classy 1930s house, with high ceilings and beautiful tile floors. Breakfast is served on the rear terrace.
HOTEL ESPAÑA €€	La Sagrada Família & L'Eixample	Clean, straightforward rooms in a Modernista building that still manages to ooze a little history.
HOTEL MAJÈSTIC €€€	La Sagrada Família & L'Eixample	This sprawling, central option with a rooftop pool, a pampering spa and European charm.
MANDARIN ORIENTAL €€€	La Sagrada Família & L'Eixample	At this imposing former bank, 98 rooms combine contemporary designer style with Eastern touches.
HOTEL OMM €€€	La Sagrada Família & L'Eixample	A wild Dalí-esque facade contains ultramodern rooms, a roof terrace and a sprawling minimalist bar.
COMTES DE BARCELONA €€	La Sagrada Família & L'Eixample	Clean, designer lines dominate, with luxurious rooms, hardwood floors and architectural touches.
HOTEL SIXTYTWO €€	La Sagrada Família & L'Eixample	Designer rooms with Bang & Olufsen TVs and expansive beds. Relax in the pretty Japanese garden.
ST MORITZ HOTEL €€	La Sagrada Família & L'Eixample	Upmarket hotel with fully equipped rooms and an elegant restaurant and terrace bar.
SUITES AVENUE €€	La Sagrada Família & L'Eixample	Apartment-style living with a terrace, gym and pool (plus a mini-museum of Hindu and Buddhist art).
FIVE ROOMS €€	La Sagrada Família & L'Eixample	Features include broad, firm beds, exposed brick walls, restored mosaic tiles and minimalist decor.
HOTEL CONSTANZA €€	La Sagrada Família & L'Eixample	Well-loved boutique stay. The terrace has fine views over the rooftops of the L'Eixample.
MARKET HOTEL €€	La Sagrada Família & L'Eixample	An attractively renovated building, around the corner from the grand old Sant Antoni market.
HOTEL D'UXELLES €€	La Sagrada Família & L'Eixample	Rooms have a charming simplicity, with wrought-iron bedsteads, flowing drapes and terraces (in some).
HOTEL PRAKTIK €€	La Sagrada Família & L'Eixample	Modernista gem with high ceilings, original tile floors and art-filled rooms, plus a chilled reading area.
HOSTAL OLIVA €€	La Sagrada Família & L'Eixample	This 4th-floor hostal is a terrific, reliable cheapie in one of the city's most expensive neighbourhoods.
URBAN SUITES €€	Montjuïc	Contemporary spot with 16 suites and four apartments. Convenient and comfortable.
HOTEL REY JUAN CARLOS I €€	Park Güell, Camp Nou & La Zona Alta	Luxury mega-hotel with more than 400 rooms, most with spectacular views.
HOTEL TURÓ DE VILANA €€	Park Güell, Camp Nou & La Zona Alta	Bright, designer hotel with 20 rooms set in the charming residential hood of Sarrià.
HOTEL CASA FUSTER €€€	Park Güell, Camp Nou & La Zona Alta	Period features and plush rooms (plus a rooftop terrace with pool) in a lovely Modernista mansion.

PRACTICALITIES	BEST FOR
☎ 902 144440; www.me-barcelona.com; Carrer de Pere IV 272-286; r €185-255; P ❄ @ 📶 🏊; M Poblenou	Sea views
☎ 93 221 26 01; www.hostalpoblenou.com; Carrer del Taulat 30; s €60, d €80-120; ❄ @ 📶; M Llacuna	*Barcelonin* charm
☎ 93 318 17 58; www.hotelespanya.com; Carrer de Sant Pau 9-11; s €100, d €125-155; ❄; M Liceu	Elegant midrange option
☎ 93 488 17 17; www.hotelmajestic.es; Passeig de Gràcia 68; d from €410; P ❄ @ 📶 🏊; M Passeig de Gràcia	Old-world sophistication
☎ 93 151 88 88; www.mandarinoriental.com; Passeig de Gràcia 38; d from €375; P ❄ @ 📶 🏊; M Passeig de Gràcia	A memorable splurge
☎ 93 445 40 00; www.hotelomm.es; Carrer de Rosselló 265; d from €360; P ❄ @ 🏊; M Diagonal	Artful design
☎ 93 445 00 00; www.condesdebarcelona.com; Passeig de Gràcia 73-75; s/d €177/260; P ❄ @ 📶 🏊; M Passeig de Gràcia	Luxury and a Modernista setting
☎ 93 272 41 80; www.sixtytwohotel.com/en; Passeig de Gràcia 62; d €170-265; P ❄ @ 📶; M Passeig de Gràcia	High-end comfort
☎ 93 481 73 50; www.hcchotels.com; Carrer de la Diputació 262bis; s/d €180/195; P ❄ @ 📶; M Passeig de Gràcia	Central L'Eixample location
☎ 93 487 41 59; www.derbyhotels.es; Passeig de Gràcia 83; apt from €192; P ❄ @ 📶 🏊; M Diagonal	Serviced apartments
☎ 93 342 78 80; www.thefiverooms.com; Carrer de Pau Claris 72; s/d from €115/135, apt from €175; ❄ @ 📶; M Urquinaona	Boutique charm
☎ 93 270 19 10; www.hotelconstanza.com; Carrer del Bruc 33; s/d €130/150; ❄ @; M Girona or Urquinaona	A romantic stay
☎ 93 325 12 05; www.forkandpillow.com; Passatge de Sant Antoni Abad 10; s €110, d €120-130, ste €145 ; ❄ @; M Sant Antoni	A colourful getaway
☎ 93 265 25 60; http://hostalduxelleshotelbarcelona.priorguest.com; Gran Via de les Corts Catalanes 688; s/d €90/109; ❄ @; M Tetuan	Catalan classic
☎ 93 343 66 90; www.hotelpraktikrambla.com; Rambla de Catalunya 27; r from €80-170; ❄ @ 📶; M Passeig de Gràcia	Refined setting
☎ 93 488 01 62; www.hostaloliva.com; Passeig de Gràcia 32; d €85, s/d without bathroom €38/66; ❄ 📶; M Passeig de Gràcia	An affordable classic
☎ 93 201 51 64; www.theurbansuites.com; Carrer de Sant Nicolau 1-3; ste from €170; P ❄ @ 📶; M Sants Estació	Self-catering
☎ 93 364 40 40; www.hrjuancarlos.com; Avinguda Diagonal 661-671; d from €130; P 🚭 ❄ @ 📶 🏊; M Zona Universitària	Amenities & great views
☎ 93 434 03 63; www.turodevilana.com; Carrer de Vilana 7; s/d from €87/97; ❄ @ 📶; 🚆 FGC Les Tres Torres, 🚌 64	Neighbourhood charm
☎ 93 255 30 00, 902 202345; www.hotelcasafuster.com; Passeig de Gràcia 132; s/d from €300/330; P ❄ @ 📶 🏊; M Diagonal	Modernista allure

Transport

Getting to Barcelona

Most travellers enter Barcelona through El Prat airport. Some budget airlines use Girona-Costa Brava airport.

Flights from North America take about eight hours from the east coast (10 to 13 hours typically, with a stopover); from the west coast count on 13 or more hours including a stopover. Flights from London take around two hours, from Western Europe it's about two to three hours.

Travelling by train is a pricier but perhaps more romantic way of reaching Catalonia from other European cities. The overnight *trenhotel* takes 12 hours from Paris to Barcelona. Long-distance trains arrive in Estació Sants, about 2.5km west of La Rambla.

Long-haul buses arrive in Estació del Nord.

Flights, tours and rail tickets can be booked online at lonelyplanet.com/bookings.

El Prat Airport

Barcelona's **El Prat airport** (902 404704; www.aena.es) lies 17km southwest of Plaça de Catalunya at El Prat de Llobregat. The airport has two main terminal buildings: the new T1 terminal and the older T2, itself divided into three terminal areas (A, B and C).

Bus

The **Aerobús** (93 415 60 20; www.aerobusbcn.com; one way €5.65) runs from both terminals to Plaça de Catalunya (single/return €5.65/9.75, 30 to 40 minutes depending on traffic) via Plaça d'Espanya, Gran Via de les Corts Catalanes (corner of Carrer del Comte d'Urgell) and Plaça de la Universitat every five to 10 minutes from 6am to 1am. Departures from Plaça de Catalunya are from 5.30am to 12.30am and stop at the corner of Carrer de Sepúlveda and Carrer del Comte d'Urgell, and Plaça d'Espanya.

Buy tickets on the bus or from agents at the bus stop.

Train

Train operator Renfe runs the R2 Nord line every half an hour from the airport (from 5.42am to 11.38pm) via several stops to Barcelona's main train station, Estació Sants, and Passeig de Gràcia in central Barcelona, after which it heads northwest out of the city. The trip between the airport and Passeig de Gràcia takes 25 minutes. A one-way ticket costs €3.60 (unless you have a multiride ticket for Barcelona public transport).

The airport railway station is about a five-minute walk from Terminal 2. Regular shuttle buses run from the station and Terminal 2 to Terminal 1 – allow for an extra 15 to 20 minutes.

Taxi

A taxi between either terminal and the city centre – about a half-hour ride depending on traffic – costs €20 to €26.

Girona-Costa Brava Airport

Girona-Costa Brava airport (902 404704; www.aena.es) is 12km south of Girona and 92km northeast of Barcelona. You'll find a tourist office, ATMs and lost-luggage desks on the ground floor.

Train (www.renfe.com) Regular services run between Girona and Barcelona (€7.50 to €10, around 1½ hours).

Bus Sagalés (902 130014; www.sagales.com) runs hourly bus services from Girona-Costa Brava airport to Girona's main bus/train station (€2.60, 30 minutes) in connection with flights. The same company runs direct **Barcelona Bus** (902 130014; www.barcelonabus.com) services to/from Estació del Nord bus station in Barcelona (one way/return €15/25, 70 minutes).

Taxi A ride into Girona from the airport costs €20 to €26. To Barcelona you would pay around €140.

Estació Sants

The main train station in Barcelona is **Estació Sants** (Plaça dels Països Catalans; Sants Estació), located 2.5km west of La Rambla. Direct overnight trains from Paris, Geneva, Milan and Zurich arrive here. From here it's a short Metro ride to the old town or L'Eixample.

Estació del Nord

Long-distance buses leave from **Estació del Nord** (📞 902 260606; www.barcelonanord.com; Carrer d'Ali Bei 80; Arc de Triomf). A plethora of companies operates to different parts of Spain, although many come under the umbrella of **Alsa** (📞 902 422242; www.alsa.es).

Eurolines (www.eurolines.es), in conjunction with local carriers all over Europe, is the main international carrier. Another carrier is **Linebús** (www.linebus.com).

Getting Around Barcelona

Barcelona has abundant options for getting around town. The excellent Metro can get you most places, with buses and trams filling in the gaps. Taxis are the best option late at night.

Ⓜ Metro & FGC

The easy-to-use **TMB Metro** (📞 010; www.tmb.net) system has 11 numbered and colour-coded lines. It runs from 5am to midnight Sunday to Thursday and holidays, from 5am to 2am on Friday and days immediately preceding holidays, and 24 hours on Saturday.

🚌 Bus

Transports Metropolitans de Barcelona (TMB; 📞 010; www.tmb.net) buses run along most city routes every few minutes from between 5am and 6.30am to between around 10pm and 11pm.

Taxi

Taxis charge €2.05 flag fall plus meter charges of €0.93 per kilometre (€1.18 from 8pm to 8am and all day on weekends). A further €3.10 is added for all trips to/from the airport, and €1 for luggage bigger than 55cm x 35cm x 35cm. The trip from Estació Sants to Plaça de Catalunya, about 3km, costs about €11.

🚲 Bicycle

Over 180km of bike lanes have been laid out across the city, making it possible to get around on two environmentally friendly wheels. A waterfront path runs northeast from Port Olímpic towards Riu Besòs.

You can transport your bicycle on the Metro on weekdays (except between 7am and 9.30am or 5pm and 8.30pm). On weekends and holidays, and during July and August, there are no restrictions. You can use FGC trains to carry your bike at any time and Renfe's *rodalies* trains from 10am to 3pm on weekdays and all day on weekends and holidays.

Hire

Countless companies around town offer bicycles (and anything remotely resembling one, from tandems to tricycle carts and more). They include the following:

BarcelonaBiking.com (Map p58; 📞 656 356300; www.barcelonabiking.com; Baixada de Sant Miquel 6; per hr/24hr €5/15; ⏲ 10am-8pm; Ⓜ Jaume I or Liceu)

Barnabike (Map p116; 📞 93 269 02 04; www.barnabike.com; Carrer del Pas de Sota la Muralla 3; per 2hr/24hr €6/15; ⏲ 10am-9.30pm; Ⓜ Barceloneta)

Biciclot (Map p116; 📞 93 221 97 78; www.biciclot.net; Passeig Marítim de la Barceloneta 33; per hr/day €5.50/€18; ⏲ 10am-3pm, longer hours in peak season; Ⓜ Ciutadella Vila Olímpica)

Bike Rental Barcelona (Map p58; 📞 666 057655; www.bikerentalbarcelona.com; Carrer d'en Rauric 20; per 3hr/24hr from €9/16 depending on type of bike; ⏲ 10am-8pm; Ⓜ Jaume I)

My Beautiful Parking (Map p58; 📞 93 304 15 80; www.mybeautifulparking.com; Carrer de Cervantes 5; per 2hr/24hr €6/15; ⏲ 10am-8pm; Ⓜ Jaume I or Liceu)

Un Cotxe Menys (📞 93 268 21 05; www.bicicletabarcelona.com; Carrer de l'Esparteria 3; per hr/day/week €5/15/55; ⏲ 9am-7pm Easter-Nov, 11am-2pm Dec-Easter; Ⓜ Jaume I)

Tickets & Targetes

The Metro, FGC trains, *rodalies/cercanías* (Renfe-run local trains) and buses come under one zoned-fare regime. Single-ride tickets on all standard transport within Zone 1 cost €2. You can save money by purchasing a Targeta T-10 ticket (10 rides for €9.25).

Climate Change & Travel

Every form of transport that relies on carbon-based fuel generates CO_2, the main cause of human-induced climate change. Modern travel is dependent on aeroplanes, which might use less fuel per kilometre per person than most cars but travel much greater distances. The altitude at which aircraft emit gases (including CO_2) and particles also contributes to their climate change impact. Many websites offer 'carbon calculators' that allow people to estimate the carbon emissions generated by their journey and, for those who wish to do so, to offset the impact of the greenhouse gases emitted with contributions to portfolios of climate-friendly initiatives throughout the world. Lonely Planet offsets the carbon footprint of all staff and author travel.

Tours

There are a range of guided tours: on foot and by bus, bicycle or scooter. Boat tours of the harbour and beaches depart daily from the waterfront.

Walking Tours

The Oficina d'Informació de Turisme de Barcelona (p240) organises guided walking tours. One explores the Barri Gòtic (adult/child €14/5); another follows in Picasso's footsteps and winds up at the Museu Picasso, to which entry is included in the price (adult/child €20/7); and a third takes in the main jewels of Modernisme (adult/child €14/5). It also offers a 'gourmet' tour of traditional purveyors of fine foodstuffs across the old city (adult/child €19/7) and a maritime-themed tour (adult/child €19/7). Stop by the tourist office, go online or call for the latest schedule. All tours last two hours and start at the tourist office.

Specialised tours can also be booked through the tourist office. Themes include running, shopping, literary Barcelona, films, birdwatching in Collserola Park, the civil war, the Gothic quarter by night and Park Güell.

Runner Bean Tours (Map p58; ☎ 636 108776; www.runnerbeantours.com; ⏱ tours 11am year-round & 4.30pm Apr-Sep) comprises several daily thematic tours. It's a pay-what-you-wish tour, with a collection taken at the end for the guide. The Old City tour explores the Roman and medieval history of Barcleona, visiting highlights in the Ciutat Vella. The Gaudí tour takes in the great works of Modernista Barcelona. It involves two hops on the metro. Both tours depart at 11am from Plaça Reial (and also at 4.30pm from April through September) and last for about two and a half hours.

Bicycle Tours

Barcelona is awash with companies offering bicycle tours. Tours typically take two to four hours and generally stick to the old city, the Sagrada Família and the beaches. Operators include the following:

Bike Tours Barcelona (Map p96; ☎ 93 268 21 05; www.bicicletabarcelona.com; Carrer de l'Esparteria 3; tour €22)

Barcelona By Bike (Map p116; ☎ 93 268 81 07; www.barcelonabybike.com; Carrer de la Marina 13; tours €22; Ⓜ Cuitadella/Vila Olimpica)

CicloTour (Map p78; ☎ 93 317 19 70; www.barcelonaciclotour.com/eng; Carrer dels Tallers 45; tours €21; ⏱ 11am daily, 4.30pm mid-Apr–Oct, 7.30pm Thu-Sun Jun-Sep)

Fat Tire Bike Tours (Map p58; ☎ 93 301 36 12; http://fattirebiketours.com/barcelona; Carrer dels Escudellers 48; tours €22)

BarcelonaBiking.com (Map p58; ☎ 656 356300; www.barcelonabiking.com; Baixada de Sant Miquel 6; per hr/24hr €5/15; ⏱ 10am-8pm; Ⓜ Jaume I or Liceu)

Bus Tours

Bus Turístic (p237) is a hop-on/hop-off service that stops at virtually all of the city's main sights. Audioguides (in 10 languages) provide running commentary on the 44 stops on three different circuits.

Boat Tours

For a trip around the harbour, board one of the **Golondrina** (☎ 93 442 31 06; www.lasgolondrinas.com; Moll de les Drassanes; adult/child €14.50/5.25; ⏱ Mar-Nov; Ⓜ Drassanes) excursion boats from Moll de les Drassanes in front of Mirador de Colom. The one-hour round trip takes you to Port Olímpic, the Fòrum and back again.

Aboard a large sailing catamaran, Orsom (p123) makes the 90-minute journey past the Port Olímpic, the beaches and out to the Fòrum and back. There are three departures per day (four on weekends in July and August), and the last is a jazz cruise, scheduled around sunset.

Directory

Business Hours

Reviews in this guide don't list business hours unless they differ from the following standards.

Restaurants lunch 1–4pm, dinner 8.30pm–midnight

Shops 10am–2pm and 4–8pm Monday–Saturday

Department stores 10am–10pm Monday–Saturday

Bars 6pm–2am

Practicalities

o Currency: the euro (€)

o Smoking: banned in restaurants and bars

Clubs midnight–6am Thursday–Saturday

Banks 8.30am–2pm Monday–Friday; some also 4–7pm Thursday or 9am–1pm Saturday

Discount Cards

Possession of a **Bus Turístic** (📞 93 285 38 32; www.barcelonaturisme.com; day ticket adult/child €24/14; ⏰ 9am–8pm) ticket entitles you to discounts to some museums.

Articket (www.articketbcn.org) gives admission to the following sights for €30 and is valid for six months. Pick it up at the tourist offices at Plaça de Catalunya, Plaça de Sant Jaume and Sants train station.

o Museu Picasso

o Museu Nacional d'Art de Catalunya

o MACBA (Museu d'Art Contemporani de Barcelona)

o Fundació Antoni Tàpies

o Centre de Cultura Contemporània de Barcelona

o Fundació Joan Miró

o La Pedrera

Barcelona Card (www.barcelonacard.com) is handy if you want to see lots in a limited time. It costs €29/35/40/47 (a little less for children aged four to 12) for two/three/four/five days. You get free transport (and 20% off the Aerobús), and discounted admission prices (up to 30% off) or free entry to many museums and other sights, as well as minor discounts on purchases at a small number of shops,

restaurants and bars. The card is available at the tourist offices and online (buying online saves you 10%).

Electricity

Spain uses 220V/230V, 50Hz, like the rest of continental Europe

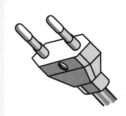

220V/230V/50Hz

Emergency

The following are the main emergency numbers:

Ambulance (📞 061)

Catalan police (Mossos d'Esquadra; 📞 088)

EU standard emergency number (📞 112)

Fire brigade (Bombers; 📞 080, 085)

Guàrdia Urbana (local police; 📞 092; La Rambla 43; Ⓜ Liceu)

Policía Nacional (national police; 091)

Internet Access
Wi-Fi Access

Many hotels offer their guests wi-fi access (not always for free). A growing array of city bars and restaurants are latching on to the service – look for the black-and-white wi-fi signs.

Places in this guide that offer wi-fi have the symbol 🛜.

Medical Services

All foreigners have the same right as Spaniards to emergency medical treatment in public hospitals. EU citizens are entitled to the full range of health-care services in public hospitals, but must present a European Health Insurance Card (enquire at your national health service) and may have to pay upfront.

Non-EU citizens have to pay for anything other than emergency treatment. Most travel-insurance policies include medical cover.

For minor health problems you can try any *farmàcia* (pharmacy), where pharmaceuticals tend to be sold more freely without prescription than in places such as the USA, Australia or the UK.

Hospitals include the following:

Hospital Clínic i Provincial (Carrer de Villarroel 170; Ⓜ Hospital Clínic)

Hospital Dos de Maig (Carrer del Dos de Maig 301; Ⓜ Sant Pau–Dos de Maig)

Some 24-hour pharmacies:

Farmàcia Castells Soler (Passeig de Gràcia 90; Ⓜ Diagonal)

Farmàcia Clapés (La Rambla 98; Ⓜ Liceu)

Farmàcia Torres (www.farmaciaabierta24h.com; Carrer d'Aribau 62; Ⓡ FGC Provença)

Money
ATMS

Barcelona abounds with banks, many of which have ATMs. ATMs are also in plentiful supply around Plaça de Catalunya, Plaça de Sant Jaume (in the Barri Gòtic) and La Rambla.

Credit Cards

Major cards such as Visa, MasterCard, Maestro and Cirrus are accepted throughout Spain. If your card is lost, stolen or swallowed by an ATM, you can telephone toll free to immediately stop its use:

Amex (902 375637)

Diners Club (900 801331)

MasterCard (900 971231)

Visa (900 991124)

Public Holidays

New Year's Day (Any Nou/Año Nuevo) 1 January

Epiphany/Three Kings' Day (Epifanía or El Dia dels Reis/Día de los Reyes Magos) 6 January

Good Friday (Divendres Sant/Viernes Santo) March/April

Easter Monday (Dilluns de Pasqua Florida) March/April

Labour Day (Dia del Treball/Fiesta del Trabajo) 1 May

Day after Pentecost Sunday (Dilluns de Pasqua Granda) May/June

Feast of St John the Baptist (Dia de Sant Joan/Día de San Juan Bautista) 24 June

Feast of the Assumption (L'Assumpció/La Asunción) 15 August

Catalonia's National Day (Diada Nacional de Catalunya) 11 September

Festes de la Mercè 24 September

Spanish National Day (Festa de la Hispanitat/Día de la Hispanidad) 12 October

All Saints Day (Dia de Tots Sants/Día de Todos los Santos) 1 November

Constitution Day (Día de la Constitución) 6 December

Feast of the Immaculate Conception (La Immaculada Concepció/La Inmaculada Concepción) 8 December

Christmas (Nadal/Navidad) 25 December

Boxing Day/St Stephen's Day (El Dia de Sant Esteve) 26 December

Safe Travel

It cannot be stressed enough that newcomers to Barcelona must be on their guard. Petty theft is a problem in the city centre, on public transport and around main sights. Report thefts to the national police. You are unlikely to recover your goods but you will need to make this formal *denuncia* (police report) for insurance purposes. There's a handy (and busy) **police station** (☎ 088; **Carrer Nou de la Rambla 80; M Paral.lel**) near La Rambla and you can also report petty crime online at www.policia.es/denuncias. You could also try the Guàrdia Urbana (p237).

Taxes & Refunds

Value-added tax, or VAT, is also known as IVA (*impuesto sobre el valor añadido*, pronounced 'EE-ba'). IVA is 8% on accommodation and restaurant prices and is usually – but not always – included in quoted prices. On most retail goods the IVA is 18%. For information about refunds, see p226.

Telephones

Public telephones
The ubiquitous blue payphones are easy to use for international and domestic calls. They accept coins, *tarjetas telefónicas* (phonecards) issued by the national phone company

Telefónica and, in some cases, credit cards. *Tarjetas telefónicas* are sold at post offices and tobacconists.

Call centres A few *Locutorios*, which also double as internet centres, are scattered around El Raval (look around Carrer de Sant Pau and Carrer de l'Hospital).

Making calls To call Barcelona from outside Spain, dial the international access code, followed by the code for Spain (☎34) and the full number (including Barcelona's area code, 93, which is an integral part of the number). To make an international call, dial the international access code (☎00), country code, area code and number.

Operator Services

International operator for reverse-charge calls ☎1408

International directory enquiries ☎11825

Domestic operator for a domestic reverse-charge call (llamada por cobro revertido) ☎1409

National directory inquiries ☎11818

Mobile Phones

Mobile-phone numbers start with 6 or 7. Numbers starting with ☎900 are national toll-free numbers, while those starting with numbers between ☎901 and ☎905 come with varying conditions. A common one is ☎902, which is a national standard-rate number. In a similar category are numbers starting with ☎803, ☎806 and ☎807.

Spain uses GSM 900/1800, compatible with the rest of Europe and Australia but not with the North American GSM 1900 or the system used in Japan. If your phone is tri- or quadriband, you will probably be fine. You can buy SIM cards and prepaid call time in Spain for your own national mobile phone (provided what you own is a GSM, dual- or tri-band cellular phone and not code-blocked). You will need your passport to open any kind of mobile-phone account, prepaid or otherwise.

Time

Spain is one hour ahead of GMT/UTC during winter, and two hours ahead during daylight saving (the last Sunday in March to the last Sunday in October). Most other western European countries are on the same time as Spain year-round. The UK, Ireland and Portugal are one hour behind. Spaniards use the 24-hour clock for official business (timetables etc) but generally switch to the 12-hour version in daily conversation.

Tourist Information

Several tourist offices operate in Barcelona. In addition to tourist offices, information booths operate at Estació del Nord bus station and at Portal de la Pau, at the foot of the Mirador de Colom at the port end of La Rambla. Others set up at various points in the city centre in summer.

Plaça de Catalunya (93 285 38 34; www. barcelonaturisme.com; underground at Plaça de Catalunya 17-S; 8.30am-8.30pm; Catalunya)

Plaça Sant Jaume (93 285 38 32; Carrer de la Ciutat 2; 8.30am-8.30pm Mon-Fri, 9am-7pm Sat, 9am-2pm Sun & holidays; Jaume I)

Estació Sants (8am-8pm; Estació Sants)

El Prat Airport (El Prat Airport, Terminal 1 arrivals, Terminal 2B arrivals hall, Terminal 2A arrivals hall; 9am-9pm)

La Rambla Information Office (www.barcelonaturisme. com; La Rambla dels Estudis 115; 8.30am-8.30pm; Liceu)

Palau Robert Regional Tourist Office (93 238 80 91, from outside Catalonia 902 400012; www.gencat.net/ probert; Passeig de Gràcia 107; 10am-8pm Mon-Sat, 10am-2.30pm Sun) A host of material on Catalonia, audiovisual resources, a bookshop and a branch of Turisme Juvenil de Catalunya (for youth travel).

●●●

Travellers with Disabilities

Some hotels and public institutions have wheelchair access. All buses in Barcelona are wheelchair accessible and a growing number of Metro stations are theoretically wheelchair accessible (generally by lift, although there have been complaints that they are only any good for parents with prams). In all, about 80% of stops have been adapted (you can check which ones by looking at a network map here: www.tmb.cat/en/ transport-accessible). Ticket vending machines in Metro stations are adapted for the disabled and have Braille options for the blind.

Several taxi companies have adapted vehicles including **Taxi Amic** (93 420 80 88; www.taxi-amic-adaptat.com), **Gestverd** (93 303 09 09) and **Radio Taxi 033** (93 303 09 09).

Most street crossings in central Barcelona are wheelchair-friendly.

For more information on what the city is doing to improve accessibility check out the council's *Accessible Barcelona Guide* in several languages (www.barcelona-access.com).

Visas

Spain is one of 25 member countries of the Schengen Convention, under which 22 EU countries (all but Bulgaria, Cyprus, Ireland, Romania and the UK) plus Iceland, Norway and Switzerland have abolished checks at common borders.

EU nationals require only their ID cards to visit Spain. Nationals of many other countries, including Australia, Canada, Israel, Japan, New Zealand and the USA, do not require visas for tourist visits to Spain of up to 90 days. Citizens of countries not mentioned above should check whether they need a visa with their Spanish consulate.

Language

Catalan and Spanish both have official-language status in Catalonia. In Barcelona, you'll hear as much Spanish as Catalan, so we've provided some Spanish to get you started. Spanish pronunciation is not difficult as most of its sounds are also found in English. You can read our pronunciation guides below as if they were English and you'll be understood just fine. And if you pronounce 'th' in our guides with a lisp and 'kh' as a throaty sound, you'll even sound like a real Spanish person.

To enhance your trip with a phrasebook, visit **lonelyplanet.com**. Lonely Planet iPhone phrasebooks are available through the Apple App store.

BASICS

Hello.
Hola.   o·la
How are you?
¿Qué tal?   ke tal
I'm fine, thanks.
Bien, gracias.   byen *gra*·thyas
Excuse me. (to get attention)
Disculpe.   dees·*kool*·pe
Yes./No.
Sí./No.   see/no
Thank you.
Gracias.   *gra*·thyas
You're welcome./That's fine.
De nada.   de *na*·da
Goodbye. /See you later.
Adiós./Hasta luego.   a·*dyos*/as·ta *lwe*·go
Do you speak English?
¿Habla inglés?   a·bla een·*gles*
I don't understand.
No entiendo.   no en·*tyen*·do
How much is this?
¿Cuánto cuesta?   *kwan*·to *kwes*·ta
Can you reduce the price a little?
¿Podría bajar un   po·*dree*·a ba·*khar* oon
poco el precio?   *po*·ko el *pre*·thyo

ACCOMMODATION

I'd like to make a booking.
Quisiera reservar   kee·*sye*·ra re·ser·*var*
una habitación.   *oo*·na a·bee·ta·*thyon*
How much is it per night?
¿Cuánto cuesta por noche?   *kwan*·to *kwes*·ta por *no*·che

EATING & DRINKING

I'd like ..., please.
Quisiera ..., por favor.   kee·*sye*·ra ... por fa·*vor*
That was delicious!
¡Estaba buenísimo!   es·*ta*·ba bwe·*nee*·see·mo
Bring the bill/check, please.
La cuenta, por favor.   la *kwen*·ta por fa·*vor*

I'm allergic to ...
Soy alérgico/a al ... (m/f)   soy a·*ler*·khee·ko/a al ...
I don't eat ...
No como ...   no *ko*·mo ...
   chicken   *pollo*   *po*·lyo
   fish   *pescado*   pes·*ka*·do
   meat   *carne*   *kar*·ne

EMERGENCIES

I'm ill.
Estoy enfermo/a. (m/f)   es·*toy* en·*fer*·mo/a
Help!
¡Socorro!   so·*ko*·ro
Call a doctor!
¡Llame a un médico!   *lya*·me a oon *me*·dee·ko
Call the police!
¡Llame a la policía!   *lya*·me a la po·lee·*thee*·a

DIRECTIONS

I'm looking for a/an/the ...
Estoy buscando ...   es·*toy* boos·*kan*·do ...
   ATM
   un cajero   oon ka·*khe*·ro
   automático   ow·to·*ma*·tee·ko
   bank
   el banco   el *ban*·ko
   ... embassy
   la embajada de ...   la em·ba·*kha*·da de ...
   market
   el mercado   el mer·*ka*·do
   museum
   el museo   el moo·*se*·o
   restaurant
   un restaurante oon res·tow·*ran*·te
   toilet
   los servicios los ser·*vee*·thyos
   tourist office
   la oficina de la o·fee·*thee*·na de
   turismo   too·*rees*·mo

Behind the Scenes

Author Thanks
Regis St Louis

I'm grateful for all the great advice from locals, expats and tourism staff. In particular, I'd like to thank Eric Mills, Sol Polo, Maria Asuncion Guardia, Margherita Bergamo Meneghini, Meritxell Checa Esteban and friends, Carine Ferry and friends, Laura of Runnerbean, and Diego in Barri Gòtic. I'd also like to thank Malén Gual, Gorka Regidor, Núria Rocamora and Gonzalo Salaya Ventura for their generous contribution to the Local Knowledge section. Finally, big hugs to my wife and daughters for their continued support.

Acknowledgments

Illustrations pp132-3 by Javier Zarracina.
Cover photographs: Front: La Sagrada Família, Dale Buckton/Lonely Planet Images ©; Back: Tapas, El Raval, Diego Lezama/ Lonely Planet Images ©

This Book

This 2nd edition of Lonely Planet's *Discover Barcelona* guidebook was coordinated by Regis St Louis and was researched and written by him, Vesna Maric and Anna Kaminski. The previous edition was written by Brendan Sainsbury and Damien Simonis. This guidebook was commissioned in Lonely Planet's London office, and produced by the following:

Commissioning Editor Dora Whitaker
Coordinating Editor Elin Berglund
Coordinating Cartographer Valeska Canas
Coordinating Layout Designer Wibowo Rusli
Managing Editors Sasha Baskett, Barbara Delissen, Anna Metcalfe
Managing Cartographers Mark Griffiths, Alison Lyall, Amanda Sierp
Managing Layout Designer Jane Hart
Assisting Editor Alan Murphy
Cover Research Naomi Parker
Internal Image Research Aude Vauconsant
Language Content Branislava Vladisavljevic
Thanks to Dan Austin, Imogen Bannister, Laura Crawford, Ryan Evans, Asha Ioculari, Jouve India, Chris Lee Ack, Annelies Mertens, Trent Paton, Derek Pinder, Martine Power, Raphael Richards, Averil Robertson, Dianne Schallmeiner, Fiona Siseman, Navin Sushil, Diana Von Holdt, Gerard Walker

NOTES

Index

See also separate subindexes for:

 Eating p251

 Drinking & Nightlife p252

 Entertainment p253

Shopping p253

 Sports & Activities p254

Sights 000
Map pages 000

Sights 000
Map pages 000

Eating

Sights 000
Map pages 000

Sights 000
Map pages 000

How to Use This Book

These symbols will help you find the listings you want:

⊙ Sights
⊗ Eating
⊖ Drinking & Nightlife

★ Entertainment
⊕ Shopping
⊕ Sports & Activities

These symbols give you the vital information for each listing:

- ☏ Telephone Numbers
- ☺ Opening Hours
- Ⓟ Parking
- ⊖ Nonsmoking
- ✳ Air-Conditioning
- @ Internet Access

- ☎ Wi-Fi Access
- ☒ Swimming Pool
- ✔ Vegetarian Selection
- 🗊 English-Language Menu
- ⊕ Family-Friendly
- ☺ Pet-Friendly

- ⊟ Bus
- ⊞ Ferry
- Ⓜ Metro
- Ⓢ Subway
- ⊟ Tram
- ⊞ Train

Reviews are organised by author preference.

Look out for these icons:

FREE — No payment required

 — A green or sustainable option

Our authors have nominated these places as demonstrating a strong commitment to sustainability – for example by supporting local communities and producers, operating in an environmentally friendly way, or supporting conservation projects.

Map Legend

Sights
- ⓑ Beach
- ⊜ Buddhist
- ⊛ Castle
- ⊕ Christian
- ⊕ Hindu
- Ⓒ Islamic
- ⊙ Jewish
- ⓞ Monument
- ⊕ Museum/Gallery
- ⊗ Ruin
- ⊗ Winery/Vineyard
- ⊗ Zoo
- ⊙ Other Sight

Sports & Activities
- ⊜ Diving/Snorkelling
- ⊜ Canoeing/Kayaking
- ⊕ Skiing
- ⊕ Surfing
- ⊗ Swimming/Pool
- ⊘ Walking
- ⊙ Windsurfing
- ⊕ Other Sports & Activities

Eating
- ⊗ Eating

Drinking & Nightlife
- ⊖ Drinking
- ⊖ Cafe

Entertainment
- ✪ Entertainment

Shopping
- ⊕ Shopping

Sleeping
- ⓘ Sleeping
- ⊕ Camping

Information
- ⊕ Post Office
- ⓘ Tourist Information

Transport
- ⊕ Airport
- ⊗ Border Crossing
- ⊕ Bus
- +⊕+ Cable Car/Funicular
- -⊛- Cycling
- -⊖- Ferry
- ⊕ Monorail
- Ⓟ Parking
- Ⓢ S-Bahn
- ⊖ Taxi
- +⊕+ Train/Railway
- ⊕ Tram
- ⊖ Tube Station
- ⓤ U-Bahn
- Ⓜ Underground Train Station
- • Other Transport

Routes
- Tollway
- Freeway
- Primary
- Secondary
- Tertiary
- Lane
- Unsealed Road
- Plaza/Mall
- Steps
-) ⹀ ⹀ Tunnel
- Pedestrian Overpass
- Walking Tour
- Walking Tour Detour
- Path

Boundaries
- — — — International
- ----- State/Province
- — — Disputed
- — ⸱ — Regional/Suburb
- Marine Park
- ⊤⊤⊤⊤ Cliff
- Wall

Geographic
- ⊕ Hut/Shelter
- ⊖ Lighthouse
- ⊜ Lookout
- ▲ Mountain/Volcano
- ⊖ Oasis
- ⊕ Park
-)(Pass
- ⊕ Picnic Area
- ⊕ Waterfall

Hydrography
- River/Creek
- Intermittent River
- Swamp/Mangrove
- Reef
- Canal
- Water
- Dry/Salt/ Intermittent Lake
- Glacier

Areas
- Beach/Desert
- Cemetery (Christian)
- Cemetery (Other)
- Park/Forest
- Sportsground
- Sight (Building)
- Top Sight (Building)

Our Story

A beat-up old car, a few dollars in the pocket and a sense of adventure. In 1972 that's all Tony and Maureen Wheeler needed for the trip of a lifetime – across Europe and Asia overland to Australia. It took several months, and at the end – broke but inspired – they sat at their kitchen table writing and stapling together their first travel guide, *Across Asia on the Cheap*. Within a week they'd sold 1500 copies. Lonely Planet was born.

Today, Lonely Planet has offices in Melbourne, London and Oakland, with more than 600 staff and writers. We share Tony's belief that 'a great guidebook should do three things: inform, educate and amuse'.

Our Writers

Regis St Louis

Coordinating Author; La Rambla & Barri Gòtic; Barceloneta & the Waterfront; Park Güell, Camp Nou & La Zona Alta Regis first fell in love with Barcelona and Catalonia on a grand journey across Iberia in the late 1990s. Since then, he's returned frequently, learning Spanish and a smattering of Catalan, and delving into the rich cultural history of this endlessly fascinating city. Favourite memories from his most recent trip include lingering over long seafood lunches with friends in Barceloneta, exploring hidden corners of La Zona Alta, catching evening concerts in the Ciutat Vella and feasting on perhaps the last *calçots* of the season. Regis is also the author of Lonely Planet's *Barcelona* guidebook, and he has contributed to *Spain, Portugal* and dozens of other titles. He lives in Brooklyn, New York.

Read more about Regis at:
lonelyplanet.com/members/regisstlouis

Vesna Maric

El Raval; La Ribera; La Sagrada Família & L'Eixample; Montjuïc; Park Güell, Camp Nou & La Zona Alta Vesna is originally from Bosnia-Herzegovina; her love of all things Spanish started when she met her partner, Rafael, 10 years ago. She has since learned the language, explored the country and fallen in love with Barcelona over and over again, returning any time she has a chance. She loves the city's beaches, incredible food markets, architecture, great nightlife and fantastic Catalan cuisine.

Anna Kaminski

Day Trips Anna's love affair with Spain began with a Spanish course in Santander in 2001, and has continued unabated in spite of a severe bout of salmonella, prompting her to return to these shores time and time again. Having adopted Barcelona as her current home, she has particularly enjoyed exploring the incredibly diverse surrounding area, wandering the same landscapes as her favourite artist, Salvador Dalí, and widening her culinary horizons (not to mention her waistline) by sampling some of the best food in the country.

Published by Lonely Planet Publications Pty Ltd
ABN 36 005 607 983
2nd edition – January 2013
ISBN 978 1 74220 623 3
© Lonely Planet 2013   Photographs © as indicated 2013
10 9 8 7 6 5 4 3 2 1
Printed in China